NEW TECHNOLOGIES IN SECONDARY EDUCATION

COUNCIL OF EUROPE

NEW TECHNOLOGIES IN SECONDARY EDUCATION

A REPORT OF THE EDUCATIONAL RESEARCH WORKSHOP
HELD IN FRASCATI, 2-5 NOVEMBER 1982

EDITED BY

THE SECRETARIAT OF THE COUNCIL OF EUROPE

1983
SWETS & ZEITLINGER – LISSE

Ministry of Education, Ontario
Information Centre, 13th Floor,
Mowat Block, Queen's Park,
Toronto, Ont.   M7A 1L2

CIP-GEGEVENS

New

New technologies in secondary education : a report of the educational research workshop held in Frascati, 2-5 November 1982 / ed. by the Secretariat of the Council of Europe ; [voorw. Michael Vorbeck]. - Lisse : Swets & Zeitlinger. - Ill.
Met lit. opg.
ISBN 90-265-0455-1
SISO 365.4 UDC 681.3.01:373.5
Trefw. : informatica ; voortgezet onderwijs.

Copyright© 1983 by
The Council of Europe, Strasbourg,
and Swets & Zeitlinger, Lisse.

Printed in The Netherlands by Offsetdrukkerij Kanters BV, Alblasserdam.

No part of this book may be reproduced in any form by print, photoprint, microfilm or any other means without permission from the publisher.

ISBN 90 265 0455 1

CONTENTS

Preface 1

PART 1: REPORTS AND COMMISSIONED PAPERS 3

1.1 Summary of the Issues Raised and Discussed
by W. R. Broderick - Rapporteur General 5

1.2 Reports of the Working Groups
by their Chairmen 14

1.3 The Austrian Experience with Microelectronics and Programming in Schools
by Dr. Helmut Aigner 19

1.4 Teaching Computer Science in the Secondary School - A Survey of Research and Evaluation in the Federal Republic of Germany
by Dr. Ulrich Bosler 29

1.5 The United Kingdom's Experience of Evaluation and Development of Computer Related Learning Systems
by W. R. Broderick 41

1.6 The Teaching of Computer Science at Secondary School - Evaluation of Experience in Spain
by Mr. E. Garcia Camarero 56

1.7 Computer Science and Education - An Overview of Experiences and Research in Italy
by Prof. M. Fierli 72

1.8 Computers in Swedish Schools - A Presentation of Experience, Research and Problems
by Dr. Anita Kollerbaur 78

PART 2: NATIONAL REPORTS 93

2.1 Austria
Computer Equipment in Austrian Secondary Schools
by Ministerialrat Dr. Johann Czemetschka 95

2.2 Belgium (Dutch Language Community)
The Situation in Belgium (Dutch Language Community)
by the Ministry of Education and Dutch Culture 99

2.3 Belgium (French Language Community)
The Situation in Belgium (French Language Community)
by M. G. De Landsheere and D. Leclerq 101

2.4 Cyprus
Introduction of Computers in Secondary Schools
by Mr. Nicos Hadjinicolas   110

2.5 Denmark
Present State of Research and Evaluation of Computer Science and
Computer-Based Teaching in Danish Secondary Schools
by Dr. Jannik Johansen   113

2.6 Finland
The Use of Microcomputers in Secondary Schools
by Prof. Jukka Lehtinen   115

2.7 France
Information Processing in French Secondary Schools
by M. Pierre Muller   117

2.8 Ireland
The Present State of Research, Development and Evaluation
by the Department of Education   123

2.9 Netherlands
Computers in Education
by Mr. Jaap Akkermans and Mr. Jef Moonen   126

2.10 Portugal
Computer Studies
by the Ministry of Education and Culture   130

2.11 Switzerland
Computers in Swiss Secondary Education
by M. Alain Bron   133

PART 3: BACKGROUND PAPERS   139

3.1 Provisional List of Ongoing Research
prepared by the Secretariat
Council of Europe   141

3.2 Provisional Bibliography
prepared by the Secretariat
Council of Europe   171

List of participants   209

PREFACE

The Workshop at Frascati is one of a series of educational research meetings which have become an important element in the programme of the Council for Cultural Co-operation (CCC) of the Council of Europe since 1975. European Co-operation in educational research aims at providing ministries of education with research findings so as to enable them to prepare their policy decisions; co-operation should also lead to a joint European evaluation of certain educational reforms. These meetings bring together educational research workers from various countries taking part in the work of the Council for Cultural Co-operation (23 countries in all). The purpose is to compare research findings with regard to a particular topic of current interest; to identify areas of research so far neglected and to discuss possibilities for joint research projects. The papers, as well as the official reports, of these meetings are in general published as a book so that ministries and interested research workers as well as a wider public (teachers, parents, press) are kept informed of the present state of research at European level.

The meeting at Frascati goes back to a suggestion made by the Italian Ministry of Education and immediately taken up by the Council of Europe. As new technologies are playing a more and more important role in almost all the countries taking part in the work of the Council for Cultural Co-operation, education, and in particular secondary education, has to prepare young people for a highly computerised employment. The Workshop was organised by the Italian Ministry of Education in co-operation with and under the auspices of the Council for Cultural Co-operation. It took place at the European Centre for Education (Centro Europeo dell'Educazione) at Villa Falconieri, Frascati. Lecturers from six countries (Austria, Federal Republic of Germany, Italy, Spain, Sweden and the United Kingdom), introduced each of the following aspects of work in plenary session, and each aspect was then discussed in three groups. The four general aspects were:

a. General introduction to computers for all pupils.

b. Computer science (informatique) as an option for specialisation.

c. Computer assisted learning.

d. Education and in-service training of teachers.

On the final day the conclusions were summed up by the Rapporteur General, Mr. William R BRODERICk. A number of individual or national reports and background papers were tabled.

Informally, in addition to the above programme, there was an exhibition of publications and materials from all over Europe, and the British delegation demonstrated various examples of the use of computers in the classroom.

The following countries were represented: Austria, Belgium, Cyprus, Denmark, Federal Republic of Germany, Finland, France, Greece, Ireland, Italy, Malta, Netherlands, Portugal, Spain, Switzerland, and the United Kingdom. UNESCO, OECD, the Commission of the European Communities, the European Institute of Education and Social Policy and a number of teacher organisations (FIPESO, WCOTP, ATEE, FISE) sent observers (see also the list of participants at the end of this book).

In particular the Council of Europe would like to thank the Italian Ministry of Education (Mr. S AVVEDUTO, Director General for International Cultural Relations, Mr F CONDO, and Mrs Ch. VACIAGO) and the European Centre for Education (the Director, Prof. A VISALBERGHI, and his staff) for their excellent work in preparing and organising the Workshop. The meeting was chaired first by Mr. AVVEDUTO and then by Mr. CONDO in a highly efficient way. The Council of Europe expresses its thanks to the two chairmen and to the Rapporteur General and the lecturers.

Strasbourg 25 March 1983

Michael VORBECK
Head of the Section for Educational
Research and Documentation
Council of Europe

PART 1: REPORTS AND COMMISSIONED PAPERS

1.1 SUMMARY OF THE ISSUES RAISED AND DISCUSSED

by

William R. BRODERICK BSc FBCS
Rapporteur General

1.1.1   INTRODUCTION

The background to this workshop was interesting. It was held at a time when budgets were increased by less than inflation and when there was increasing unemployment, and yet there was a widely recognised need to launch a new educational initiative in this field. Members of the workshop recognised that this was not the only priority in education, but were encouraged by the interest and support from international and supranational organisations (Council of Europe, UNESCO, OECD and the European Community).

1.1.2   GENERAL INTRODUCTION TO COMPUTER STUDIES FOR ALL PUPILS

It was almost universally recognised that all students should know about the implications, applications and limitations of computers, but there was widespread agreement they should know "enough but not too much". It was widely agreed that teaching programming was only appropriate for about 20% of all pupils, and schools should be more prepared to use ready-made packages and should be strongly advised to avoid the pitfalls of teaching "the transient technology".

Evaluation of work was a fundamental theme of the workshop, and a model of evaluation which was widely referred to by delegates as both acceptable and practicable is given in Section 5 below.

The role of the teacher in evaluation was frequently discussed both when considering this section, and others. Many delegates with extensive experience in the field emphasised that the teachers needed and wished to be involved in the evaluation, and that they could feel anxious if they were excluded from the evaluation process. It was widely held that teachers are supportive of evaluation projects if they are involved in them, and that they recognise that external evaluation must be seen as part of total evaluation of an activity. The majority of delegates felt that imposing computer studies and evaluation from above may lead to failure - the phrase "top down is upside down" was coined, but at least one delegation felt that the "top down" approach was the most acceptable in their context.

It was recognised that the expectations of the general public about new technology varied tremendously. However, it was felt important that people should be made realistic, and one should avoid being over-optimistic. It was considered important to recognise that Ministers of Education are chosen from the general public: they are frequently not specialists in the area of computing and they need sound and realistic advice. It was widely recognised that their advisers should examine, in the national context, how government policy might best influence work in the classroom and enable appropriate developments to take place. It was also felt important to recognise that one has to be realistic about pupils - they forget much of the detail of what they are taught.

Social Issues

There was almost universal agreement that teachers need have no anxiety: they will not be replaced by microcomputers, but they will have to learn to use them as another weapon in their armoury as teachers. It was commented (with particular reference to the UK experience) that subjects such as Art, Cookery and Geography were sometimes replaced by Computer Studies. It was virtually universally recognised that schools have a responsibility to educate the whole man, and therefore they must ensure that there is an appropriate balance between the subjects and the contents of the subjects. It was also emphasised that when school timetables were being created, it was important to ensure that pupil activities were well balanced over the day.

Strategies for Introducing Computer Studies

The most appropriate strategy is bound to depend upon local circumstances, and therefore schools should look at models tried elsewhere and then adapt them to their local situation. Likewise, it was considered important to use local strengths (for instance educational broadcasting and Open University in the United Kingdom) to support developments. Without any doubt at all, it was considered important to use proven and well established methods of communication, as well as innovative ones to educate and inform others. On the other hand, it was recognised that it was equally vital to recognise local weaknesses and to underpin them and try to overcome them. Without doubt, it was felt that practice must be related to the needs and abilities of pupils in the classroom, for failure to do this would undermine the educational value of any project.

1.1.3   COMPUTER SCIENCE

The workshop drew a careful distinction between Computer Studies and Computer Science, the latter being a more specialised and academic study. It was emphasised, however, that it was necessary to avoid too much specialisation, as otherwise the students would not be employable, despite the fact that it was estimated that in about fifteen years' time, 50% of all jobs would be affected by computers. It was also recognised that some educational systems separate for vocational and academic education whilst others combine them. It was agreed that in both cases, Computer Science should be offered. The syllabus content for the subject as used in the United Kingdom appeared to be acceptable to many, but not all, the participants, and it was accepted that it was relatively easy to choose locally appropriate sub-sets from the syllabus.

Teachers of Computer Science

It was emphasised that they needed a suitable academic and professional training to teach the subject to this degree of specialisation. Additionally, a carefully structured syllabus appropriate to local needs and supported by texts books and other teaching material (which must be flexible) are necessary before the subject will be widely taught. There was considerable discussion as to whether it was better to integrate Computer Science into the various other disciplines or to offer it as a specialisation in its own right. It was accepted that this was a national issue and the decision taken will reflect national priorities and educational philosophies. It was thought to be essential that teachers of Computer Science should be very well versed in the possible applications of computers, not just in an academic sense, but also in a practical sense, and a period of industrial experience was considered most important as a technique for bringing a very practical perspective into classroom work.

Pupils

It was again reiterated that it was necessary to educate the whole man and therefore essential to avoid too much specialisation too early. It was emphasised that the pupils need some knowledge of Computer Science before choosing it as an option, otherwise they may become very disillusioned. Some pupils become over-enthusiastic for computing, perhaps to the detriment of their other work, and teachers need to use their professional skills to ensure that students develop a balanced approach to their studies. It was notable that there had been an explosion in pupil interest in Great Britain. In 1974 there were just 7,000 students doing Computing Science - this figure had risen to 54,000 in 1981. There may be a parallel explosion in other countries.

Scope of Computer Science

It was considered essential that Computer Science should reflect real life practice as well as the academic side of this subject. Topics generally considered appropriate include logic and arithmetic; data structures; system architecture; system software; system design (with an emphasis on real life practices); approaches to programming (with an emphasis on developing sound rituals); a comparative study of programming languages; control technology.

1.1.4 COMPUTER ASSISTED LEARNING

It was felt that the bad experiences with programmed instruction in the late 1960s and early 1970s had been an inhibiting factor in many countries, and it was strongly emphasised that computer assisted learning was different from programmed instruction in many vital respects. It was considered vital that teachers should adapt technology to education rather than education to technology, whilst schools may influence industry to produce adequate hardware, software and teaching materials, it would not be a good idea if hardware was produced exclusively for use in schools. Given the right conditions, educational consumers can be a powerful market influence and, because of the importance of this subject to a nation's economic development, can have a powerful political influence. It was again emphasised how important it was to keep the student experience gained from CAL realistic. It was also emphasised that CAL must work in real classrooms for real children and that theoretical models, which were operationally inadequate, financially unviable and technically unrealistic, should not progress beyond the design or pilot stage without radical modification in these respects.

The Design of CAL

It is considered essential to study who is in control of the CAL activity. It may be the learner (who in response to prompts puts in data and relates this data to other data already in the system, thus creating his own knowledge based system), it may be the teacher (who uses a particular simulation relating multiple causes and multiple effects and who then steers the children to consider particular perspectives of this model), or it may be the designer who builds a particular instructional strategy into a programme (eg drill and practice). There is no right or wrong model, but it is important to know why the locus of control rests with the person it rests with. Again flexibility was considered to be very important here. Under appropriate circumstances, allowing the teacher to change the model or adapt the system to his own particular needs was considered essential to the long term success of CAL. The "not invented here" syndrome was to be avoided. Teachers must learn to be open to innovations such as CAL, but their confidence must be won by involving them in design, development and evaluation, and again it was emphasised that the "top down" approach was rarely successful.

Consideration was given to who should write the computer programmes, and examples involving all possible combinations of pupils, teachers and professional programmers were given. The lesson was clear - choose the means most likely to meet your objectives.

Simulations

The use of the computer to provide simulations of real life situations has many advantages. Simulations are quicker, cheaper, safer and often socially more acceptable than traditional experiments. They also help modernise the curriculum and make it more relevant. Many examples were quoted by delegates of the successful use of simulations that achieve these objectives. It was emphasised that whilst simulations provide an obviously rich source of learning, other simpler techniques such as structured dialogue or drill and practice can produce relevant and appropriate learning environments. Again the message was clear - choose the most appropriate means to meet your objectives.

Information Retrieval

The use of information retrieval with a variety of data bases provides a powerful learning tool. It requires a great deal of logical thinking without requiring any programming knowledge and, because the data bases can span a wide range (eg from chemical data to historical census data), can be used in a wide range of educational contexts. Consideration was given to the different ranges of equipment considered for use in the CAL context. The utility of the pocket calculator was a controversial issue.

CAL and the Teacher

CAL may be used well or badly - it depends on the skill of the teacher. If the right use of the computer system is made, then CAL is an important weapon in the teacher's armoury. It is our task to see that proper use is made of CAL. There should be no fear of CAL because it requires teachers to be even more professional. They will no longer be the prime source of information in the classroom, but skilfully used CAL will support their work. In general CAL systems will give teachers more work to do, not less. They will help them develop new skills and new teaching styles and allow them to use processes which are parallel to those used in the outside world, thus enhancing their status.

1.1.5   TEACHER EDUCATION TRAINING

It is considered essential that all teachers should be given some introduction (20/40 hours) to computers and their possible use in education in their initial training. Teachers teaching Computer Science will need more thorough training, often up to degree level.

In-service Education and Training of Teachers (INSET)

It was considered possible to use the computer in all subjects, and teachers and systems' designers should be reminded that given a suitable environment (for example, an information retrieval system), teachers can prepare much of their own teaching material. Again it was emphasised that teachers should be involved in curriculum design, development, innovation and evaluation. This way they are unlikely to reject the outcomes. Using appropriate authoring systems, teachers can be taught to build their own programs, evaluate and disseminate them. Although the quality of such "home built" educational software can be variable, such software frequently embodies ideas and teaching strategies which are well worth spending time and money to formalise, professionalise and distribute more widely. To lay the foundation for good classroom practice and curriculum development, INSET should embrace the technical, methodological and pedagogical aspects of the use of computers in education.

General Training Issues

The training of all teachers will certainly not be cheap, although the long-term rewards of the initial investment in pre-service training are obvious. Good in-service education and training, in the experience of the UK, produces almost insatiable demands. There are, however, remarkable similarities between the in-service training issues in many countries. Broadly speaking, at any one time, 10% of teachers are in training and 90% are in post, but the INSET efforts should consider the age pyramid of the teachers in post. In most countries the current situation is that few teachers can be recruited, and few will retire because most teachers are relatively young. It was emphasised that INSET should be based upon inculcation rather than indoctrination: "Convince the man against his will - he'll be of the same opinion still".

INSET Models

School based INSET is very helpful because it is difficult to avoid and therefore involves more teachers. The "Cascade" model is popular and cheap. A few trainers are trained centrally, and these act as regional or local trainers and train others. The model has been found to be attractive and effective. It ensures local involvement, local adaptation to local needs, yet permits and disseminates a central core of knowledge and practice. Of course, training models will have to be adapted to nationally established patterns and should build upon local strengths (such as well established educational broadcasting systems). It must be recognised that support materials and also support for teachers during innovation all make vital contributions to the quality of the change in classroom practice which results from in-service training. It was recognised that incentives need not be financial or material, but personal and professional development is an important factor in motivating teachers. Of course, INSET is inseparable from curriculum development. Again it was emphasised that a "top down" approach should be avoided.

1.1.6   RESEARCH AND EVALUATION

This was the main theme of the workshop. There is very little pure and academic research on computer related instruction. On the other hand, applied research is very common - it is also essential and involves and motivates teachers. One delegation emphasised the importance of pure research and a "top down" implementation strategy based on this. This view was not supported by those delegates with most practical experience in this field. As all computer related learning systems must work satisfactorily in the real world, operational and financial evaluation are necessary to ensure widespread acceptability. Overall, it was emphasised that it is important to look at children's needs. Teachers, research workers and evaluators have to adapt towards children's needs and to learn from children.

Evaluation: Classical Models of Education Evaluation with Presupposed Clearly Stated Objectives

Illuminative models relate to these objectives to practice out of the classroom and try to explain how and why something has happened rather than just measuring whether it has happened or not. It is considered important to look at the children in the classroom, to see whether you can actually see any change in their behaviour and performance. If the answer is "yes", then the system you are testing is good, and if you can't detect any change, then it is failing and could well be a candidate for being discarded. It was again reiterated that it was important to have teacher feedback from evaluation. While statistical techniques often do not provide very much real information to record, report and discuss the work involved with all the participants, researchers, teachers, parents, etc is a vital aspect of modern education evaluation, and will provide much information which will lead towards the success of projects.

1.1.7   FUTURE ACTIONS

There have been some spectacularly successful software and curriculum development projects. Information about these and other methodology should be widely disseminated. Exchanges of complete case studies should be promoted and may be found to be very valuable. Encouraging and supporting meetings among researchers, developers and teachers involved in aspects of computer related education can prove a valuable supplement to the exchange of documentation.

A curriculum development model might look as follows:

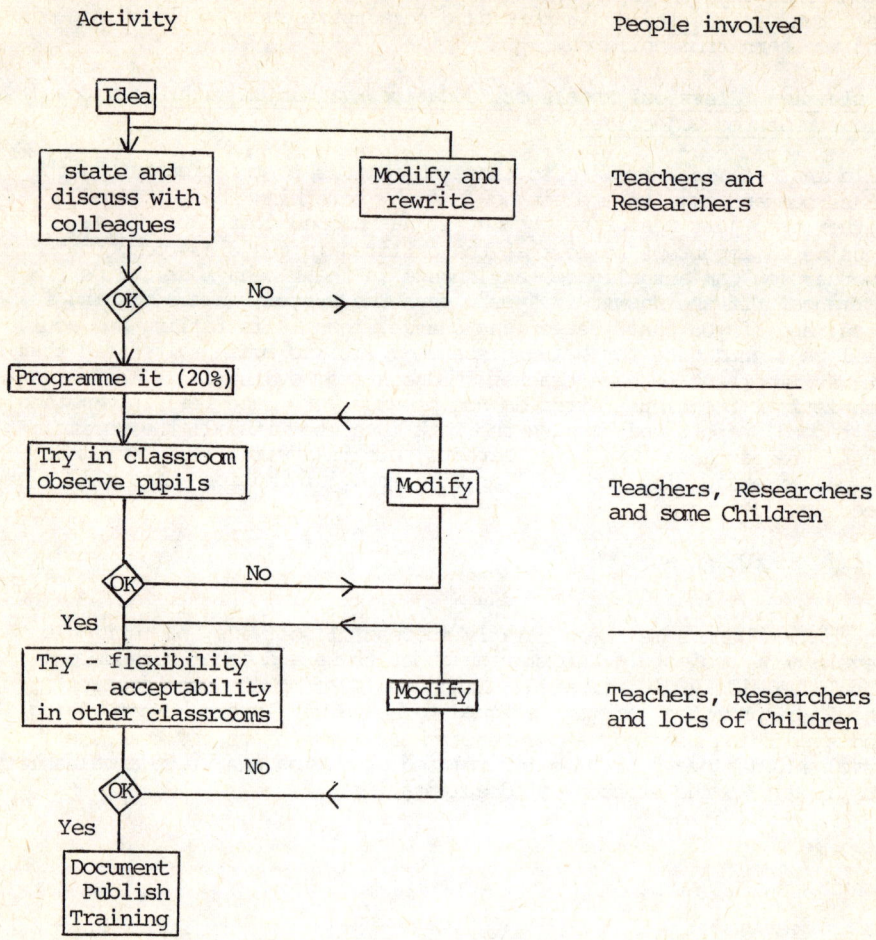

1.1.8   SUMMARY

There were some clearly consistent and widely (not necessarily universally) accepted statements which came out of the workshop. These were:

a. Those not yet involved in computer related education should be encouraged to take a big leap forward.

b. There is no need to re-invent the wheel. Developments from elsewhere can be adopted and adapted to local circumstances.

c. Teachers should be involved in research, evaluation and design of materials.

d. A "top down" approach is not the best one to adopt.

e. Ecclectic evaluation can prove more successful than classical and statistical models.

f. There is a classroom hierarchy which places the needs of children above those of teachers, and both above those of researchers when it comes to learning in the classroom.

The contents of this report reflect not only the plenary discussions on the various topics, but also a more detailed work done in the three groups, the reports of which are reproduced separately. These group reports complement this report on the plenary sessions, and contain many valuable statements. Some scepticism was expressed that the picture represented by this report may present too optimistic a view of the world to those countries who have not already embarked on work in this field at a significant level. Some participants did not accept the idea of computer literacy, and others drew attention to the fact that the factors which had inhibited the spread of audio-visual aids in the classroom in the 1960s and 1970s may also inhibit the spread of computer related learning in the 1980s. This argument was countered by the suggestion that we should have learnt from difficulties in the past, and therefore be more effective as disseminators of new technologies in our schools.

1.2 REPORTS OF THE WORKING GROUPS

by

their Chairmen

1.2.1   THE REPORT OF WORKING GROUP A   Chairman: Mr. P Muller
                                            Rapporteur: Mr. A Bron

Computer studies (informatique) comprise three notions:

- subject matter (discipline)
- instrument
- culture

a.   An introduction to computer studies is essential for all pupils in compulsory education. Two approaches might supplement each other: on the one hand proper computer courses (eg the 24 Hours Minimum Programme presented by Switzerland) and on the other didactical applications of the computer in the various other subjects.

b.   As regards vocational education, it is obvious that there will have to be proper training for the various careers in addition to a general introduction. This type of training must be distinguished from offering computer science as an optional subject which would have to be offered in general education. The aim of this option would not be to train computer specialists but to deepen the basic knowledge of those pupils who take a particular interest in the subject of computers; it would be an option parallel to subjects such as Latin, modern languages, etc.

c.   The use of computers as a tool in the teaching of other subjects must not be restricted to computer assisted learning but should mean genuine computer applications supporting teaching and learning. The use of the computer as a tool implies the integration of the computer as a helpful device as well as the use of different types of software (eg simulations, calculation aids, etc). The computer should also be a help to the teacher (eg text processing, access to data banks, etc).

d.   Pocket calculators should not be used before the children have acquired the basic skills of calculation. In no case would pocket calculators render genuine computer studies superfluous.

The didactical use of computers in the various disciplines implies research on the subject concerned, training teachers in the new methodologies, and the existence of quality software, accompanied by good documentation. Such software should be flexible as regards its use and transportable so that it may be distributed easily. Thus teachers can continue to be masters of their own teaching. Interdisciplinary work becomes easier as a result of computer based learning.

e. Any newly recruited teacher should have had a minimum of computer education, covering three aspects: the technical, the methodological, and the educational (pedagogical) aspect. Those teachers who want to teach computer science must necessarily have a more in-depth education in computer science in addition to education in their chosen subject matter.

In-service education and training should be promoted and developed, using computer based learning when appropriate so as to make the computer's possible uses more widely known. If in-service education and training is to be fully successful, the teachers must be given the necessary support, (eg material and educational leave during term).

f. In all fields concerned research should be encouraged and developed in co-operation with the teachers in the classroom. The results of research should be made known as widely as possible. Perhaps the Council of Europe could help here. Any experiments should be properly evaluated (see 1.5).

1.2.2   THE REPORT OF WORKING GROUP B   Chairman: Mr. J Johansen
                                         Rapporteur: Mr. L Sack

a. General introduction to computers is a must for every citizen. Nationally sponsored programmes are recommended. Everybody should be able to extract information from computers and to run programs. The impact of computers on society should also be included.

The analysis of problems and synthesis of solutions, a new topic in secondary education, should also be included. Educators should fight computer illiteracy. The scheme of evaluation put forward by Mr. Broderick (see 1.5) was supported. Case studies are considered more important than formal evaluation. Evaluation should be an integral part of projects, and the responsibility of the teacher(s).

b. Computer studies should be offered as an option to all students in secondary education. There is no evidence that computer studies as an optional subject was combined with more technical subjects.

c. The computer has changed working life and the applications of many subjects outside the school, so it must lead to a change in syllabus.

The concept of Computer Assisted Learning (CAL) has changed tremendously during the last 15 years. The teacher is now seen as an integral part and the cost has gone down. It is recommended that new approach to CAL must go far beyond the electronic page-turning. For example, the student should be putting questions to the computer - not always vice versa.

In simulations the ideology behind the different models should be clearly expressed. Simulations should not replace practice in classroom but should extend it (eg Millikens experiment).

d. Teacher training should be appropriate to the teacher's needs in the classroom. Software and curriculum material should be developed. A teacher with a degree in computer science would be an asset in every school. Only through teacher training can one remove the fear of the computer that many teachers feel. Although there are wide national differences the overall view is that there is a lot of teacher training taking place. Good students may become good programmers and by working in collaboration with the teacher may lead to the production of good software (eg Five Ways project in the UK).

1.2.3   THE REPORT OF WORKING GROUP C   Chairman: Mr. R Fothergill
Rapporteur: Mr. C O'Caoimh

a. Computer studies

Tomorrow's world will demand of its population the ability to think, to communicate and to adapt.

In general education a minimum level computer studies must hence be available to all secondary pupils; to each according to ability. Pupils must know

i. how to store information, how to retrieve it and how to structure it in order to deal with problem solving. This, perhaps, leads to a redefinition of what is meant by knowledge.

ii. how to explore a number of applications of microelectronics in business and industry. As a consequence they will have some ideas of the implications for society and for their careers and be able to cope with the emotional problems that may arise.

The aim of the above is to ensure that all children can live successfully in our future society.

The use of the computer in an integrated mode may need to await the replacement of a subject oriented curriculum by equivalent topics.

Since it may take some considerable time to give all teachers a satisfactory competence in computers, a compulsory stand alone subject called computer studies is necessary now until the integrated approach is feasible.

b. **Computer science**

A detailed study of computer science should be available as an option to all pupils of both sexes at some stage in their schooling. This will depend on different national approaches to the curriculum.

This subject should include information technology and maybe information theory, telecommunications, automation, electronics, programming, simulations, principles of computer operations, practical applications and the influence on society.

A good syllabus is a listing of fundamental ideas, only, so that it is flexible, open to change and up to date. To support this approach teachers will need a constant supply of materials describing relevant modern activities and developments.

Computer studies must of necessity influence the discarding of outmoded topics in vocational schools.

c. **Using the computer in other subjects**

There was general support for the use of the computer as an aid to learning all subjects.

There are at least two types of material:

i. that for demonstration purposes

ii. that for interactive use by the pupil.

However many other systems of categorisation are possible.

Not only is it difficult to produce good material, it is also very expensive. Teachers must be closely involved in the development, and the programs should be flexible and capable of amendment to match particular uses.

Particularly valuable areas which were highlighted included remedial work, word processing and the use of databases to introduce new conceptual approaches. There should also be more programs in which the models are created and amended by students, rather than just responding to altered parameters.

Materials should follow closely the theories of learning so as to avoid the situation in which the pupil can answer questions but learn little. Group work by children should also be fostered.

Children can benefit from programs from a young age, for example from making use of databases, but the use of the computer as a teaching aid could benefit from further research at all levels of use.

d. Teacher training

There are two levels of training required, one for those who will be responsible for teaching computer science, the other for all teachers of every subject.

For those teaching computer science, full training is necessary but timing and strategy will depend on the systems of different countries, and has to take account of union regulations.

All teachers must experience the general education knowledge of computer studies that is given to all pupils (see Aspect 1). They should also have sufficient competence to amend programs in simple ways (change "data" for example), but not necessarily be expected to write their own programs. They should, however, be able to explain their needs to people who can write programs.

Studies should build on pedagogic theory, enabling them to be able to choose whether the computer is useful to them. Their role in the classroom and in society may be altered and they should appreciate how and what this means. As an activity, a computer centre may affect the general culture of the school also. Teachers also need to learn how to evaluate software.

e. Evaluation

There was agreement that Mr. Broderick's analysis (see 1.5) was a useful one among several available strategies. Evaluation of programs, in-service training courses and even the total school environment was essential and necessary. The results should be used to improve the activities and materials.

Too much and too lengthy evaluation could be counter-productive and destroy the value of the original experiment. In this field, descriptive or illuminative evaluation was especially valuable, and the absence of quantitative results should not invalidate it. Indeed, the opposite, for the effects of this work may well benefit from the absence of quantitative techniques.

1.3 THE AUSTRIAN EXPERIENCE WITH MICROELECTRONICS AND PROGRAMMING IN SCHOOLS

by

Dr. Helmut AIGNER
Federal Ministry of
Education and Culture, Vienna

1.3.1   SYSTEM PARAMETERS

1.   Structure of the school system

Austrian post-compulsory education comprises

- general schools (four years' study providing university access) and
- technical and vocational schools.

Technical and vocational schools are grouped into industrial, commercial, agricultural, tourist-trade and domestic-science schools with a large number of further subdivisions (specialisations). They are also divided by level into:

- technical schools (five years' study providing university access, training to engineering-technician or middle-management level);
- full-time vocational schools (three to four years' study, supplementing training to skilled-worker level);
- part-time vocational schools (typically three years' study, supplementing training to skilled-worker level).

The system is characterised by:

- a high degree of centralisation: there are nationwide curricula, which are also binding on private schools;
- lockstep learning: pupils in a class stay together for instruction in virtually all subjects, the main exception being split classes for practical work;
- a fairly large number (12 to 20) of subjects studied in a given year, with correspondingly little teaching time assigned to each (the number of weekly fifty-minute periods in compulsory subjects is 34 in the general schools, 32 to 41 in technical and full-time vocational schools and nine in part-time vocational schools).

2. Current curricular provisions for microelectronics and programming.

A separate subject termed "data processing" or "electronic data processing" exists in the following schools:

- as an optional subject with or without assessment of student achievement in some general schools (three or four years respectively at two periods per week);

- as an elective subject in certain general schools (2 x 2 or 1 x 4 periods per week);

- as a compulsory subject in all schools of technical level in commercial and industrial fields (1 x 4 and 1 x 2 periods per week respectively, 2 x 2 periods in production engineering and in electronics);

- as an optional subject in all commercial full-time vocational schools (1 x 3 periods per week);

- as an optional subject in all (except girls') schools of technical level in agriculture and forestry (1 x 3 periods per week), two schools have yet to implement this course.

Some knowledge and skills in microelectronics and programming are integrated into traditional subjects as follows:

- mathematics in scientifically oriented curricula of general schools, as well as in domestic-science and tourist-trade schools of technical level;

- physics and chemistry in all schools where these subjects are taught;

- accounting in commercial schools of technical and full-time vocational level;

- a course comprising shorthand, typing and word processing in the same schools (a total of ten class periods being assigned to word processing);

- economics in the part-time vocational schools;

- subjects dealing with measurement, communication and control in industrial schools of all levels.

Curricula with major accent on data processing are rare:

- a school of data processing at technical level, opened in September 1982, stresses commercial rather than industrial applications and aims at skills in the software field as well as in organisation;

- four schools offer courses on microcomputer technology (both hardware and software) to graduates of technical schools of electrical engineering and electronics (two one-semester units);

- two commercial schools at full-time vocational level feature a certain slant towards data processing;

- two schools offer software skills to persons over 17 who have passed an aptitude test;

- one school, opened in September 1982, offers a two-year course (three years in evening classes) to graduates of general schools, aiming at the same qualification as the five-year technical curriculum.

There is virtually no instance of computer-assisted instruction outside the previously listed subjects. Some schools do, however, use their computers not only for instruction but also for administrative purposes, with one centre in Vienna running a nationwide system concerned with free textbooks for pupils and with student grants.

3. Teachers.

Teachers at Austrian post-compulsory school fall into the following three categories:

- teachers of general subjects, who have taken a master's degree in one or two of these subjects together with education;

- teachers of technical subjects, who have taken an appropriate master's degree, followed by several years' practice in business or industry;

- teachers of vocational subjects, who have qualifications at engineering technician or master craftsman level, followed by several years' practice.

None of these categories would admit a university graduate in "informatics" without additional qualifications.

Most teachers currently in the system have not taken courses in microelectronics at the university (first and second categories) or vocational teachers' academy. A large proportion of those teaching in the field are self-taught. In many instances their qualifications come from jobs previously held or from the part-time jobs which they are encouraged to hold during their teaching careers.

Further teacher training in Austria is compulsory in principle but optional with regard to a given course. It is organised by the Federal Ministry of Education for teachers at general schools, and by a further-training institute in each of the nine provinces for teachers at technical and vocational schools (the latter model is expected to be extended to the general schools). In the field of microelectronics and data processing, the following four types of courses are offered (not all of them for every type of school):

a. introductory courses for interested teachers of all subjects;

b. users' courses for teachers of subjects where software packages are commonly used (accounting, word processing);

c. training courses for teachers of data processing and for teachers of subjects dealing with measurement, communication and control;

d. updating courses for the teachers of group (c).

4. The mechanism of curricular change.

Major curricular changes - down to a change in the canon of general subjects in any type of school - require a two-thirds majority in parliament. Changes in the content of a subject can be decreed by the Minister of Education after submitting the draft for comment to the nine provincial school boards (by law) and to a considerable number of interest groups (by custom). Pilot projects are possible at any time, but in strictly limited numbers.

The stimulus for changes in curricula may come from teachers, heads of schools, inspectors, ministry staff, and/or from employers' and employees' organisations. The same groups contribute to the formulation of the new curricula, with the two basic issues of relevance and attainability decided on the basis of experience and common sense rather than research. The universities are only involved in the case of subjects prerequisite for university admission. Pupils are not involved except through informal feedback.

1.3.2 THE CONTRIBUTION OF MICROELECTRONICS AND DATA PROCESSING TO GENERAL EDUCATION

1. The pocket calculator.

Austrian schoolchildren must not use a pocket calculator before grade 7, although many of them do so illegally. It is argued that thorough skills in unaided arithmetic should be acquired before computational aids are used. A minority view tends to compare these skills to the ability of telling time by the sun, the stars and the flora before timepieces came into common use. The introduction of the pocket calculator in grade 7 is justified by the Pythagorean theorem and computations involving π, where the time saved through the calculator is considerable.

While teachers at lower secondary level still have the nominal option of introducing the slide-rule, use of the pocket calculator is universal. The type chosen will generally have keys for square root, reciprocal and π, but many pupils will buy more advanced models to save buying another calculator later, or merely for fun or even for status. Calculators with an algebraic operating system are preferred over those featuring reverse Polish notation because they are both cheaper and more natural to operate. This type of calculator will frequently accompany a pupil through his years at a vocational school.

A more advanced calculator is required in the upper secondary general school; it will typically feature circular and hyperbolic, exponential and logarithmic functions, as well as some memory storage; in some cases, statistical functions are also included.

2. The role of mathematics, physics and chemistry.

In the general school, mathematics and the sciences are expected to be supported by, rather than contribute to an understanding of, the new technologies. The pocket calculator has taken the drudgery out of the mathematics lesson, permitting more time to be devoted to models of problem-solving and the like; knowledge of the physical and chemical basis of semi-conductor technology contributes to an overall understanding of the structure of the physical world. Even so, the computer age has put its stamp on school mathematics: the disappearance of the concept of the two-valued or multi-valued function is at least partly due to the way in which functions can be implemented in a computer. While Boolean algebra has been placed on the curriculum of science-oriented general schools mainly for theoretical reasons, the addition of statistics and probability with their useful applications has only become possible since computations need no longer be performed by hand.

3. Electronic data processing in the general school.

General schools will offer instruction in electronic data processing if there is a qualified and interested teacher and if there is sufficient pupil interest. The avowed aim is the ability to enter into intelligent dialogue with data-processing staff.

The syllabus (created in 1976) provides for the learning of an assembly-language and a higher level language, treatment of both numerical and non-numerical problems, and some knowledge of hardware and its operation. The assembly language is currently used as a means to keep the number of pupils' programmes down to a level that can be handled by the small number of micro-computers currently installed. The assembly language is expected to be dropped as more micro-computers are purchased.

In the past, the subject was occasionally taught without access to any machine, and ALGOL was the preferred language in these instances. At present, BASIC seems to be vastly preferred, but newly acquired micro-computers must also be able to handle either FORTRAN or PASCAL.

A pilot project of "enhanced mathematics" (extra teaching time for data processing integrated into mathematics) was abandoned because it tended to widen rather than narrow the gulf between the best pupils and the under-achievers.

4. Computer-assisted instruction.

The notion of computer-assisted instruction has never had many advocates in Austria because of

- the expense involved;

- the bottleneck of software production and the high costs involved;

- a general conviction that teachers are paid for teaching rather than for letting machines do the work.

Therefore no schemes of programmed instruction have been implemented, even though there was a stillborn attempt at an industrial school of technical level, where the self-produced hardware did not prove sturdy enough nor the self-produced software sufficient in either quality or quantity.

This does not, of course, preclude the use of micro-processors, micro-computers and software packages in subject areas where they are also used in practice: laboratory equipment, machine-tools, television sets, typewriters, accounting machines, word processors.

1.3.3 MICRO-ELECTRONICS AND PROGRAMMING FOR VOCATIONAL PURPOSES

1. The following types of requirements must be met by various technical and vocational curricula:

- ability to write, debug and run simple technical programmes and to use relevant software packages (all industrial and some agricultural schools at technical level, vocational schools of electronics);

- ability to write, debug and run simple commercial programmes and to use relevant software packages (commercial, agricultural, domestic-science and tourist-trade schools at technical and full-time vocational levels);

- ability to use commercial software packages (part-time vocational schools for commercial trades and for crafts, the latter because they are characterised by very small enterprises);

- ability to work with numerically controlled machine-tools (schools of mechanical engineering at all levels);

- ability to assemble microprocessors (schools of electrical and electronic engineering at all levels);

- ability to write simple programmes in statistics and operations research (technical schools of production engineering);

- skill in organising the solution of commercial problems, particularly with the help of data processing (all technical schools except in the industrial sector).

The above aims have been arrived at by the processes outlined in section 1.3.1-4.

2. Equipment.

In most cases, the pocket calculators brought to the technical or vocational school by pupils are not sufficient for the solution of more advanced problems. While at the domestic-science and tourist-trade schools the calculator is banned during the first year in order to permit remedial arithmetic, a calculator of the advanced type described in section 1.3.2-1 is purchased in many schools. Programmable calculators are expected to become the rule in the near future in the industrial technical schools if prices continue to fall. In the commercial schools calculators featuring at least 10 digits, memory storage, fixed-point mode and fast keyboards are required, supplemented after the first year, which has no mathematics, by a mathematical calculator of the advanced type described.

Data processing instruction started in the technical schools in the mid-sixties, and the schools used what machines they could get. Mainframes (even of the first generation), minis, time-sharing systems and bought (or begged) computer time were used, and some of them are still in use. In recent years, however, all schools have been equipped with micro-computers at rates between 2 and 12 per school, with groups of 3 to 6 sharing a common printer. Exact numbers depend on the size of the school and on the importance of data processing for its curricula. Most industrial schools will continue to use minis.

3. Software.

An assembler language is only taught at some commercial technical schools; elsewhere one higher-level language (exceptionally two) is the rule. While in the past the available hardware sometimes necessitated the use of a less common language (eg FOCAL), the advent of the micro-computer has tended to favour BASIC, mainly because the programmer need not bother with details that are marginal to the problem. FORTRAN 77 and PASCAL are runners-up for technical applications, whilst COBOL is similarly placed in the commercial sector.

Some programmes are, of course, developed by the pupils, but most schools or individual teachers also have libraries of teacher-developed programmes that are used for demonstration purposes and as models for the production of variants by pupils, saving time over the writing of lengthy programmes by pupils. Teacher-produced software, not unexpectedly, has its problems. At any moment, programmes for roughly the same purpose are being developed by dozens of teachers all over Austria; but attempts at programme exchange have so far failed, partly because of hardware differences and partly for lack of agreement on just what the programme should be able to do (but this is not unheard of in industry, either).

4. Evaluation.

Are the aims of micro-electronics and programming instruction in Austrian technical and vocational education as outlined in section 3.1 sufficient, and are they being attained? The answers, which Austrians expect to come from employers rather than from researchers (see section 1.3.1-4), seem to be a qualified "no" to the first question and an emphatic "yes" to the second. In other words, business and industry need more and better qualified micro-electronics and data processing experts than the school (and university) system can currently produce. Of course in many jobs data processing, while not negligible, plays a fairly marginal role, and holders of these jobs (say, building technologists, junior executives, farmers) seem to be getting by and large what they need. The real difficulty lies with the microelectronics and data processing specialists, who are, according to a consensus of manpower experts, unlikely to be trainable below university level. The pool of potential specialists in this field seems to be strictly limited by talent, so that the current software bottleneck in data processing, which is ultimately a liveware bottleneck, may be here to stay.

In recognition of this limitation, the school authorities have tried to keep the number of schools entirely devoted to data processing quite low. A five-year technical school of pulse technology and data processing had to be discontinued because the concepts involved proved to be too difficult at the secondary level, and the special courses arranged for graduates of technical schools (see latter part of section 1.3.1-2) are characterised by extremely high drop-out rates. The success of the two recently opened schools (actually different curricula offered by the same school) is yet to be evaluated.

One field where the current teaching time assigned to data processing seems to be insufficient is at the industrial technical schools. Curricular changes in technical and vocational education being fairly frequent (in step with technical progress), the continuation of the two class periods per week currently provided at these schools into a second year, either on a compulsory or on an optional basis, is already in the planning stage. When implemented, the new curriculum is expected to stress algorithms during the first year and engineering applications and possibly a second language, during the second.

In the long run, the labour market will probably need more people who know a lot about computers (and it is doubtful whether the school will ever be able completely to fill this need) but possibly fewer people who know only a little. If this should turn out to be true, the computer may well join the motor car as a gadget that is taught to some specialists but not to all boys and girls.

1.3.4 TEACHERS

1. Computer science v. informatics.

The question of who should teach computer-related subjects is tightly bound up with the philosophy held concerning the nature of these subjects. While in countries where Romance languages are spoken the concept of *informatics* as a way of thinking takes pride of place, the English term *computer science*, even by referring to an actual machine, tends to be more applications-oriented. In Austria both schools of thought have had their vociferous advocates, with informatics mainly winning out in the universities and computer science elsewhere.

Clearly, an applications-oriented approach is *de rigueur* in technical and vocational education if it wants to find jobs for its graduates. This is why teachers of programming must, in addition to programming, also know enough about one of the major subjects of the school concerned to be able to solve its typical problems, even manually without a computer. Lack of this qualification has so far been the major obstacle to professional success of informatics graduates, not only as teachers but also in business and industry. A comparable impediment might be thought to apply to mathematics graduates, but most of them tend to acquire considerable knowledge of technology while at the industrial school (less so in the case of business knowledge at the commercial schools).

In fact, the teachers of data processing at Austrian schools all teach other subjects as well, viz,

- at general schools: mathematics;

- at industrial schools: mathematics (2/3), engineering (1/3);

- at commercial schools: business subjects (95%), mathematics (5%);

- at domestic science and tourist-trade schools, where data processing is or will be integrated into mathematics: mathematics (mainly), commercial subjects (including tourism);

- at agricultural schools: mathematics (mainly), agricultural subjects, guest teachers (from commercial schools);

- at part-time schools, where data processing will be integrated into theoretical technical subjects: vocational subjects.

2. Recruitment.

In general, tenured teachers may not be motivated to undertake teaching a new subject requiring a good deal of retraining and intensive work. Besides the intrinsic motivation that is unusually high for data processing "addicts" (they exist among the pupils as well as among the teachers), teachers are attracted into the new subject by offers of paid overtime and by the legal provision by which data processing classes are split. As the legal limit of class size is 36 and actual numbers closer to 25 by the time data processing is taught, there is typically one teacher per dozen pupils. Not infrequently the class is only divided as needed, and there are two teachers presenting the theory together to the whole class.

3. Further training.

The typical further training course lasts one week (see end of section 1.3.1-3). The courses for teachers in general education combine the functions (a) and (c), offering group work according to levels of previous knowledge; they are held during the summer holidays. Courses in technical and vocational education are of all four types; they are held during the school year, with teachers given paid leave from their schools and paid a per-diem allowance. They take place at schools, at further-training institutes or on the premises of computer companies.

Further training courses for agricultural teachers also cater to their dual role as advisers to the farming community. Functions (a) and (b) tend to be combined in these courses.

1.3.5   NOTE

This paper is based on

- the published syllabuses of Austrian schools (*Bundesgesetzblatt* = Federal Gazette);

- interviews with the heads of departments in the Federal Ministry of Education and Arts in charge of the various types of schools;

- experience gained and discussions held in the course of a curriculum development programme;

- experience as a teacher and textbook author in the field of data processing.

1.4 TEACHING COMPUTER SCIENCE IN THE SECONDARY SCHOOL

A Survey of Research and Evaluation
in the Federal Republic of Germany

by

Dr. Ulrich BOSLER
Institute for Science Education, Kiel

1.4.1   SUMMARY

The article deals with the effects various promotional measures such as EDP programme II and Modellversuche have in the Federal Republic of Germany.

Section 2 describes in detail the content of computer science at general and vocational schools. Most activities at general schools take place on the secondary level II where most of the Bundesländer have introduced an optional course "computer science". There are greater difficulties at vocational schools because of the laborious development of nationwide outline curricula for data processing.

The availability of hardware, the suitability of programming languages, the current standing of teaching materials, journals suited for school use and teacher training are discussed.

The third section concerns changes due to the advancement of microcomputers. The curriculum conference on microcomputers, the Zeitungskolleg and some samples of instruction are described in brief.

The article closes with the addresses of important institutions of education in the Federal Republic of Germany.

1.4.2   SURVEY

The term "computer science" has been used in the title of this paper. In Germany people also often speak of "informatics". For the schools this usually means an algorithm- or application orientated approach. The concepts of microelectronics and microcomputers will be used very carefully here, particularly in connection with the control and regulation of operations.

1. Conditions relating to school

The educational system in the Federal Republic of Germany primarily still characterised by its three branches "Hauptschule", "Realschule" and "Gymnasium", with comprehensive reforms applied up to now to upper secondary education at the Gymnasium. There a system of courses has been introduced which provides for various optional subjects. Experiments involving Gesamtschulen (comprehensive schools) are only very moderately supported, and the reform of the vocational school system is still forthcoming.

A federally structured school system might facilitate a variety of different individual experiments. This possibility is only partly made use of.

Reforms are sometimes hampered by the federal system with its inherent problems of responsibility at various levels. The federal government has only indirect influence, through such activities as research grants for example. The autonomy of individual schools is markedly restricted by way of guidelines issued by the respective Länder, and is so far not comparable with that of American or English schools. Only upper secondary education has enough flexibility to introduce new subjects.

The traditional subjects offered within the German school system are not very flexible. It seems easier today to introduce an entirely new subject, such as computer science into the secondary school rather than to integrate vital EDP (electronic data processing) components into other subjects.

2. EDP promotion

Apart from some regional support, national research support took the form of two substantial EDP programmes: EDP I from 1967 to 1970, and EDP II from 1971 to 1975. One objective of the EDP I programme was, among others, to build up informatics at the university. The EDP II programme mainly supported the application of EDP. One of the areas of EDP usage was the field of computers in education (1).

So far, the major consequences I see from the EDP II programme are:

a. A market for a national EDP industry needs to be created.

b. Only research was financed by the Federal Ministry of Technology, not the dissemination into schools.

c. Computers in education were introduced from the top via CAI (computer-assisted instruction) and administration (plans in 1971 provided for two-thirds CAI and one-third administration; informatics at school was not systematically supported).

d. The CAI efforts stagnated and informatics was not sufficiently developed between 1971 and 1975.

Expectations with regard to CAI had been much too high with the result that supporters were greatly disappointed when the expected success failed to come. CAI using large computers was too expensive and the dissemination into the schools was missing. Now that the EDP II programme has come to an end there are no longer any federally promoted CAI programmes worth mentioning.

3. Pilot experiments (Modellversuche)

As regards the development of a new school subject "computer science" pilot experiments funded by the federal government and usually one Land played an important part. For example: the objective of one pilot experiment had been the development of teaching materials for a three-year course of computer science at upper secondary education in Schleswig-Holstein. This material was prepared at one school and tested in four others. Guidance was provided by the IPN in its capacity as institute for science education. Important results of the pilot experiment even went beyond the original objectives: hardware was procured; there was close co-operation among the teachers themselves as well as among teachers and persons acting as scientific advisers. Intensive training of the participating teachers resulted from the preparation of their own teaching materials. Infrastructure was developed in one region of the Federal Republic of Germany.

Examples are the development of a curriculum for computer science in Rhineland-Palatinate (25), the development of teaching materials in North Rhine-Westphalia (8), for the 9th and 10th grades in Berlin (7) and a supraregional pilot experiment co-ordinated by the IPN in which programming languages were tested and teaching materials prepared (13).

In the past pilot experiments have been the most important - but also the most expensive - instrument for institutionalisation and recognition of computer science teaching. Due to financial constraints and greater reference of the Länder to their educational autonomy there will hardly be any more pilot experiments in the coming years.

4. Individual work

With the increasing availability of microcomputers, the use of computers supported by individual communities is rising. The number of these projects is difficult to estimate and the quality of efforts varies greatly.

1.4.3 TEACHING COMPUTER SCIENCE AT SCHOOL

According to a rough estimate about 30-40 per cent of schools (not of students!) in general education (especially in general upper secondary education) are equipped with computers of some kind or have access to a large computer.

1. Curricula contents in general education

As early as 1969 initiatives were started in Bavaria to integrate computer science elements into general schools.

Since then, computer science is taught in all Länder including Berlin, as part of mathematics education and as a subject of its own at the Upper Level of Gymnasium (upper secondary education). Most Länder have introduced computer science as an optional course in its own right which often emphasises applications related to other subjects such as mathematics, physics and biology.

a. Primary education

There are no known efforts with respect to computer science education at primary school.

b. Lower secondary education

In lower secondary education computer science is usually offered in connection with other subjects (eg pre-vocational training, technology). In Berlin computer science can, on request, be taught mainly as a subject of its own at comprehensive schools within the range of optional courses (2), (3).

There are considerable efforts in Bavaria - promoted by the Zentralstelle für programmierten Unterricht und Computer im Unterricht (Centre for Programmed Instruction and Computers in Education) - to introduce EDP contents into lower secondary education.

c. Upper secondary education

A course system has been introduced providing for the choice of various subjects. Only upper secondary education with computer science as an optional subject provides enough flexibility to introduce new subjects.

Since computer science is a newly emerging field, curricula in the different Länder vary a lot as regards the topics, their sequence and the time allotted. From the point of view of content the available curricula and draft curricula can be assigned mainly to three approaches to curriculum (cf (4)):

- hardware oriented;

- algorithm-oriented;

- application oriented.

The hardware-oriented approach is based on the hardware development of the fifties and sixties and has influenced particularly the first curricula for computer science. Here it is considered to be mainly a technical discipline; conveying the mathematical/technical foundations of data processing is the main objective.

Within a short space of time computer science went beyond the more technical dimension and developed into a structural science. With the algorithm-oriented approach "there resulted a fundamental change of the objectives and contents of education in computer science: the systematic search for algorithmic solutions to problems and the formulation of algorithmic solutions to problems as programmes were to be learned (cf. (5))". The structured solution to problems is what matters. The computer is just given the role of an instrument. Its structure and manner of functioning are dealt with only to the extent that this is absolutely necessary. The mathematical/technical foundations are of less importance. Problem solving is developed "top down" (cf. (6)) according to step by step refinement (see (4)).

The application-oriented approach derives from the development of curriculum reform, whereby "it was declared that the traditional concept of teaching, structured around separate subjects was no longer compatible with the educating and training function of the general school. The objective of conceiving education as the tool for mastering real life situations resulted in a demand for situation-oriented curriculum development as was formulated eg by (23)" (see (4), p 43).

"Learning the method of problem solving in the course of computer science education must take place within the context of the application of data processing in administration, industry and research, ie within the context of the applications which appeal to the students as a result of his being actually affected" (see (4), p 43).

The older hardware-oriented syllabuses have often been supplemented with respect to their content via the addition of algorithm- or application-oriented approaches.

Hardware-oriented curricula can be found up to the year 1975. Recommendations of the Society for Computer Science which became known early in 1974 in preliminary form (5) had significant effect on the subsequent plans which were initially algorithm-oriented.

Application-oriented components can be found in more recent curricula of the Länder of Berlin (7), North Rhine-Westphalia (pilot experiment Gelsenkirchen) (8), Schleswig-Holstein (pilot experiment (10)).

The curricula allot 60 or 120 hours, often 160-200 hours to computer science in some of the Länder. Details may be found in the survey of computer science curricula (11).

2. Contents in vocational education

The vocational sector is highly diversified as regards types of schools and specialisations offered. There are two types of educational provision:

Full-time vocational schools under the exclusive educational responsibility of the Ministers of Education and

the dual part-time system where the responsibility of Ministries of Education is limited to the vocational aspect.

a. Full-time vocational school

EDP-related topics are found particularly at business schools. The treatment and introduction of EDP topics in instruction at such schools is partly analogous to the developments described in Section 1.4.3-1 (c) pertaining to computer science at general schools. The revision of the curricula with regard to algorithm or application-oriented approaches, however, lags considerably behind general education. Details may be found under (11).

b. Basic vocational training

The firm in co-operation with the vocational school is responsible for passing on abilities and knowledge defined in the regulations for vocational training. Besides a dualism of learning places ("school" and "firm"), this implies a dual training responsibility.

In order to co-ordinate these two sectors the Conference of Ministers of Education is preparing a nationwide framework curriculum (eg (2)). This is difficult and takes time. Since such a syllabus often does not provide enough flexibility, outdated knowledge is often declared as being relevant for instruction later on. There are more than 20 framework curricula affecting about 15% of the 1.4 million trainees. With 80% the greater part of the co-ordinated framework curricula.

Details may be found under (11).

The time allotted for data processing instruction is often insufficient. Often only 30 hours are foreseen for data processing at vocational schools.

In contrast to general schools, a hardware-oriented approach is more often the case than an application-oriented one. This is particularly due to the difficulties and the time involved in developing framework curricula.

Details may be found under (11).

3. Programming languages

A lively discussion has been going on about an appropriate teaching and learning language, underscoring the fact that the language strongly influences the type of problem selected and its method of solution. This discussion could be settled by a large pilot experiment (13).

The choice of the language strongly depends on the time available. If you have less time, an extended - often commercially-oriented - BASIC is useful. If you have more time, languages like ELAN, LOGO and PASCAL are helpful.

The pilot experiment made it clear, how important it is for the student to establish good communication with the computer.

PASCAL is spreading in the Federal Republic of Germany. Denmark has had good experience with COMAL. In the Federal Republic of Germany there has been too little experience with it.

4. Teaching material, journals and teacher training

Gradually teaching materials have been made available through pilot experiments and some books suited for schools have been prepared (eg (14), (15)).

Teacher training is unsatisfactory. The classical forms of in-service training do not help since in-service training presupposes relevant basic education which is lacking.

So far some teacher training is offered at university level. There are possibilities for future teachers in Berlin and at the Open University of Hagen. The best training has resulted from the pilot experiments mentioned above.

Advanced training for teachers exists in the Länder on a limited scale. Individual and partly combined courses are usually offered. In some Länder (ie Berlin, Lower Saxony and Rhineland-Palatinate) a complete schedule of courses was established.

Some in-service training is taken care of by recently published journals. Since the beginning of 1981 the Oldenbourg Publishing Company issues a journal called LOG IN which is edited by the IPN, the Free University of Berlin and 5 other institutions. The journal BUS is geared mainly to Bavaria. The editor is the

Centre for Programmed Instruction and Computers in Education; it is published by the Bavarian Textbook Publishing Company. These journals can contribute greatly toward establishing computer science education in the Federal Republic of Germany by way of educational contributions and samples of instruction.

1.4.4   NEW OPPORTUNITIES FOR COMPUTER SCIENCE EDUCATION THROUGH THE USE OF MICROCOMPUTERS

Cheap microcomputers are being used increasingly at school. There are even pupils having their own microcomputer. Does this change the content structure of computer science education?

No and yes.

No: no new logical dimension is introduced via microelectronics if no concrete control and regulation problems are dealt with. Usually this equipment is used as the EDP computers were earlier. It is just that it is less expensive and smaller. Now the schools can afford these microcomputers.

Yes: EDP computers used to be found mainly in "aseptic" computing centres serviced by EDP specialists. Microcomputers, on the other hand, land on the table of the clerks. Their value for control and regulation operations is incalculable. Expansion of the application aspect and increased inclusion in instruction of topics such as control and regulation of operations, problems of text processing, communication, etc are necessary (cf. (17), p 239).

"The introduction of microelectronics does not, however, imply any essential change with respect to conveying hardware content in computer science education or the expansion of algorithm-oriented content. Instead, the links of microelectronics to different areas of application will have consequences for instruction so that the objective of the school, ie to raise mature students with a good comprehension of their world, is fulfilled. Computer science education must keep in mind the principles of microcomputers and the structures of its application potential within the framework of the overall use of data processing. In particular this means:

- expansion of an algorithm-oriented into an application-oriented approach to instruction;

- ample treatment of case studies and project-oriented instruction;

- expansion of case studies and projects to the control and regulation of operations;

- reservation of space in the curriculum (ca. 50%) for carrying out self-sufficient projects at secondary level II and for the possibility of the flexible orientation of instruction by the teacher.

The importance of microelectronics will probably change the priority given to computer science education at school with respect, firstly, to the increased recognition of computer sciences as a subject of its own and, secondly, as instruction principle in different subjects. Computer science education could acquire a similar significance to that of mathematics instruction: on the one hand, as a subject of its own and, on the other hand, as complementary subject to other subjects. If the effects of microelectronics are to be taken seriously, it is necessary to offer elements of computer science at lower secondary education.

The treatment of the applications of microelectronics, particularly the realisation of control and regulation operations, still raises several problems which hamper adequate work. Thus, there are no known programming languages appropriate for schools - languages which provide simple operation processing language elements. Limitation to a few interfaces for application at school is recommended.

It is conceivable that already existing languages suggested for school use can be extended to include the appropriate operation processing language elements which fulfill the requirements of school languages" (see (16)).

1. Fundamental publications

A comprehensive compilation of effects on job descriptions and qualifications can be found in the Battelle Study (18). The relationship between microelectronics, social change and education was discussed in detail at the Lüdenscheid Conference in January 1980 and described in (19).

2. Curriculum Conference: Field of microcomputers

Subsequent to the Lüdenscheid Conference, Professor Frey of the IPN raised the question of computer literacy, including microelectronics. The following question was the basis of the curriculum conference: how should general vocational education look for those in whose field of activity microcomputers play a role (eg bank clerk, auto mechanic, salesman at a supermarket, etc)?

The field of application of microcomputers and the differing evaluation of this application were to be consciously included in the curriculum conference.

It was not microcomputer specialists who were to develop the curriculum but 12 persons from different fields with extensive experience in education and some experience with microcomputers. EDP experts served as their advisers.

The model of the curriculum conference was meant to link the integration of knowledge about microcomputers to the training aspirations of those who were confronted with microcomputers at their jobs.

The course of events and findings are documented in (20).

3. <u>Zeitungskolleg (The Newspaper Courses)</u>

The most important source of information for laymen about the use of computers are articles and contributions in daily newspapers and journals. This fact was made use of by the Zeitungskolleg. From March to June 1980 it printed 12 newspaper articles on the topic "Microprocessors, the Electronic Revolution". A journalist revised the "comprehensibly" written articles of computer specialists. About 100 German dailies printed these articles once a week. Various institutions of adult education offered accompanying courses. In addition to the 12 newspaper articles, a collection of texts and a study guide on this topic were prepared by the German Institute for Correspondence Courses at the University of Tübingen (21).

4. <u>Control and regulation in general education</u>

In the Federal Republic of Germany there have hitherto been only a few documented examples. An example is the operation of a gantry crane via a microcomputer.

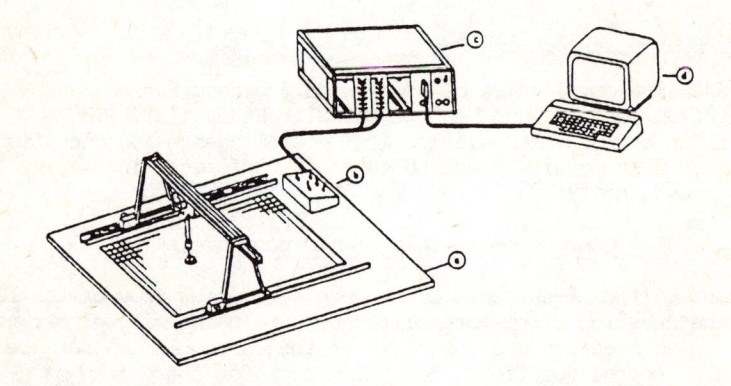

Fig. 1: Operation of a gantry crane via a microcomputer
(from: (9), p 223).

At the IPN studies have been prepared by Mr Hansen on a unit of instruction "elevator operation", "regulation of a greenhouse", "regulation of a disc with solar collectors". These examples and others can be found in (22).

1.4.5   REFERENCES

(1) DER BUNDESMINISTER FÜR BILDUNG UND WISSENSCHAFT: Erstes und zweites Datenverarbeitungsprogramm der Bundes- regierung, 1967 und 1971.

(2) ARLT, W: ECIS - Modellversuch zur Entwicklung und Erprobung von Curriculumelementen für das Fach Informatik in der 5./6. Klassenstufe in der Sekundarstufe I. In: ARLT, W (Ed): Beiträge zur ACU-Tagung 2/77 an der Pädagogischen Hochschule Berlin. Berlin, 1977.

(3) ARLT, W (Ed): EDV-Einsatz in Schule und Ausbildung - Modelle und Erfahrungen. Datenverarbeitung im Bildungswesen, Band 1. München/Wien: Oldenbourg, 1978.

(4) SCHULZ-ZANDER, R: Analyse curricularer Ansätze für das Schulfach Informatik. In: ARLT, W (Ed): EDV-Einsatz in Schule und Ausbildung - Modelle und Erfahrungen. Datenverarbeitung im Bildungswesen. Band 1. München/Wien: Oldenbourg, 1978, pp 40-49.

(5) GESELLSCHAFT FÜR INFORMATIK (Ed): Zielsetzungen und Lerninhalte des Informatikunterrichts. Stuttgart: Klett, 1976.

(6) BAUER, F L: Top-down Teaching of Informatics in Secondary Schools. In: Computers in Education. Proceedings of IFIP Conference Marseille. Amsterdam: North Holland Publishing Company, 1975, pp 53-61.

(7) SENATOR FOR SCHULWESEN BERLIN (Ed): Informatik. Entwurf von 5 Grundkursen für die Neugestaltung der gymnasialen Oberstufe in der Sekundarstufe II. Berlin, 1978.

(8) DRESCH, FROBEL, KOSCHORREK, TEUFEL; Eds: HAUF, A, STURM, L: Kursmaterialien Informatik.
    Kurs 2: Algorithmik I
    Kurs 3: Struktur und Arbeitsweise einer DV-Anlage
    Kurs 4: Algorithmik II: Datenstrukturen
    Aufgabensammlung
    Gelsenkirchen: Gesamtschule Berger Feld/Paderborn: FEoLL, 1978.

(9) HAUF, A: Überlegungen zur Behandlung des Themas "Prozesssteuerung" im Informatikunterricht allgemeinbildender Schulen. In: (19), pp 219-231.

(10) DER KULTUSMINISTER DES LANDES SCHLESWIG-HOLSTEIN (Ed.): Lehrplan Gymnasien Informatik - Erprobungsfassung für einen Modellversuch. AZ XL 120 - 3243.074. Kiel, 1979.

(11) BOSLER, U, CLAUSS, TH, DERLIEN, TH: Informatik-Lehrpläne, Stand 1978/79. Köln: Aulis, 1980.

(12) STÄNDIGE KONFERENZ DER KULTUSMINISTER DER LÄNDER IN DER BUNDESREPUBLIK DEUTSCHLAND (Ed): Rahmenlehrplanentwurf Bankkaufmann vom 26.6.1978.

(13) SCHULZ-ZANDER, R: Länderübergreifender Modellversuch "überregionale Erprobung und Vergleich von schulspezifischen Programmiersprachen für den Informatik- und Datenverarbeitungsunterricht". In: ARLT, W (Ed): Informatik als Schulfach. Reihe: Datenverarbeitung Informatik im Bildungsbereich Bd. 4. München/Wien: Oldenbourg, 1981.

(14) OCKER, SCHÖTTLE, SIMON: Informatik. Algorithmen und ihre Programmierung. München: Oldenbourg, 1979.

(15) BAUMANN, R: Programmieren mit PASCAL. Einstieg für Schüler, Hobbyprogrammierer, Volkshochschüler. Würzburg: Vogel, 1980.

(16) BOSLER, U, KOERBER, B: Mikroelektronik und das Schulfach Informatik. In: LOG IN 3 (1981) 1, pp 25-28.

(17) KOERBER, B: Mikroelektronik und das Schulfach Informatik. In: (19), pp 237-243.

(18) GIZYCKI, W, WIELER, U: Auswirkungen einer breiten Einführung von Mikroprozessoren auf die Bildungs- und Berufsqualifizierungspolitik. Battelle-Institut, Frankfurt, 1979.

(19) BOSLER, U, HANSEN, K-H (Eds): Mikroelektronik, sozialer Wandel und Bildung. Bericht über eine Fachtagung in Lüdenscheid, Weinheim/Basel: Beltz, 1981.

(20) FREY, K (Ed): Curriculum-Konferenz: Gebiet Mikroprozessor. Arbeitsbericht Nr. 45. Kiel: IPN, 1981.

(21) ZEITUNGSKOLLEG (Eds): Mikroprozessoren - Die elektronische Revolution. Tübingen: Deutsches Institut für Fernstudien an der Universität Tübingen, 1980.

(22) HANSEN, K-H, BOSLER, U (Eds): Materialsammlung zum IPN-Seminar 24 "Mikrocomputer im Unterricht". Polyscript. Kiel: IPN, 1981.

(23) ROBINSOHN, S: Bildungsreform als Reform des Curriculum. Neuwied/Berlin: Luchterhand, 1971.

(24) GORNY, P: New Information Technologies in Education in Germany. Polyscript. Brussel: Association for Teacher Education in Europe, 1981.

(25) KULTUSMINISTERIUM RHEINLAND-PFALZ (Ed): Modellversuch zum Computereinsatz in Unterricht und Verwaltung. Entwurf eines lernzielorientierten Lehrplans - Informatik Grundfach. Mainz: Hase & Köhler, 1978.

1.5 THE UNITED KINGDOM'S EXPERIENCE OF EVALUATION AND DEVELOPMENT OF COMPUTER RELATED LEARNING SYSTEMS

by

William R. BRODERICK BSc FBCS
Adviser for Computing Services and
Head of the Educational Computer Centre
London Borough of Havering

1.5.1   INTRODUCTION

Interest in computer related learning systems in the United Kingdom developed in the 1960s. At the start of that decade there were computers in all the United Kingdom's universities and it was natural that interest in their use should expand beyond the narrow confines of science and research into supporting the teaching role of an institution. At the same time a few school teachers were experimenting with teaching students programming and by 1965 the first computer was installed in a school (1). By the end of the decade a number of schools had computers or had formal and reliable access to them. These initiatives, which were spawned from the interest, energy and enthusiasm of teachers were supported by three national bodies, the Science Research Council, the Social Science Research Council and the National Council for Educational Technology. Whilst the research councils naturally tended to have a greater interest in pure research, the emphasis on applied research, which had its origins in the National Council for Educational Technology, affected their policies sufficiently to ensure that a number of applied research projects received research funding.

The 1970s was a decade of development. The Department of Education and Science funded a national development programme in computer assisted learning (2). This programme, which preceded the advent of microcomputers, concentrated on higher education with some school involvement. Cost effectiveness and institutionalisation of computer based learning systems were two of its prime emphases (6). This small but effective programme laid a strong foundation for a second Department of Education and Science funded initiative, the Micro-electronics Education Programme (MEP), to build upon for the 1980s.

The Micro-electronics Education Programme, currently funded until 1984, is a school based programme which has as its objective to foster the development of education about micro-electronics and through micro-electronics in schools throughout the country. It is concentrating on setting up regional organisations involving local education authorities and grant-aiding both in-service training and curriculum development work. Further details of the national scenario in the United Kingdom are given in 1.5.7.

However, it is against this background with over two decades of development and evaluation of computer assisted learning that teachers and students are becoming involved in one of the most exciting and potentially revolutionary developments that we have seen in education.

1.5.2   COMPUTER RELATED LEARNING SYSTEMS

The term computer related learning systems spans a spectrum of activities which flows from the use of computers in control and technology through education about computers, simulation and gaming, computer managed learning systems, to studies of the electronic office and information systems such as Prestel. Work at the extremities of the spectrum, in schools at least, is a relatively new activity. Until the advent of cheap, fast micro-processors in the industrial context there was not the support, nor the perceived need, for inculcating to our students that the method of control of any process may be extended from the familiar mechanical and electrical components to a micro-computer. The most up-to-date report on this work (7) gives a significant insight into the development of work in this area in some UK schools. Likewise until networks of micro-computers, public and private view data systems had been developed their educational potential was only casually considered.

The first developments in teaching using computers at university and secondary school level were naturally teaching people how to programme computers. In parallel with much of this work the use of the computer in association with the solution of mathematical problems generated a greater understanding of the value of an algorithmic approach to problem solving. The undisputed value of this work has been responsible for much of the initial orientation of computing journals solving problems of a mathematical form. Care must be taken in the swing away from the association of computing and mathematics to ensure that the intrinsic value of the algorithm approval to problem solving is not lost. The rapid feedback provided by computer systems helped improve performance of student programmers and quite rapidly led to the development of a number of simulations of machines designed to illuminate the user's understanding of both the contents of registers and the dataflow between them. This led rapidly to an interest in the development of computer based simulations of other processes. The computer clearly provided facilities whereby the student could at first hand study some processes which previously he could only read about. In genetics some experiments were limited by time or ethical considerations. In environmental science, social consciences prevented the pollution of rivers and lakes purely for students to study the effects of pollution on game fish. In physics convenience and safety inhibited the study of the mechanically complex experiments (eg Miliken's oil drop experiment) or those associated with nuclear science. In other cases, whilst the experiment could be conveniently performed in the laboratory, it all happened so quickly that the student had no real demonstration nor opportunity to study the internal mechanics of it. The computer provided a solution to this and other problems which had been concerning teachers for years.

Whilst some development groups concerned themselves with teaching small elements of the curriculum, others focused upon the management of learning and how the computer could be used as a powerful resource to help teachers learn more about both individuals in their classes, the profile of a class as a whole, and the effectiveness of their own techniques. Finally, there were also a group of programmes developed which did not fit into any of the foregoing neat compartments but were basically designed to analyse data and through this analysis help students learn more about the topics being studied. Computer related learning systems in the United Kingdom cover this whole spectrum and there are available some fine exemplars in each sphere of activity.

1.5.3   DEVELOPMENT

The micro-computer of the early 1980s differs in two fundamental respects from its mainframe and timesharing predecessors of the two previous decades. Firstly, it is cheap and, therefore, widely affordable. Secondly, the screen of the Visual Display is memory mapped and thus it provides powerful graphics facilities. In other respects today's micro-computer is not fundamentally different to its predecessors. However, it is these two differences which have done so much to broaden today's micro-computers educational application. The current state of development of education about computers is that the subject is now studied both informally and for examinations (at ages 16 and 18) and, of course, at degree level. The annual rise in examination entries gives some idea of the growth of computer studies in schools in the last 8 years.

YEAR	CSE	O	A	TOTAL
1974	5,487	400	1,000	6,887
1976	13,181	3,333	1,512	18,026
1978	15,489	8,928	2,032	26,419
1980	17,901	15,956	3,454	37,311

Despite the large number of students who are on such courses, relatively little work is being done to foster the development of the use of simulations in teaching the subject beyond the level of language and machine emulators. There is still an untapped potential for development in the field of helping many students and less formal users of computers to understand better the processes of computing science. No doubt this lack of development has its origins in the fact that heretofore most students of computing science and users of computing science were relatively sophisticated learners and, therefore, needed few practical aids. However, the wider availability of computers and the vast interest created opens up a whole new potential area of the development of simulations and operational models.

In the field of simulations and other interactive computer assisted learning (CAL) work the micro-computer has, in most applications, replaced the interactive terminal connected to a mini or large mainframe system. This change in technology has been accompanied by a change in style.

Greater attention has been paid to the interaction between the user and the micro-computer and graphics have been used to communicate more effectively some of the complex ideas involved.

Despite the changed external appearances of much of this CAL work, most of that which is currently available is very heavily dependent upon work done in the 1970s, the only real changes made being those to accommodate and adapt to the new technology.

The ITMA project, which was initiated with the arrival of micro-computers, is based upon careful programme design, very thorough evaluation of performance and transactions with the programme in the classroom. This has led to the production of high quality, very exceptional programmes which, because they have been prepared very thoroughly, are also quite expensive to produce. It will indeed be interesting to observe over the next few years how such work is received in comparison with that from other projects which are working to tighter time scales and less rigorous formative evaluation procedures, yet still producing programmes which look attractive and would appear to appeal to teachers in the classroom.

During the 1970s three computer managed learning (CML) systems were carefully developed and evaluated. Historically the first one was the Havering Computer Managed Learning System (3) (of which the author was the co-designer) which was funded from 1970 to 1976 by grants from the Social Science Research Council. This work resulted in the production of a computer independent and curriculum independent computer managed learning system which ultimately was used by a number of authorities in the United Kingdom and overseas. The focus of the research in this system was upon methods of structuring materials, routing students through the network or knowledge which forms the curriculum and discovering the respective roles of the computer teacher and student in generation of successful learning environments using such a system. After more than ten years of use it is currently being restructured as a two-level system to provide immediate responses and short-term routing and file retention on a micro-computer. The mainframe support for long-term routing and file retention via a remote job entry link.

This project's development outside its initial sphere has been interesting: it has led to the development of parallel systems in Canada and in Scotland. The work in Scotland, which started as a joint project to extend the test banking facets of the system to embrace item banking has now devolved into an entirely independent and very valuable item banking project. The hub is based upon the development of a test generation and evaluation system based upon the Godfrey Thompson Unit at Edinburgh University with satellite projects established in a number of institutions throughout Scotland. There is no doubt about the influence of the Munn and Dunning reports upon these developments.

The second CML system, the Hertfordshire Computer Managed Mathematics Project (4) (HCMMP) was designed to aid the teacher of mathematics in teaching the subject to mixed ability students during their first two years in secondary school (12 and 13 years old). Structured teaching material was supported with careful in-service training and extensive use of video tapes. The computer programmes were originally run on the mainframe system but during the latter part of the 1970s were converted to run on microcomputers for easy classroom use on a "cafeteria" basis. The system is still extensively used in Hertfordshire and consideration is being given to its extension to other curriculum areas.

The third system, "CAMOL", was designed under the auspices of NDPCAL to provide a second generation of CML system based upon the experience gathered from the Havering and Hertfordshire work. A number of users were identified and programming work was done by ICL, but only ever implemented by ICL equipment. The author does not know of any institutions currently using the system. One of its main contributions to research was that because it was used in the New University of Ulster Education Department a considerable amount of work was done studying the role of CML in the more independent learning environment of a university, compared with the school environments used by its two predecessors.

In addition to the above-mentioned system which fit neatly into the classifications, there are a number of "stand alone systems" which are CAL programmes designed for a variety of applications. A typical example of such a system would be the JIIG/CAL (Job Ideas and Information Generator/Computer Assisted Learning) System (5) of which the author is a co-designer. This system is designed for careers education and guidance as a joint project between the London Borough of Havering Educational Computer Centre and the Department of Business Studies at Edinburgh University. The system is based on the research and development conducted at these two centres during the previous decade. In Edinburgh, Dr. Closs' research covered careers guidance issues with specific focus on occupational interests. An interest test - the APU Occupational Interests Guide - was the main result of this research and was first published in 1969. It it used in the UK and overseas and English and French versions of it are available. The system acts as a resource for the careers officer, teacher and others concerned with careers education and guidance for young people. It provides both the pupil and careers adviser with ideas for relevant job titles which can be explored as possible careers. JIIG/CAL also supplies information about each job in the form of brief descriptions of what work is involved, together with any details of skills, personal qualities and qualifications required, plus notes on other relevant features, extensive references to related careers publications through which the pupil is encouraged to find more about each job for himself.

The design of the system, which was both a massive computing and curriculum development exercise, took three years and included a lot of formative evaluation. A further three year research project will be completed in March 1983 but interim results have been published. In the two and a half years since it was made publicly available over 35 local authorities in England and Wales have taken out licences to use this system. A micro-computer version is being prepared but due to the limitations of micro-computers, will only provide a restricted range of facilities.

Another typical example of the "stand alone" CAL programme is the Diet Analysis programme. There are a number of versions of this programme currently available, but they have broadly the same characterisitics. The programme accesses a large database which breaks down the food into its constitutent component parts. The user inputs, for exmaple, what he has eaten during a day or over a period of time and also a description of his or her lifestyle. The computer analyses the user's data and provides information about the amount of minerals, vitamins, proteins, etc in the diet and highlights any areas of deficiency. It is frequently used by more senior students of home economics. A third example of the "stand alone" CAL programme is the information retrieval package. Probably the best known is query, again developed in Hertfordshire; query allows the user to create and access a database by means of a simple set of commands. It can be used easily by teachers and students who are not familiar with computing or computers. Databases have already been prepared to cover a number of subject areas including such topics as meteorology (reports from weather stations for a period of time), history (from parish documents covering a number of years), and geography (demographic information about towns, villages and traffic flow in an area).

It is essential to recognise the exciting developments taking place in the primary area of education. Work on LOGO has been developed in both Edinburgh University and at a number of centres in South-East England. Likewise there has been a variety of encouraging initiatives that have focused on the broadly based use of computers in primary education: the main focus has been on encouraging and developing thinking skills and analysing students' behaviour rather than drill and practice.

The foregoing description of the national background and the range of recent developments in computer related learning systems provides a starting point to look at the evaluation techniques that are most useful at this stage of the development of the art in the United Kingdom.

1.5.4   PROJECT BASED EVALUATION

The development of computer related learning systems in the United Kingdom is based upon small projects. The outcome of these projects are (usually) computer programmes, student texts, teacher texts and support materials. These materials are developed by the project team in a relatively enclosed environment and then disseminated to other audiences either informally ie responding to requests, or formally through the project establishing a distribution mechanism, or commercially using commercial publishers to advertise and market the materials. As the emphasis of these days is upon spreading the considerable investment in developing materials over a relatively large number of users, there is considerable pressure to ensure that materials as they are developed, are properly evaluated. Many of the project teams, whilst experienced in the curriculum development field, meet evaluation in any formal sense for the first time in the context of such projects.

The Oxford English Dictionary includes in its definition of education "bringing up the young, development of character or mental powers, systematic instruction", and most of us would consider that good educational practice embraces all of these functions. As education is a complex process its evaluation must be an interdisciplinary task for the evaluation embraces many facets of the measurement of man's behaviour. In order for a project to formulate an evaluation policy, it must decide on the purposes of its evaluation and for whom the evaluation is being conducted.

We can draw up some criteria which any evaluation or assessment procedure should satisfy, eg:

1. Informative - will provide useful information for potential audience.

2. Sensitive - it will detect changes of a sub-acute nature and be useful in relating these to potential causes.

3. Predictive - will provide information which a competent evaluator will be able to replicate.

4. Objective - will provide information which will be independent of the observer or his attitude.

5. Acceptable - will be conceptually and operationally acceptable to all parties involved.

Certainly, when assessing computer related learning materials, one would expect to address issues in the following areas:

a. Academic - has the student actually learned something from using these materials and, if so, was this what materials set out to teach him.

b. Social - has the student's attitude, behaviour and view been broadened by using these materials.

c. Financial - can we afford to use these materials to teach children the objectives they are designed to teach?

d. Operational - does using this material create a classroom environment in which the teacher can operate effectively without introducing so many problems that the teacher wonders whether the whole exercise was worthwhile in the first place.

In a formal testing environment the classical evaluation model usually depends upon pre and post testing the population. Part of the population are subjected to the experiment treatment and part of them are not. The evaluator then attempts to state whether or not the differences between the two groups were significant at the end of the experiment and he attempts to relate these differences to differences in the experimental and the control treatments. Given large samples of students and sophisticated experimental design, relationships between pupil performance and variables such as sex, age, test scores, can be deduced by statistical analysis. This approach to evaluation is most useful when the objectives are clear, the extraneous influences are insignificant or controllable and where the need to understand what happens in the learning environment is minimal. This classical model of evaluation is based upon the model of experimental work in hypothesis testing and in the natural sciences. In this sense it is nomothetic in that its methods are concerned with formulating laws. On the other hand, illuminative evaluation has as its objectives generating an understanding of the learning process and as its methods an intensive study of individuals. Alas the literature and discussions of illuminative evaluation tend to get cluttered with the jargon of sociology and psychology. Techniques are best understood by looking at the methods used by the evaluators.

The evaluator studies the activities and transactions that take place, eg what is the student doing, reading, using apparatus, writing answers. What transactions are taking place, student-teacher communication, student-student communication, etc. The objective is then to study the role of the component activities and transactions in the learning milieu to see how they contribute to the total activity of the classroom. This brief description of illuminative evaluation would be criticised by many exponents as over-simplified and too scientific. Specifically, they would attack the concept of breaking up learning into its component parts. It has been argued that it is not a "standard methodological package" but a way of trying to understand the learning milieu. The evaluator usually starts by looking at the phenomenon of student learning in terms which are appropriate to its context (eg learning in that classroom is not independent of the pupil, teacher, headteacher, school methods, etc).

Evaluators study the knowledge structure of the student in relationship with his total learning environment. The product of illuminative evaluation should be a report containing the facts and reason deductions that help the reader understand the learning and the learning process.

The fire of controversy over classical and illuminative evaluation never dies and rarely ever drops below the level of an inferno. The divisions between the ideographic and nomothetic philosophies appear irreconcilable. They are not helped by reference to opposites as synonyms, eg hard (classical) and soft (illuminative) evaluation. In the author's view an electric approach using both models at appropriate times serves the purposes best when one is evaluating a complex learning package such as CAL material.

Clearly, effects of components, eg using the computer programme, can be well illustrated by classical evaluation techniques. The student can be asked a set of questions before and after using the package and the evaluator can learn in many contexts, but not all contexts, about the student's increased knowledge and, perhaps, even understanding, by these methods. However, CAL materials do not exist in isolation. If a package is going to be well used in a school it is likely that it will form part of an educational continuum. The teacher will build up to using the package, create the background structure against which it is going to be used, pose the problems which the student is going to use the package to develop a better understanding of, and afterwards ensure that the materials are not just forgotten but carefully woven into a course to be built upon and to be reinforced. Therefore, to evaluate a package which consists of both computer materials, student and teacher texts, one would have to study the package in an elongated teaching context and adduce from this study whether the in-service training preparing the teachers, the teachers' materials, the students' texts, the exercises and the resource materials were well suited to the tasks which they were required to perform. Where illuminative evaluation techniques are used, they provide specially valuable information where the CAL material is not in the scientific area but is a package concerned with social behaviour, eg Huntington 2 Malaria Eradication Programme MALAR, or Huntington 2 Pollution Programme POLUT.

The strategies associated with evaluation are essential to projects. Summative evaluation - which looks at a state at the end of a process - is not usually applied by the project itself, but more often by external agencies, the questions asked being of the form - was this worth doing? has the process achieved its objectives? etc. Formative evaluation - where the project team looks at aspects of its own work and looks at the success or otherwise of its materials at various stages through their development cycle - is essential. Without formative evaluation one tends to find weak materials produced which reflects initial ideas not modified by experience. Alternatively one tends to find interminable arguments in project teams about the changes being made because insufficient evidence has been gathered to support various bases for making these changes.

Designing and building formative evaluation practice into the development aspect of the project is, therefore, essential and makes a significant contribution to the quality of the end product.

Operational evaluation is equally essential, and often a neglected aspect of the total evaluation process. If the teacher can't operate the package in a classroom without a great deal of extra work, (work which frequently is not providing benefits commensurate with the effort), then the project materials will not be used after an initial spurt of enthusiasm. Typical operational issues that require consideration are:

a. The availability of equipment - is the equipment required easily available or does the teacher have to go searching all over the school for it?

b. Reliability of equipment - are the materials designed to work with equipment which is reliable or does the teacher end up in the classroom with all the equipment and then discover, just as the lesson is about to start, that it won't work?

c. Do the materials support changes in classroom procedure - is, for example, a change from teacher-centred learning to child-centred learning given a satisfactory level of support so that even the less experienced and skilled teachers can use the materials without classroom chaos? If the materials require one or more students sitting down at a micro-computer is there adequate support material to provide activities for the other 27 children in the classroom? Where batch systems are being used are the requirements posed by classroom organisation for turn round etc. acceptable? Do materials that need to be given out cost so much that they can't be afforded on normal school budgets? If optical mark reading techniques are involved is it necessary to use specialised pens which may not be freely available?

In doing an operational analysis it is necessary to look both at the normal working environment and also the extra changes imposed on it by the project itself. A project must be sensitive to the context in which it is being used and not the specialised context in which it is being developed if the projects outcomes are to be acceptable in a wide range of classrooms.

1.5.5 FINANCIAL EVALUATION

Where the introduction of computer based learning systems requires the use of resources which are not normally available in a school, or the reallocation of resources on a greater scale than is normally prevalent in a school context, sooner or later the questions about the cost of using such a system are going to be asked. It is wise that these questions are asked by the designers and developers at the very earliest stages so that where decisions are made affecting the resources required, they can be made in the context of a reasonable knowledge of what current costs are and a knowledge of what can be

changed through the discretion of the head of department or the
headteacher, and what facets of the work will demand that local and
national authorities need to be involved and, perhaps, prevailed upon
to provide new, additional or different services. As operational
decisions make a considerable impact upon financial implications, it
is worthwhile keeping the two facets of evaluation going hand-in-hand.

These, then, are the evaluation tools which the project team need
to have available for their work in developing computer related
learning materials. The needs for formative evaluation should be
taken into account in the original project design and budgeting.
Evaluation is a time consuming exercise. It inevitably leads to the
reworking of some aspects of the project's materials and is a right
and proper part of any development exercise and needs resourcing
accordingly.

1.5.6   CURRICULUM DEVELOPMENT ISSUES AND PRACTICE

The strategies for curriculum development within projects are
intrinsically entwined with strategies for evaluation. Formative
evaluation and curriculum development in a project cannot be
separated. Within the United Kingdom a model (upon which there are
a large number of variations) has emerged. This general model is
not perfect. The derived models which have emerged in individual
circumstances reflect both the skills of individuals within a project
and the needs of that project. The use of these models has led to the
development of some high quality educational software.

Without doubt, the starting point for any curriculum development
activity must be the classroom. Ideally, one needs not one classroom
but a number of classrooms and a group of teachers. If the curriculum
development is to be widely accepted amongst the teaching population
of the country, then the original idea must be based upon meeting the
overt (and less obvious) needs of a large group of teachers. The
rationales for such development are as varied as the development
themselves. In careers education and guidance teachers and careers
officers were frustrated by the lack of support and resources for their
work. In physics, teachers were frustrated by the difficulties of
setting up Miliken's oil drop experiment for class use. In ecology,
teachers were frustrated by the constraints on demonstrating the
effects of pollution on rivers and lakes and therefore needed
simulation for the subject. The computer is being used to solve
problems which cannot be solved sensibly by any other means. If the
problem can be solved sensibly by other means, then serious
consideration should usually be given to the other means as long as
they are cheaper and equally effective.

Let us assume that a problem has been identified and the group of
teachers and the co-ordinator who is going to be involved with the
project are satisfied that the use of the computer system is a
potentially viable way of tackling this educational problem. The
group firstly need to write a specification of: (a) what they intend
to do to define what input they intend to put into the programme;

(b) what options should be available for the teachers to select for running the programme; (c) how the data supplied will be processed by the programme and what the exact format is of the output from the programme. This may sound like a trivial idea. One man must sit down and write a specification, if not on the back of a postcard, on a couple of sheets of paper. By the time this has been discussed with a group of teachers and the gaps in the specification filled, the assumptions made about the user audience have been specified and the format of the output has been agreed, then the two page specification may well have developed into a 20 or 40 page specification. Then draft out the supporting materials. Do not despair at this stage, for this will be the longest and most difficult stage of the curriculum development exercise. Expose the specification to groups of teachers involved in teaching the subject. Listen to what they say. Differentiate between ingrained attitudes and constructive criticism. Take heed of all the new ideas in the teachers' statements. Then go back and rewrite (starting with an open mind) your specification again.

Writing the programme is the easy part. Study your local standards for programming, for availability of equipment and for interaction between programmes and students and write your programmes. Write them according to professional standards in a modular manner - this may appear to be a burden initially, but it will pay tremendous dividends during the development stage.

The next thing to do is to take the programmes (after they have been tested thoroughly with the test data in the curriculum development/computing departments) and put them on school trials.

It is suggested that these school trials should take place in a relatively small number of schools initially, that the programmes should be slotted into their proper educational context and that the teachers used to trial this material should span the spectrum of interest, enthusiasm and ability. In the end the programmes have to work with the normal distribution of the teaching population, not just the keen, enthusiastic supporters of computer related learning systems. A member of the development team should observe pupils using the materials and make detailed notes, particularly of any difficulties that they have. After the trials the teacher should be interviewed and detailed notes of their difficulties made. After the series of trials the specification will have been modified and the programmes modified to match the specification - the importance of this procedure is to ensure well structured programmes overall - once the programmes have been modified they should be retested until there is a high level of certainty that the number of iterations through this expensive and time-consuming loop have ensured that the law of diminishing returns is coming into play. One can always carry on improving programmes, one can always carry on improving student texts, but we do not live in a perfect world with the infinite resources required to meet perfection. Judgement by the Project Directorate is necessary to ensure that the trial population is satisfactory, that the materials have met the requirements of the trial population in a satisfactory manner and that they are then ready for public release.

Public release will depend upon the strategies adopted by the project for dissemination, but will usually result in publication in some form or other, plus distribution of software either for specific machines or in a machine independent form, it being recognised that machine independent is a difficult ideal to achieve.

The adaptation of the above models for the individual purposes must be sensitive to the needs and resources of individual projects. There can be cases, for instance, for small or micro-computer projects based upon individual developments where the developer is also the source of the computing expertise being most economically and effectively achieved through much curtailed procedure. The effectiveness of this method, however, is dependent upon the quality of the individual rather than the procedure itself. A more normal model will consist of the group of broadly experienced computing and curriculum experts, maybe only four or five in number, developing the initial specification, followed by their consulting more local curriculum development groups and then involving a relatively small team of perhaps two or three people implementing the ideas, observing classroom practice, conducting the formative evaluation and subsequent system modification and producing, using again computer means, eg word processors etc, the final computer related learning materials.

Whatever happens it is necessary to ensure the quality of the resources available for project development. The initial model proposed in this paper may well be a dinosaur. There are certainly circumstances in which it can be reduced to the scale of a greyhound, but there is no merit in doing this unless the greyhound is a winner.

The above paper reflects some of the experience in the United Kingdom in the last 15 years. It is put forward in the spirit of offering the United Kingdom's experience of evaluation and development of computer based learning systems as a model upon which others can base and develop their own work. In the end it is more important that it works in your school with your children and it works in one only in the United Kingdom!

1.5.7 FOOTNOTE ON THE DEVELOPMENT OF MICROELECTRONICS EDUCATION IN THE UNITED KINGDOM - 1982

There are two schemes for microelectronics education in the United Kingdom. The major one covers England, Wales and Northern Ireland and is funded by the Department of Education and Science. This microelectronics education programme has divided the United Kingdom part into 14 regions. Each region is a geographical grouping of local education authorities who have chosen to work together to foster the developments of microelectronics education. Each region, in order to receive central support, needs to meet certain basic criteria (eg there is an element of "core curriculum" in the in-service training). There are (very low) minimum contact times specified for in-service training and curriculum development work is subject to monitoring (to prevent duplication) and evaluation. Local control is exercised by a regional committee, usually consisting of educational administrators and school advisers or inspectors. Local education authorities in a region are providing both direct and indirect support to augment central government funds and to channel these so as to best meet local needs.

The work of the microelectronics education programme has been divided up into four domains:

1. That of microelectronics and control, which really spans those aspects of the application of micro-electronics in other aspects of science education as well as the introduction of ideas related to the use of microelectronics instead of other control and voluntary mechanisms in engineering.

2. Computer based learning systems - that domain spans the area covered by computer related learning systems in this paper.

3. Education about computers - this domain is concerned not only with education about hardware, but software and applications and general appreciation and awareness both for teachers and students.

4. Communications and information systems - this not only covers such activities as the electronic office, word processing, electronic mail, but also private and public viewdata systems and other integrated information systems.

The work in the four domains is divided into two areas, in-service training and curriculum development. The in-service training element is for the training of teachers already in post and in each region there is an in-service training co-ordinator associated with each domain. His job is to foster and develop in-service training courses throughout the region in that domain. In some cases the same person also co-ordinates and sponsors the curriculum development work, for which there is grant aid. The purpose of the curriculum development work is to ensure that there is a strong foundation of locally developed educational software which can be published either formally or informally.

Evaluation work is an essential element of all in-service education and curriculum development work. The style of the evaluation varies from project to project and, in some cases, is quite formal, whilst in others it is much less so. One gains the impression that regions do not feel coerced into externally imposed evaluation procedures but feel encouraged to evaluate their work in a way which matches local skills and interests.

The second development, funded separately by the Scottish Education Department and known as the Scottish Micro-electronic Development Programme (SMDP) is broadly similar in aims to the MEP, although because it started from a different initial position has proceeded slightly differently. Whereas MEP has concentrated its initial efforts on setting up regional structures, SMDP has provided equipment for classroom use and used this stimulus to encourage individual local education authorities to set up their own in-service training and information centre. The net result of the two projects in the long run is likely to be similar and their curriculum development activities are seen as complementary in many instances.

1.5.8   REFERENCES

(1)   BRODERICK W R (1968): The Computer in School, Bodley Head, London.

(2)   HOOPER R & TOYE I (1975): Computer Assisted Learning in the United Kingdom, Council for Educational Technology, London.

(3)   BRODERICK W R (1975): The Havering Computer Managed Learning System, Hooper & Toye (2).

(4)   AUCBE (1981): Hertfordshire Computer Managed Mathematics Project.

(5)   CLOSS S J (1980): Manual for the JIIG/CAL System, Hodder & Stoughton.

(6)   FIELDEN J & PEARSON P K (1978): The Cost of Learning with Computers, Council for Educational Technology, London.

(7)   DEPARTMENT OF EDUCATION AND SCIENCE (1982): Technology in Schools - Developments in Craft, Design and Technology Departments, HMSO.

1.6 THE TEACHING OF COMPUTER SCIENCE AT SECONDARY SCHOOL –
Evaluation of Experience in Spain

by

E. Garcia CAMARERO
Computer Centre,
Complutense University Madrid

1.6.1   INTRODUCTION

This paper deals with the activities, experience and results recorded in the teaching of computer science at secondary school in Spain. My first task will accordingly be to outline what I mean by secondary education in the Spanish school system, and also to relate the teaching of computer science at this level to its counterparts at university and in vocational training.

Roughly speaking, the Spanish education system is divided into three levels:

a.   General basic education (EGB)

   covers eight classes, spread over three levels:

1.   elementary level (classes 1 and 2) for 6-7 year olds,

2.   intermediate level (3, 4 and 5) for 8-10 year olds.

3.   upper level (6, 7 and 8) for 11-13 year olds,

b.   Secondary education certificate (BUP) and vocational training

1.   The general secondary education certificate (BUP)

   is a general course covering three classes (1, 2 and 3) for 14-16 year olds;

2.   Vocational training (FP)

   caters for the same ages as the BUP, but trains skilled workers and craftsmen in various trades;

c.   University education is divided into three levels:

1. <u>undergraduate level 1</u> which lasts three academic years
    (1st, 2nd and 3rd - college or university) and leads to
    a "diploma";

2. <u>undergraduate level 2</u>, which lasts two years (4th and 5th -
    university) and leads to a "degree";

3. <u>postgraduate level</u>, which lasts two years and leads to a
    "doctorate".

Within this general framework I shall take secondary education to mean the EGB intermediate and upper levels and the BUP. Though this paper does not deal with vocational training, I shall allude to it briefly.

The teaching of computer science at university level began in Spain in 1969 with the setting up of the Computer Science Institute and of a Computer Science Department in the Science Faculty of the University of Madrid. Special courses had previously been offered in various faculties, engineering schools and other higher education establishments, and also in university computing centres. In 1977 computer science faculties were set up in various universities and the Computer Science Institute disappeared. Today, advanced computer science studies are well established at the three university levels and a growing number of universities are including them in their curricula.

In 1976 regulations were introduced to make computer science a part of vocational training (FP) and in 1977 the subject was included in administration, commerce, electricity and electronics courses. The curricula were approved in 1978.

I shall discuss the actual subject of this paper - experience and activities in the sphere of computer science teaching at secondary school - from three angles:

a. the establishments working on it;

b. the meetings, seminars and conferences which focussed on the problems raised by the introduction of computer science into secondary schools and their possible solutions;

c. the groups of people which have been experimenting in this field.

1.6.2   FIRST STEPS

The Spanish delegation to the Western European Symposium on Computer Education, held in London in March 1969 under the auspices of IFIP, briefly reported on the teaching of computer science at secondary school, which amounted to the inclusion of a few optional computer science subjects in the University Orientation

Course (COU) in order to attract students to that particular branch.

At that time, a number of Spanish higher education establishments were considering research and experiments on the use of computers in education. At the Instituto Quimico del Sarria, Garcia Ramos had developed programmes for the automatic correction of multiple choice examinations and the construction of reading machines for the chemical analysis laboratory; meanwhile, at the Universidad Laboral de Alcala de Henares, a group of teachers (including B Fernand, Maria Luisa Zavala, M Pascua Piquera and Maria Paz Ovejero) were working out CAI programmes (Computer Assisted Instruction) to teach various subjects and an introduction to a few computer science subjects.

However, the first national experiment aimed at introducing computer science into secondary schools took place at the end of 1969, when a seminar was held at the Computing Centre of the University of Madrid under my direction. Its purpose was to establish which computer science subjects should be taught at secondary school and to devise a suitable methodology. The experiment was conducted with the help of Irene Fernandez Florez, Isidro Ramos, Javier Arlegui and Mariano Solanas, computer scientists from the computing centres of the Universities of Madrid and Saragossa, the above-mentioned teachers from the Universidad Laboral de Alcala de Henares and the Instituto Quimico de Sarria and secondary school teachers Mercedes Civantos (Instituto Ramiro de Maeztu, Madrid), Augusto Sanchez (Instituto Ortega y Gasset, Madrid), Mr Jesus Arroyo (Colegio de Santa Ana, Saragossa), Javier Ayestaran (Colegio del Pilar, Saragossa), J Casulleras Regas (Instituto Mila y Fontanals, Barcelona), Roser Pujades Duran (Inspectorate for Intermediate Education, Barcelona), V Torra Ferré (Instituto de Cornella) and a few others.

The aim was to convey the essentials of computer science to pupils between the ages of 11 and 13. It was decided to do this with a "70/13 virtual computer" whose internal structure could be studied by the pupils, and a machine-oriented programming language (which would compel them to refer to each of the computer units) codified in natural language to make the meaning of the instructions clear. The computer had to be very simply constructed while possessing the basic units of any real computer: input and output units, a memory (of limited capacity, to enable the children to represent all the locations on a piece of paper), the registers required for the control unit (instructions and sequence control), an accumulator and an arithmetic unit.

A "Computer Science Handbook for Children" was written and published for schools. It contained a description of the 70/13 machine and the programming language used, with instructions in natural language and in abbreviated or codified form; it also included an introduction to flow charts and a collection of programming exercises with answers.

During the final stage of the experiment, classes were taught to children of various ages in Madrid, Saragossa, Barcelona and Alcala de Henares. They were usually preceded by a visit to the town's university computing centre, where the children heard a series of lectures to arouse their interest in the subject; afterwards, at their school or institute, they attended a course of 20-30 hours with practice in programming the "virtual" machine (the 70/13) simulated on the IBM 1620 at the Science Faculty of the University of Saragossa and the IBM 1130 at the Instituto Quimico de Sarria.

The results of the experiment were extremely positive. The following points stood out:

a. the principle of arranging meetings between computer scientists and secondary school teachers to study the problem and work out the project together;

b. the facility with which secondary school pupils took to computer science, relating to computers in a much more natural manner than adults;

c. plans to include the subject in curricula on a regular basis in view of the interest shown by the dozen or so schools and institutes that took part in the experiment.

It was agreed that if computer science was to be included in official secondary school curricula, the following steps would have to be taken:

1. decide whether to include new computer science subjects in the curricula or expand existing subjects (eg mathematics, languages), and fix the number of hours for each level;

2. draw up training programmes for the teachers in charge of these subjects;

3. equip educational establishments with the computer hardware needed for practical work.

In view of the importance and scope of these three points, a broader experimental phase was recommended, in which a series of pilot centres would be required to find solution to the three problems.

As a result of these recommendations a series of national seminars and meetings were held over the next few years to meet the aforesaid requirements, and groups of interested teachers appeared in several parts of Spain. In section 1.6.3, I shall discuss the aims and conclusions of these meetings, and in section 1.6.4, the results of the experiments about which I have received information.

1.6.3   DEVISING A METHODOLOGY

The problems of teaching computer science at secondary school have been studied over the past few years by the National Institute for Educational Science (INICIE), the Educational Science Institutes (ICE) of several universities and a number of foundations. Several BUP institutes and secondary schools and a few university computing centres have co-operated with them and done the experimenting.

The Foundation for the Social Development of Communications (FUNDESCO, attached to the Spanish National Telephone Company) has always paid special attention to educational problems and new technologies. In March 1975 it held a symposium on "Computers and Education" at the Ground Satellite Communications Station in Buitrago, with delegates from the United States (W F Atchison, Sylvia Sharp, C Johnson), Denmark (U Brondum), the United Kingdom (R Buckingham, R Lewis, F Lovis, D Tagg, J D Tinsley) and Spain (F Cano, E Garcia Camarero, J Minguet, M Rico, J Sanchez Izquierdo). The discussions centred on the present and future of computers in education, Spain's experience with computers in education, computers as teaching aids and computers' impact on society through education.

After IFIP's Second International Conference on Computers and Education in Marseilles in September 1975, the CITEMA and FUNDESCO foundations, taking advantage of the presence in Europe of several Latin American experts, held a symposium in Madrid on "Education and Computer Science" from the viewpoint of a shared language and culture. The discussions focused on some aspects of the relationship between education and computer science in Spain and Latin America, including computer science subjects at secondary school.

In April 1981 FUNDESCO held a seminar at Buitrago on "Computer Studies as Part of General Education" to foster an exchange of views and experience, define educational objectives for the teaching of computer science at EGB and BUP level, study methodologies, plan a teacher training course for a pilot project and a further course for pupils, and set up a group to observe and assess the experiments. The seminar was attended by nearly 50 people. The final report contained a definition of objectives, a study of the adoption of computer science subjects at the various educational levels, proposals for methodology and details of the equipment (eg programmable pocket calculators, micro-computers) and human resources (recruitment and training of teachers) required.

The seminar brought together the various groups which were experimenting separately with the teaching of computer science at secondary school. The outcome was a whole series of activities throughout 1981-82, many of them co-ordinated by the former INCIE and a number of ICEs.

The INCIE, a national centre operating under the Ministry of Education, was responsible for co-ordinating the activities of the ICEs institutes for the development of educational techniques attached to the universities. Much of the INCIE's and ICE's work has focused on the uses of computer science, especially in CAI. Over the past few years the INCIE has sponsored several meetings on the inclusion of computer science in the BUP and has helped organise numerous computer science courses for BUP teachers (which I shall discuss in the next paragraph). Three of these meetings took place last year, in 1981.

The first, held at the ICE of the Technical University of Madrid in June, was entitled "Computer Science in the BUP" and directed by Mr Luisa Pacios Jimenez. It was agreed that the teaching of computer science at BUP level should aim to:

1. teach the basic computer science vocabulary and concepts in current use;

2. teach pupils to express with proper clarity the various techniques or algorithms used in solving problems;

3. teach them to handle information, however profuse and complex, for dealing with daily problems;

4. prepare them to use new forms of language and communicate with computers;

5. prepare them to select the most effective techniques for solving problems.

It was thought that these objectives could be achieved on the basis of a systematic official plan, on condition that teachers were suitably trained and the teaching process properly organised. The inclusion of computer science in the curricula could take three forms:

a. establish computer science as a new subject;

b. introduce specific computer science subjects into mathematics and physics syllabi;

c. include "An Introduction to Computer Science" as an optional subject among the EATP (Technical and Occupational Courses and Activities).

Alternative (c) was considered the most realistic step to start with, leading to alternative (a) in the medium term.

It was accordingly agreed that a co-ordinating body should be set up to:

1. plan the supply of hardware to educational establishments;

2. support and forward the initiatives taken by these establishments;

3. draw up a teacher training programme;

4. plan the full introduction of computer science into the BUP.

The second meeting, held by the ICE of the University of Santiago and entitled "Symposium on Computer Education in Schools", took place in September 1981 under the auspices of the Barrie de la Maza and FUNDESCO foundations. The participants decided to establish a plan of action for 1981-82 and set up a management committee to:

1. study how best to introduce computer science into the EGB and intermediate level curricula;

2.   pay practical attention to experiments in progress;

3.   equip some establishments with hardware and make use of university computing centres, local companies and so on.

Though the seminar was held at Santiago de Compostela and most of the participants came from the Gallega region, many were also from other areas: Alava, Leon, Logrono, Madrid, Murcia, Segovia etc.

In November 1981 a study session on "Computer Education in Schools" was held in Madrid by the Office of the Undersecretary to the Minister of Education, assisted by the ICE of the University of Santiago de Compostela and the Barrie de la Maza and FUNDESCO foundations. The following steps were recommended:

1.   preparation and distribution of a report on the current situation (and developments over the past 10 years) as regards the teaching of computer science and its uses at school, within the Spanish context;

2.   launching of activities to inform and arouse the awareness of educational circles, especially teaching staff;

3.   organisation of advanced training courses and programmes for EGB and BUP teachers, to enable them to transmit the "computer mentality" to their pupils;

4.   inclusion of computer science as a special optional subject among the Technical and Occupational Courses and Activities (EATP).

1.6.4   EXPERIMENTS

Apart from those discussed under "First steps", the experiments aimed at introducing computer science subjects into secondary schools were launched on the initiative of several BUP teachers who wished pupils receiving a general education to acquire some knowledge of a subject with a considerable impact on the modern world. Most of them have taken place in Madrid, Barcelona and La Coruna; however, many other areas like the Basque country, Saragossa or Murcia have also been extremely active in this field. It must nevertheless be pointed out that there is no national policy to stimulate, develop and co-ordinate this type of work: the guidelines for the development of the various activities carried no executive weight, being adopted on a purely advisory basis at the meetings and seminars described above.

In Madrid the most active group has undoubtedly been the one formed by the teachers of the "Herrera Oria" BUP Institute, Ricardo Aguado, Agustin Blanco, Javier Zavala and Ricardo Zamarreno. In 1973 they began experimenting with pocket calculators in mathematics classes, both to counterbalance "modern mathematics" by teaching pupils practical computing techniques that would enable them to apply the theories and focus on reality, and to go deeper into the calculations which had always been beyond BUP pupils because of the difficult algorithms. This led to methodology changes in certain subjects in the official curriculum and the introduction of some basic computer science concepts. In 1979 the institute acquired a micro-computer, which enabled it to start teaching programming languages and solving new problems. Another micro-computer was acquired in 1980. However, as computer science is not a part of official BUP curricula, programming classes had to be given outside school hours to a small group of volunteers. To remedy this, computer science was included among the Technical and Occupational Courses and Activities (EATP) and given comparable academic status to all the subjects taught under that heading. On the course, which involves two hours' tuition a week, pupils learn to handle the micro-computer and master the BASIC programming language, the basic concepts of computer science (eg organigramme, programme, algorithm) and their elementary uses in technology and management. This group of teachers has produced a considerable number of publications describing their experiments in detail and explaining their views on how to introduce computer science into secondary education.

Several other BUP institutes and schools have carried out similar experiments, including a number of institutes in Madrid - the "Quevedo" (Antonio Rolda and Juan Manuel Garcia, Dozagart), "Garcia Morato" (Jose Maria Cortes Cato), "Ramiro de Maeztu" (Ana Garcia Azcarate), "Calderon de la Barca" (Eduardo Abad, Manuel Aviles), "Emilo Pardo Bazan" (Enrique Rubiales) - and other institutes in the Cuidad Real province, such as the "Francisco de Quevedo" Institute in Villanueva de los Infantes (Jesus Romero, Juan Antonio Izarra) and the "Damaso Alonso" Institute in Puertollano (Felix Carrasco).

Almost all these establishments have a certain amount of hardware (COMMODORE and APPLE II micro-computers) and offer programming courses, usually in BASIC, for pupils of BUP 2nd and 3rd classes, as part of the EATP.

Besides the work done in BUP schools, introductory and training courses for teachers have been held in Madrid, for instance by the ICE's of the various universities: the Autonomous University ("Calculators and Micro-computers as Teaching Aids" and "BASIC Programming for BUP Teachers"), the Technical University ("Computer Science for BUP Teachers") and Alcala de Henares ("The Uses of Computers in Education"). Others have been organised by the National BUP by Correspondence Institute (INDAD), ("BASIC Course for BUP Teachers"), the Colegio Oficial de Doctores y Licenciados ("Calculators in Class") the Centro de Calculo de la Universidad Complutense (Seminar on "Computer Science at Secondary School").

In Barcelona, the group that first studied the introduction of computer science subjects into secondary schools worked at the Technical University of Barcelona Computing Centre (CCUPB) under the direction of Martin Verges, assisted by Jordi Castell and others. The Schools' Programming Tournament, which was successfully organised in 1979-80 and spread throughout Spain in 1981 with the IFIP's World Congress on Education and Computers, helped to heighten interest in computer science studies at secondary school level. Likewise, the

the projects and courses devised at the CCUPB played a decisive role in developing computer science classes in secondary schools and institutes.

Also active in the field is the Instituto Quimico de Sarria, thanks to the efforts of Luis A Garcia Ramos, who recently set up a nationwide association (GREI) for the teaching of computer science, to link up all those working for the inclusion of computer science in secondary schools.

A number of secondary schools and institutes in Catalonia are experimenting with computer science teaching, such as the Academia Sagrada Familia in Villafranca del Panedes (I Salinas), the Berga BUP Institute (Fernando Ruiz Tarrago), Colegio Claret and Colegio Aula (Jordi Castell, Juan Ilary). All these establishments have a certain amount of micro-computer hardware on which pupils practise programming, usually in BASIC.

In Barcelona, the Science Museum has set aside a room for demonstration of the handling and uses of micro-computers, using educational programmes drawn up with the help of the industrial laboratory of the city's Industrial Engineering School (Vazquez Magan, Ruiz Bruner). The Colegio Oficial de Licenciados y Doctores offers courses on computer science at BUP level.

The ICEs of the Barcelona universities have also worked on the subject. Thus, the Central University has held courses on "Computer Education and Social Sciences", "Introduction to PL/1 and FORTRAN Programming" and "Micro-computer Programming in BASIC", and the Autonomous University on "Teacher Training in Computer Techniques", "Introduction to the Use of Computers at School" and "The Use of Computers in Chemistry Classes".

Work has likewise been underway in Galicia for a number of years. Prof. Luengo of the Colegio Santa Maria del Mar ran computer science seminars for several years, starting in 1973, for COU pupils. The courses lasted 40 hours, half of them devoted to the study of the FORTRAN language and the rest to other aspects of computer science such as hardware, history, computer science and society, etc. Programming was practised on an IBM 1130 computer. At present, BASIC is taught as part of the EATP in the BUP 2nd and 3rd classes and practicals are done on a micro-computer set up in the school. For younger pupils, activities have been devised on the basis of models closely linked to computer science and a programme suited to the EGB is currently being studied.

Courses offered by the ICE of the University of Santiago here included: "Introduction to Computer Science for BUP and EGB 8th Class Teachers", Practical Introduction to Micro-computers", "Introduction to Computer Science in Education" and "Introduction to Computer Science for EGB Teachers". An "Introductory Seminar on Computer Science in Education" is being held simultaneously at La Coruna, Orense, Lugo and Vigo, and a "National Introductory Course on Computer Science in Education" is also operating.

In the Basque Country, a "Pilot Scheme for the Teaching of Computer Science at Secondary School" has been launched by the Computer Science Faculty of the University of the Basque country under the direction of Luis Guruchaga. The aim is to equip ten institutes in the province of Guipuzcoa with micro-computers, devise programmes for their classes and train the teaching staff to teach them. The University ICE has also held a course entitled "Introduction to Computer Handling".

In Valencia, at the Centro de Informatica de la Universidad Literaria (Isidro Ramos), various experiments have been made with teaching the PASCAL language at secondary level. The ICE has held courses entitled "Introduction to the PASCAL Programming Language: Computer Science in the BUP" and "PASCAL Language: An Advanced Course".

The ICEs of several other universities are also working on the subject. The ICE of the University of Murcia has offered courses on "Computer Science at Upper EGB Level", "Computer Science and Education in FP and the BUP", "Computer Science and Education at EGB Level" and "Computer Science in EGB Teacher Training Colleges"; the ICE of the University of Seville, on "Computer Aids for Teaching Mathematics in the BUP 2nd Class", "Introduction to Micro-Processors", "Introduction to Computer Science and Basic Programming" and "Introducing Computer Science into Intermediate Education through Mathematics"; the ICE of the University of Saragossa, on "Microcomputers and an Introduction to BASIC" and "Introduction to the Use of Programmable Calculators and Programming"; the University of La Laguna, "Calculators in Class", "Introduction to Computer Science for Teachers" and "Advanced Course in Computer Science"; and the University of Alicante, on "Micro-computers and their uses in Teaching Physics and Chemistry at BUP and COU levels" and "Programming in BASIC and its uses at BUP and COU levels"; other courses have been held by the ICEs of the Universities of Santander, Malaga and Valladolid.

1.6.5 REFERENCES

AGUADO-MUNOZ, R
"Las calculadoras de bolsillo en la enseñanza de las matemáticas", in "Cursillos sobre Didáctica Matemática", vol. XI, CSIC Madrid 1976.

AGUADO-MUNOZ, R
"De la calculadora al microordenador", contribution to the Buitrago Symposium. 1981.

AGUADO-MUNOZ, R
"La informática en el bachillerato", in "El País", 9.1.82 (Tribuna Libre).

AGUADO-MUNOZ, R + BLANCO, A + ZAMARRENO, R
"El aula de la informática", in "La Educación informática en la Enseñanza General". Buitrago, 1981 (Fundesco).

AGUADO-MUNOZ, R + BLANCO, A + ZAMARRENO, R
"Un ayudante en la clase de Matemáticas", in the journal

"Numéros", No. 3 1982, pp 103-106.

AGUADO-MUNOZ, R + BLANCO, A + ZABALA, J + ZAMERRENO, R

"Basic Básico. Programación de ordenadores", published by the authors, 1982.

AGUADO-MUNOZ, R + BLANCO, A + ZAMARRENO, R

"Las calculadoras en el aula", in "Revista de Bachillerato", No. 17, Madrid, 1978, pp 51-55.

AGUADO-MUNOZ, R + BLANCO, A, + ZAMARRENO, R

"Las calculadoras en el aula", Amaya Publications, 1982 (book).

AGUADO-MUNOZ, R, + BLANCO, A, + ZAMARRENO, R

"De la Calculadora al Ordenador", in "La educación informática en la Enseñanza General", Buitrago, 1981 (Fundesco).

AGUADO-MUNOZ, R, + BLANCO, A, + ZAMARRENO, R

"La informática integrada en el bachillerato como EATP", in "La educación informática en la Enseñanza General", Buitrago 2-4 April 1981 (Fundesco).

AGUADO-MUNOZ, R, + BLANCO, A, + ZAMARRENO, R

"Microordenadores y Eduación" in "Revista de Bachillerato", No. 17, pp 12-15.

AGUADO-MUNOZ, R, + BLANCO, A, + ZAMARRENO, R

"si Arquimides hubiera tenido calculadora", in "Il Jornadas de grupos de Matemáticos", Seville, April 1982, 9 p.

AGUADO-MUNOZ, R, + BLANCO, A, + ZAMARRENO, R

"Simulaciones alcatorias", in "Revista Bachillerato", special issue on mathematics, Madrid, 1980, pp 72-77.

ALDEANUEVA, Antonio

"Proyección del ordenador en la educación", in "Actas del Primer Congreso Hispano-Luso de Informática", Madrid, 1971, pp 231-233.

BLANCO, Agustin

"Aula de informática en los Institutos de Bachillerato", contribution to the Buitrage Symposium, 1981.

BANCO RUIZ, A, + REVILLA GONZALEZ, F

"Sistema de apoyo gráfico para la ensenanza de la Geografía", INB Herrera Oria, 1982.

CANO SEVILLA, Francisco

    "Enseñanza con Ordenador", Cuadernos Fundesco, No. 11, pp 114-119, 1975.

CASULLERAS REGAS, J, + GARCIA RAMOS, L, + PUJADES DURAN, R, + TORRA FERRE, V

    Reseña sobre actividades en Barcelona del grupo de trabajo sobre enseñanza de ordenadores en secundaría, in "ordenadores en la Escuela Secundaria", Madrid, 1971, pp 141-184.

CIVANTOS, M; + SANCHEZ, A, + GARCIA CAMARERO, E

    Reseña de la experiencia didactica sobre ordenadores realizada en Madrid, in "Ordenadores en la Escuela Secundaria", Madrid, 1971, pp 35-48.

COELLO GARAU, Gloria

    "Comparación de algoritmos en Bachillerato", INB Herrera Oria, 1982.

COMISION ESPAÑOLA DE LA IFIP

    Informo sobre sus deliberaciones y recomendaciones (Western European Symposium on Computer Education), Madrid, CCUM, 1969, 37 p.

ESTEBAN, M A, + REBOLLEDO, M A, + ARLEGUI, F J

    El simulador MED de la 70/13 en la IBI-1620, in "Ordenadores en la Escuela Secundaria", Madrid, 1971, pp 123-139.

FERNANDEZ FLOREZ, I, + RAMOS, I

    70/13 Translator, in "Ordenadores en la Escuela Secundaria", Madrid, 1971, pp 49-65.

FERNAUD, B, + ZAVALA, M L, + PASCUA PIQUERA, M

    Resumen sobre el curso de ordenadores impartido en la Universidad laboral de Alcalá de Henares, in "Ordenadores en la Escuela Secundaria", Madrid, 1971, pp 185-204.

FUNDESCO

    La informática aplicada a la educación. Madrid, Cuadernos Fundesco. (1978).

FUNDESCO

    El ordenador y la Educación (Actas de las Jornadas sobre Ordenadores y Eduación), Cuadernos Fundesco, No. 11.

GARCIA CAMARERO, E

"An experiment in Computer Education in Secondary Schools", in "1972 Conference on Computers in Undergraduate Curricula", Atlanta, Georgia, 1972.

GARCIA CAMARERO, E

"Educación en informática", in "Novatecnia", 23-1, 1970.

GARCIA CAMARERO, E

"L'enseignement de l'informatique dans l'école secondaire: L'entrainement des professeurs", in "Les politiques de formation des informaticiens", OECD, Paris, May 1973.

GARCIA CAMARERO, E, + BUJOSA, A

La enseñanza de la informatica, in "Automatica", No. 6, Madrid, 1969.

GARCIA CAMARERO, E

"Enseñanza de la Informática", Cuadernos Fundesco, No. 11, pp 120-151, 1975.

GARCIA CAMARERO, E

"La enseñanza de la informática en la escuela secundaria: La preparación de profesores", in "Informática", January 1974.

GARCIA CAMARERO, E

Enseñanza de Ordenadores en la Escuela, in "Ordenadores en la Escuela Secundaría", Madrid, 1971, pp 1-34.

GARCIA CAMARERO, E

La enseñanza de ordenadores en la Escuela Secundaria", in "Boletin CCUCM", No. 7, pp 5-7, Madrid, 1969.

GARCIA CAMARERO, E

La enseñanza de ordenadores en Secundaria, in "Boletin CCUCM", No. 12, pp 1-9, Madrid, 1970.

GARCIA CAMARERO, E

"La enseñanza del ordenador", in "El Ordenador y la Enseñanza", No. 16, pp 64-83, 1975.

GARCIA CAMARERO, E

"Informatics as a basic discipline", in "The Rio Symposium on Computer Education for Developing Countries", Rio de Janeiro, 1972, pp S.5.20-23.

GARCIA CAMARERO, E

    "Informatica en la Educacion Basica", in "Actas del Primer Congreso Hispano-Luso de Informatica", Madrid, 1971, pp. 21-219.

GARCIA CAMARERO, E

    Manuel de Informatica para niños, Madrid, 1971, 68 pp.

GARCIA CAMARERO, E

    La Máquina didáctica 70/13, in "Boletín CCUCM", nos. 8 and 9, pp. 28-31, Madrid, 1970.

GARCIA CAMARERO, E

    Ordenadores en la Enseñanza Secundaria", in "Informática", no. 12, pp. 3-5, Madrid, 1970.

GARCIA CAMARERO, E

    "Programa de un Curso de Informática para BUP", in "La educación informática en la Enseñanza General", Buitrago 2-4 April 1981 (Fundesco).

GARCIA CAMARERO, E and FERNANDEZ FLOREZ, I, and RAMOS, I

    "A basic language oriented to secondary school", in "Information Processing 71", North-Holland, Amsterdam, 1972.

GRUPO DE PROFESORES ZONA SANTIAGO

    Proyecto de dotación de ordenadores en Centros escolares de EGB y BUP.

HEREDIA, Zacarias

    La evaluación mediante ordenador, in "Communidad Educativa", no. 18, January 1972.

ICE Universidad Politécnica de Madrid

    "Estudio para la utilización del ordenador en la formación del Profesorado de EGB" cf: La informática aplicada a la educación, p. 33.

IGUACEN, Felix

    La técnica al servicio de la educación, in "Comunidad Educativa", no. 18, January 1972.

"Investigaciones en curso pertenecientes al plan Nacional 1978(VIII) de la red INCIE-ICES". Cf: La informática aplicada a la educación, p. 32.

ITURRINO, Ignacio

"Algunos trabajos de Fundesco en relación con la enseñanza y el ordenador", Cuadernos Fundesco, no. 16, pp. 56, 1975.

MINGUET, Jesús

"El ordenador y la gestión educativa", Caudernos Fundesco, no. 11, pp. 186-213, 1975.

MINGUET, Jésus

"Gestión educativa", in Cuadernos Fundesco, no. 16, pp. 84-98.

ORTIZ BERROCAL, Luis

"Enseñanza con ordenador", in "El ordenador y la Enseñanza", Cuadernos Fundesco, no. 16, pp. 45-55, 1975.

PACIOS JIMENEZ, M Luisa

La informática en el bachillerato, Madrid, June 1981, 8 p.

RICO, Marcos

"El ordenador como incentivo a la investigación", Cuadernos Fundesco, no. 11, pp. 151-185, 1975.

SOLANOS, M, and ARROYO, M J, and AYESTARAN, J, and ARLEGUI, J

Experiencia en Zaragoza sobre ordenadores en la enseñanza secundaria, in "Ordenadores en la Escuela Secundaria", Madrid, 1971, pp. 67-121.

RUBIALES CAMINO, Enrique

"Las calculadoras de bolsillo de cuatro operaciones, científicas y programables en el BUP y en el COU", study awarded the National Prize for Educational Research with honours in 1979.

RUBIALES CAMINO, E, and ZABALA CAMARERO-NUNEZ, J

"Programa de informática como EATP en Segundo y Tercero de BUP", en II Jornadas de Grupos de Matemáticos", Seville, April, 1982, 9 pp.

SAEZ VACAS, Fernando

"Educación social e informática", in "Actas del Primer Congreso Hispano-Luso de Informática", Madrid, 1971, pp. 235-240.

SANCHEZ IZQUIERDO, Jesús

"Equipos especiales para la enseñanza", Cuadernos Fundesco, no. 11, pp. 213-224, 1975.

SCALA, J J

"Informatics in primary and secondary education in developing countries", in "Computers in education", North Holland, 1975, pp. 135-143.

ZAMERRENO, Ricardo

"La informática integrada en el Bachillerato como Enseñanza y Actividad Técnico Profesional", contribution to the Buitrago symposium, 1978.

1.7 COMPUTER SCIENCE AND EDUCATION
An Overview of Experiences and Research in Italy

by

Prof M. FIERLI
Interregional Board of Education
for Lazio and Umbria

1.7.1   INTRODUCTION

Before approaching the theme of the workshop a few items of information about the Italian school system are given.

The structure of the system is described below:

1. Compulsory education (8 years)

-   Primary school (Scuola Elementare)   (5 years, age 6-10)

-   Lower secondary school (Scuola Media) (3 years, age 11-13)

Both the Scuola Elementare and the Scuola Media have a fixed curriculum and options are not allowed within it.

2. Upper secondary school

There are three different sub-systems:

a. General education

-   Liceo Classico (5 years, age 14-18)

-   Liceo Scientifico (5 years, age 14-18)

-   Istituto Magistrale (4 years, age 14-17)

b. Technical school (Istituto Tecnico) (5 years, age 14-18)

The Istituto Tecnico gives scientific and technical instruction in specific fields (electricity, electronics, computer science, agriculture, administration etc), but it includes also an important component of general education: about 80% of the school time in the 1st and 2nd years and 30% in the last three.

c. Vocational education (Istituto Professionale) (3 years, age 14-16)

The Istituto Professionale are for vocational training in very specific fields and the general education component is reduced to the minimum. It is possible to complete the curriculum in two extra school years.

Centralisation is one of the characteristics of the Italian school system. Curricula, for instance, are fixed at national level. Nevertheless the system is not extremely rigid. For instance, the curriculum of the Scuola Media (which has been revised recently) explicitly states the responsibility of every single school for the selection of topics within the suggested syllabus and for the planning of school activities. The same flexibility exists for the Elementary School, while the curricula of the Upper Secondary school are more prescriptive.

Recently the entire system has been modified with the introduction of several institutions dedicated to educational research, teacher training and experimentation with new curricula. Two of them operate at national level: the CEDE (Centro Europeo dell'Educazione) in Frascati and the BDP (Biblioteca di Documentazione Pedagogica) in Florence. The IRRSAE are regional institutes that promote experimentation at local level. Every single school may experiment: it is possible, that a school adopts new methods or new topics within the traditional subjects (termed "methodological experimentation") or a new curriculum completely different from the national one (termed) "structural experimentation"). Structure experimentation requires a special decree from the Ministry.

These mechanisms to provide flexibility are principally adopted by upper secondary schools because this school level has remained stable since the early sixties so that methodological or structural experimentation is the only channel for innovation. Presently about 10% of upper secondary schools adopt structural experimentation. When referring to the introduction of information technologies in the upper secondary school, we must distinguish between traditional and experimental curricula.

1.7.2   COMPUTER SCIENCE IN THE GENERAL EDUCATION

In the national curricula both at primary and secondary level there are no specific subjects supporting new information technologies as an autonomous component of general education. Even in the traditional subjects, such as mathematics, natural sciences, physics, etc, there are very few references to them.

It is not very common that specific topics of information science (eg theory of algorithms), are explicitly covered in mathematics courses. In many cases there is an implicit use of simple concepts or instruments from computer science (such as flow-charts for the representation of procedures) and it is very common to find in textbooks chapters dedicated to the pocket calculators. Computer science topics, however, are generally introduced in subordinate aspects of mathematics: information, languages and computing are not considered a new scientific area that needs separate treatment.

The only relevant case where information technologies are explictly suggested as a topic in a national curriculum, is in technical education in the Scuola Media. This subject has been recently introduced as compulsory and some teachers are introducing some elements about computers and communication technologies.

Because of the flexibility of curricula in the Scuola Media and the experiments in the upper secondary school, an increasing number of teachers are trying to introduce information science as a separate subject or as a topic within other subjects. It is not easy to give an exhaustive view of these experiences, especially when they involve only non-structural experimentation. There are three main developments. The first is the introduction of programming skills generally for scientific and technical computing. The second is the introduction of the more complex skills of system design and analysis. The third is the introduction of some ideas and models from the theoretical background of information science (such as automata, formal languages and communication), in the context of the analysis of simple natural and artificial systems.

There has been very little research into the introduction of information science in general education. Some developments have given a great emphasis to the study of skills such as observation, analysis and problem solving.

Previously all the developments have been limited and uncoordinated, but now there are some large scale projects, principally supported by public institutions, which provide more systematic action in this field. The most relevant is perhaps the project of the Centro Europeo dell'Educazione (CEDE) at Frascati. The project, (named IRIS), is at an initial stage and a committee has just finished the preliminary work of defining the objectives, the organisation and the timetable. IRIS will produce and experiment with a set of didactic units at primary, lower secondary and upper secondary level. A national sample of schools will be involved in the experiments starting in the 1983/84 academic year. The project includes the creation, at regional level, of a permanent group of teachers involved in the experimentation and supported by the regional institutes for educational research and experimentation (IRRSAE). IRIS is not just a central group of researchers and experts, but draws on practically all the research groups interested in the uses of computers in education (see section 1.7.4). The CEDE has a co-ordinating function.

1.7.3 COMPUTER SCIENCE IN THE TECHNICAL EDUCATION

Technical education in the upper secondary school is the area in which there has been most specific and systematic work towards the introduction of computers and computer science.

There are two curricula specially devoted to the Electronic Data Processing and its applications. The first is orientated to the study of computers and to their industrial applications; this includes a large set of specific subjects, eg computer science, electronics, automatic systems, statistics and operational research. The second is orientated to administrative applications and includes only one specific subject: computer science: but in some of the traditional subjects (eg management and accountancy) the analysis and automation of administrative systems are very important topics. Both the above curricula were set up in the academic year 1967/68 and in this period the number of schools involved has grown rapidly.

	1967/68	1982/83
Industrial applications course	4	52
Administrative applications course	4	76

All these schools are, or soon will be, equipped with computers. The typical configuration has been a minicomputer with 3-8 terminals, the number depending on the number of classes involved. In the industrial applications course systems for the study and the development of electronic programmable devices are widely used. Now new configurations are being installed, consisting of a network of personal computers sharing common disks, printers and plotters.

In addition to the important task of training a number of technicians, these courses have given the opportunity for many interesting methodological innovations. For example in mathematics teaching such new topics have been introduced as formal logic and numerical analysis and the use of computers as aids for learning has been formally established. Unfortunately there is resistance to the transfer of experiences from the specialised courses to the others: even in the same school there is in general little osmosis between the computer specialists and the other students.

A more general process of transformation of all the technical courses has started. More schools, for instance, are adopting experimental curricula that introduce major changes in the existing electronic and telecommunication topic. A reform law for the upper secondary school, that the parliament is discussing this year, provides a specific section of the curriculum for mathematics and computer science and several topics, including administration and electronics, in which information technologies will be an important component.

1.7.4 COMPUTER BASED LEARNING

In the late sixties and early seventies educational technology, including Computer Based Learning, became very popular in Italy. Many conferences were organised and much research conducted. The impact on schools, however, was practically nil. The only effective large scale application was in the computer industries own industrial training. In four or five years interest in educational technology decreased very rapidly and only two or three research groups continued work principally developing courses at the university level.

More recently, in the last two or three years, Computer Based Learning (CBL) has gained new supporters. The Italian Association for Automatic Computing (AICA), for instance, has established a specific working group concerned with the educational uses of computers. The research is no longer exclusively orientated to university courses, and there are interesting, but still limited, experiences involving secondary schools. At the same time the concept of CBL has expanded from simple programmed instruction to a wider range of learning activities including simulation, discovery and the testing of models.

The IRIS project (see Section 1.7.2), whilst principally dedicated to the introduction of computer science into the curricula, provides some units using CBL methodologies for mathematics, physics, statistics. The use of computers for mathematics teaching in technical schools is moving in the same direction: the interesting concept of the "mathematics laboratory" has been born.

Previously in Italy there has not existed any commercial production and supply of CBL packages. The conditions for this commercial development are being created just now: personal and home computers are spreading over the country very rapidly and major publishers are planning the production of educational software.

1.7.5 TEACHERS' TRAINING AND SENSIBILISATION

As for many other educational innovations, teacher training is a key element in the introduction of new technologies in our schools. A central initiative has been taken by the Ministry of Education for in-service training of teachers of specialised schools (see Section 1.7.3). A structured set of courses has been organised and repeated for many years and teachers of specific subjects attend them. The co-ordination of teacher training and curriculum development is giving very good results.

There are also some opportunities for non-specialist teachers. At least three regional institutes (see Section 1.7.1) are promoting important programmes for the familiarisation and training of teachers of various traditional subjects.

An important familiarisation project for teachers' sensibilisation has been prepared for the Ministry of Education by a private company operating in the field of vocational training and counselling about new information technologies. The project provides for the production and the distribution to a very large number of secondary schools of a self-instructional multi-media package, including textbooks, audiocassettes but not computer programs.

The last initiative to be mentioned is that of the working group on the educational uses of computer of the Italian Association for Automatic Computing (see section 1.7.4). The group organised its first summer school, in September 1982, for teachers interested in studying CBL techniques.

The IRIS project provides systematic training of teachers engaged in their experiments.

1.8 COMPUTERS IN SWEDISH SCHOOLS
A Presentation of Experience, Research and Problems

by

Dr Anita KOLLERBAUR
Department of Information Processing
and Computer Science, University of Stockholm

1.8.1   SUMMARY

Research and development in Sweden relating to computers in schools have been divided into three main sections.

1.   Instruction concerning computers and their use in society.

2.   The use of computers in schools to modernise teaching content in various subjects.

3.   The use of computers as an aid to learning.

Sections 1 and 2 are dealt with separately from section 3 in this paper.

Knowledge concerning the way in which teaching about and with computers should be designed has been gained primarily by empirical means. A general description is given of the arrangement and follow-up of the experimental activities which have been conducted. The various questions discussed in the paper are considered in the light of experience accruing from this experimentation.

Some important standpoints concerning the content and organisation of teaching are presented and discussed. The attitudes of teachers and pupils towards the teaching are considered, as well as the results achieved.

The following are required to facilitate the introduction of teaching in schools:

-   Teacher - In-service Education and Training (INSET).

-   Access to adequate teaching materials, including software and hardware.

A general description is given of the Swedish approach and of the current debate in a number of problem areas.

A number of prerequisites of viable teaching over a longer period of time are discussed.

In the context of Computer Assisted Learning (CAL), the approach which has been chosen for study in Sweden is presented together with the current state of research.

1.8.2 INTRODUCTION

The computer can be applied to a wide variety of purposes in the school sector. It can be used for such administrative tasks as timetabling, resource distribution etc or to support teaching in various ways. It can also be used for general instruction concerning computers and their utilisation in the community.

Research, development and the introduction of computers in schools in Sweden are considered under three headings.

1. Instruction concerning computers and their utilisation in the community, in short: computer appreciation.

2. The use of computers in schools as a means of modernising teaching subjects, eg the computer as a calculating aid. In short: subject-related computer utilisation.

3. The use of computers as an aid to learning. In short: computer-assisted learning (CAL).

The first of these headings implies general instruction for all pupils at the senior level of compulsory school (grade 9 at present) and in all lines of grade 1 of upper secondary school. The rule is that computers are to be used as calculation aids and as a means of illustrating computer utilisation in various upper secondary school disciplines. R & D work relating to these two fields was undertaken between 1974 and 1979 in the DIS project (DIS being the Swedish abbreviation of "Computers in schools"). The results of that project are now being applied to everyday school activities.

Within the CAL sector, research is still continuing under the PRINCESS project (Project for Research on INteractive Computer-based Education Systems), which will be concluded in 1982.

The present paper deals then primarily with the first and second of the above-mentioned fields and contains a general account of working method used, standpoints adopted, experience gained and problems encountered.

1.8.3 EXPERIMENTATION - A FIRST ESSENTIAL

Analyses of similar instruction in Sweden and abroad revealed that no international experience was directly applicable to Swedish schools. Knowledge concerning the way in which instruction should be designed and deployed has been gained primarily through practical experimentation. Teachers and EDP specialists have, for example, formulated and revised ideas concerning syllabi, the construction of experimental teaching materials in several iterations interspersed with experimental activities.

Experiments have been conducted, at both levels, in schools having access to computer equipment of various makes and in schools having no such equipment at all. Syllabi, teaching materials, teaching methods and INSET have all been studied in the course of the experiments, which have involved a total of some 450 teachers and 8,000 pupils, divided between computer appreciation (300 teachers and 5,000 pupils approx.) and subject related computer utilisation (about 150 teachers and 3,000 pupils). No systematic investigation has been made of the spill-over of the experiments, but as every teacher teaches several classes in the concerned subjects, the number of involved students are much higher.

The experiments were evaluated by means of questionnaires distributed to pupils and teachers, through discussions at conferences of teachers and pupils, and in field trips to various schools. This evaluation was above all aimed at identifying the advantages and drawbacks of computer appreciation.

All municipalities and county councils have been invited to take part in these experiments, and the level of interest has been such that participants have had to be selected. Selection criteria have varied according to the particular problems to be studied, but one aim has been to distribute the experiments geographically and, within the municipalities taking part, to conduct them in both compulsory and upper secondary schools.

The teachers taking part in the experimental activities were given a week's INSET during the summer holidays. They had various reasons for taking part in the experiments. Most of them did so spontaneously, while others were persuaded by colleagues. Others again were put down for participation by their Local Education Authorities (LEAs). The group as a whole was presumably rather more favourably disposed than the average teacher would be towards teaching with and about computers.

The computer appreciation syllabi were revised no less than three times. The first syllabus was tried out in 1974/75, the second and third in 1975/76 and 1976/77 respectively. The experience accruing from these experiments formed the basis of a concluding round of experimentation in 1977/78, on which standpoints concerning the way in which Swedish schools are to be provided with general instructions about computers and their use were thus based.

During the experiments, the teachers devoted between 20 and 40 lessons to computer appreciation.

1.8.4 INSTRUCTION CONCERNING COMPUTERS AND THEIR USE IN SOCIETY - ARRANGEMENT, EXPERIENCE AND PROBLEMS

Sweden has decided to integrate general instruction about computers and their use with various teaching subjects, instead of introducing a new teaching subject. There were two main reasons for this.

1. It is unrealistic to create new subjects parallel to changes in the community at large. The tendency in Swedish schools is more in favour of projects or thematic studies.

2. Instead of equipping pupils with specialised knowledge, the intention was to present the computer as an aid for various purposes.

Computer appreciation could have been integrated with a vast number of subjects, from Swedish to mathematics, but for practical reasons this integration has been confined mostly to mathematics and civics. These subjects are taken by all compulsory school pupils, and they are also included in most lines of upper secondary school.

The purpose of computer appreciation has never been debated. The aim throughout has been to convey knowledge which will make it easier for pupils to appraise and influence the use of computers in society.

On the other hand, when the DIS project started, opinions were divided concerning the detailed teaching content required in order to confer this knowledge. The slant which the project team wanted to give to computer appreciation differed from the approach adopted in other European countries and the United States, in that it was far more societally oriented. But many Swedish specialists at the time would also have preferred a more technical emphasis than was proposed.

Apart from the approach to be adopted, the level at which instruction was to be provided and the detailed content with which it was to be invested were also debated points. Should this instruction come at the senior level of compulsory school or in the first grade of upper secondary school? Some people maintained that compulsory school pupils were insufficiently mature for computer appreciation. (Pupils leave compulsory school at age 15 or 16.)

The experiments showed that instruction could be introduced at the senior level of compulsory school, and computer appreciation is now a compulsory feature of the mathematics and social subjects syllabi. It is also mentioned in the natural science syllabus.

Compulsory school pupils are introduced to the various fields of computer processing which exist today and may conceivably come into being in the community at large. This introduction serves to make them aware of the consequences of computerisation in relation to the individual and society. This instruction also conveys an idea of computerised data processing and of the potentialities and limitations of different ways of designing data systems. It also includes a general presentation of legislation governing the use of computers.

Programming has not been made a compulsory teaching subject in compulsory school, partly for financial reasons but also for reasons connected with the subject itself. This is a somewhat controversial matter, and there is a debate in progress concerning the value of BASIC programming in relation to the goals laid down for this instruction. Some protagonists argue that programming needs to be taught so as to bring the whole subject down to earth and facilitate a proper understanding of the various sections of computer appreciation, while others maintain that no such knowledge is needed.

During the experiments, most of the pupils at the senior level of compulsory school were against practical training in programming. This may, of course, have been due to the number of computer work stations being insufficient. Discussions with teachers have shown that a small number of pupils are genuinely interested, while others are content to "play" with ready-made programmes, which should ultimately constitute an important element. The instruction also includes practical features in the form of field trips to industry and public administration.

In the debate for and against programming, it should also be borne in mind that simple BASIC programming is easier to teach than the consequences of computerisation.

Some portions of the general instruction were too difficult for pupils at the senior level of compulsory school. This was particularly true of sections concerning structural change in society, international perspectives, advanced studies of detailed points, implications for the individual, problems relating to privacy and secrecy etc. These sections have therefore been transferred to upper secondary school.

The instruction given in upper secondary school is designed to give the student an appreciation of the way in which computerisation affects the social structure and also of the apportionment of responsibilities. Special emphasis has to be laid on the use of the information network and on the role and opportunities of the individual in connection with the introduction and use of computer systems at various workplaces. Students in the three and four-year theoretical streams of upper secondary school must be able to use computers for problem solving by writing programmes of their own in a high level language.

The experiments conducted in vocational lines of upper secondary school have shown that instruction should be given more of a practical slant, so as to provide the students with the knowledge they need concerning the impact of data processing on a particular occupation or field, and so as to prepare them for activities within that field.

The teachers have found some sections heavier going than others. This applies particularly to sections dealing with problems relating to the development and introduction of EDP systems. Inter-subject integration has failed to work in some cases. The general introduction to computers has been treated as a separate section and has sometimes within the subjects been inadequately planned and adapted. Otherwise pupils and teachers have found this integration tremendously rewarding. Normally there is no planning co-ordination between these subjects.

Both teachers and pupils feel that computer appreciation should be jointly based on mathematics and civics. Computer appreciation has proved feasible within these subjects without any detrimental effect on the subjects themselves. In upper secondary school mathematics, students have actually been found to acquire a more positive attitude towards the subject, and by using the computer in problem solving they have developed their capacity for formalising and solving problems.

Both teacher and pupils have been asked concerning their attitudes towards computer appreciation and the use of computers in society. After receiving this instruction, 73 per cent of the pupils find computer appreciation fairly or very interesting, while the remainder are indifferent and find the subject fairly or very tedious. 82 per cent of the pupils agree, wholly or partially, that our society needs computers, while the remainder are indifferent or disagree to a greater or lesser extent. All teachers feel that computer appreciation should be put on the school timetable and that the proposed syllabus is a good one. The conditions for introducing computer appreciation were consequently advantageous.

The effects of the experiments were favourable. The instruction has increased the pupils' knowledge of facts concerning computerisation, and it has improved their ability to adopt standpoints to statements concerning the use of computers in society and to follow the current debate. The experiments have also shown this instruction to provide natural opportunities for project and problem-oriented teaching. The pupils for their part find the instruction pre-eminently realistic, due of course to such activities as field trips to workplaces where computers are used. Computer appreciation also provides opportunities of varying working methods from individual studies to group work.

1.8.5 THE USE OF COMPUTERS AS A MEANS OF MODERNISING TEACHING SUBJECTS

The DIS project also had the task of investigating potential uses of the computer in schools as an aid to calculation and methods at upper secondary level, above all in the illustration of computerisation by means of practical examples. Development work was confined to mathematics, physics, business economics and various groups of technical subjects. These activities presupposed that the upper secondary school students had been taught computer appreciation before starting to use computers in various subjects.

Special attention will be devoted here to the experience gained concerning mathematics and the use of the computer in commercial subjects.

Two main approaches are involved where commercial subjects are concerned. One of these is to develop special computer programmes for school teaching ie programmes which often provide a miniature depiction of the activities concerned. The other entails using programmes from companies and organisations which are only slightly modified to suit the teaching situation, eg by means of specially formulated instructions and simplified communication with the programme.

The students greatly appreciated using software coming straight from real life, while some of the teachers found it difficult to integrate these programmes with their own teaching. Existing teaching activities have to be extensively replanned, and the teacher himself has to be highly proficient in the use of the programme. The programmes which have been developed for schools are easier for teachers to handle but appear to generate less motivation on the part of students. More will be said below concerning the level of programmes.

In mathematics, numerical methods have been integrated with teaching by means of computer support. These experiments showed eg:

- Pupils can work experimentally in order to discover mathematical relationships.

- Subject matter can be made more concrete.

- The pupils acquire a more solid foundation for the analytical aspects of mathematics.

- Greater co-ordination can be achieved between physics and mathematics.

- Numerical methods can be used in other subjects, especially technical ones.

1.8.6   IN-SERVICE TRAINING

One week's INSET was provided in connection with the experiment. Teachers were then expected to be able to provide instruction as per the syllabus on the strength of independent studies and planned collaboration with their colleagues, as regards both computer appreciation and the subject-related use of computers. This INSET, of course, was far too short, and under an INSET reform which took effect in the summer of 1982, the participating compulsory school teachers will be given three weeks' training and their upper secondary school counterparts at least five weeks' training.

Various models have been discussed for this INSET, but for quality reasons the choice has fallen on direct INSET, which means that the teachers will be trained by special subject and methods experts. The method at present being used is for the teachers to take place in a course at a college or in distance teaching conducted by a college. The goal is that approximately 30,000 teachers will be trained by 1986. This will probably not be fulfilled due to lack of resources of various kinds.

Experience of this INSET model has been limited so far. Experimental activities based on the model have shown that the teachers are prepared to engage in the training envisaged after the course; in other words, the volume of training appears to be correct.

The teachers are able to study during working hours, and they can choose between studying part time and full time. Most of the teachers taking part in the experiments preferred half time, however, because they felt that this way they would assimilate things better. The Union, on the other hand, felt in principle that studies should be conducted on a full time basis.

INSET has been given essentially the same content as the instruction to be given to the pupils, though in greater depth in some respects.

1.8.7   TEACHING MATERIALS

Computer appreciation and computer utilisation demand new teaching materials in schools, viz computer programs - software, and computer equipment - hardware. This in turn raises a number of questions. What software and hardware are needed for teaching? How are these acquisitions to be financed? And so on.

The simplest solution to the school computer problem is to develop a national computer which all schools have to install. This eliminates the problems of purchasing, of software immobility, of close and compelling links between a particular computer make and printed teaching materials etc.

But is this the best solution? This question need not be decided in Sweden for the time being, as computer equipment is purchased at local (municipal) level. In addition, the general opinion among those responsible for such matters in schools is that the individual school and municipality must be free to choose their teaching materials and that this is an advantage from the instructional viewpoint. But of course, a national school computer can compete in the procurement process, which should result in the choice of the best computer at the lowest price.

A technology procurement project has been started in Sweden with the aim of giving Swedish enterprise and industry a better chance of competing in the school computer market, and this may result in a Swedish school computer. Swedish firms have been invited to tender a (new?) product on the basis of a detailed specification drawn up jointly by representatives of schools, research and industry.

Examples of the functional stipulations made concerning computer equipment are that each individual station must be capable of development for future applications and the base system function, must embody graphics with a resolution of about 500 x 500 points. In addition, each work station must have facilities for communicating with another, larger computer, either for running programs on the latter or for shifting data and programs between the systems. The requirements also include detailed specifications concerning software and types of documentation. Ergonomic aspects of computer equipment and software have been taken into account. Procurement will begin during the autumn of 1982.

Thus Sweden still has the problem of different schools/municipalities having to do their own purchasing of computers and software. This requires support. A large number of different schools precludes centrally formulated standard specifications. To assist schools in the business of procurement, a detailed report has been compiled by the PRODIS project (Software and computer equipment in schools) at the National Board of Education (NBE). This report deals with requirements concerning computer equipment for different subjects, general stipulations to be made concerning computers and software and schools, operating problems, how to draw up a specification of requirements etc. In addition, staff receive central guidance from the NBE (through the DUN project - DUN being short for "The computer in teaching") and from the Swedish Association of Local Authorities.

But even if "good" purchasing is within the bounds of possibility, there are still problems. Often no specification is made of requirements. Instead an approach is simply made to a supplier who is said to have suitable equipment (purchased, perhaps, by a school in the neighbouring municipality). Representatives of different subjects differ in their awareness and influence when a school is about to purchase a computer. If the mathematics teacher dominates his school, this can result in the purchase of equipment which makes poor provision for the requirements of economics subjects.

Another problem concerns the difficulties involved in forecasting needs both quantitatively, ie in terms of the number of computer work stations, and qualitatively, ie in terms of the way in which the computer will be used. In 1979, for example, five work stations per school was considered a minimum requirement. This had already risen to 10, preferably 15 work stations per school by 1981. (Needless to say, the number of work stations had to be adjusted to the size of the school concerned.)

In addition, greater demands are being made concerning facilities for the use of advanced software. For example, teachers illustrating data processing in the community at large want to be able to show data base handling, and this makes special demands on the equipment.

BASIC is at present practically the sole language used for pupil programming and for developing applications programs for schools. It is agreed, however, that this is not a very happy state of affairs. BASIC has many advantages. It is easy to learn and can be used with practically any kind of computer. On the other hand, it is a non-structured language and therefore does not directly support a natural way of solving problems.

No systematic efforts have yet been made to use other languages besides BASIC. As part of the research activities of the CLEA (Computer-based LEArning environments) centre, work has begun on the analysis of different languages with reference to the requirements for a school language.

Another problem connected with software and hardware is that of who is to develop and distribute applications programs for schools. At present this is done almost exclusively by producers of teaching materials. A certain amount of development is being financed by the State, and these programs are of course available free. Various methods of encouraging teachers to develop their own programmes have been tried in Sweden, and attempts have also been made to devise ways of distributing information about these various programs. But it has not been possible for example, to create a common data base for programs developed by teachers who have been unwilling, for various reasons, to part with their software.

1.8.8 INTEGRATION OF THE EDUCATIONAL AND ADMINISTRATIVE USE OF COMPUTERS

The integration of the administrative and educational use of computers in schools has been a much discussed topic in Sweden. When research and development began in the DIS and PRINCESS projects in 1973, the widely accepted view was that financial considerations would lead to the integration of the educational and administrative use of computers in schools. This, it was argued, was the only possible way of putting computing resources at the disposal of schools, and the rationalisation benefits thus obtained in the administrative context would finance the use of computers for teaching purposes. A careful inquiry was undertaken with a view to this type of integrated solution, and it had been proposed that a model experiment should be mounted in one municipality. Thus it was hoped that the actual procurement of computer hardware for schools would not require any new resources. The DIS project, however, took a critical view of this solution and began by drawing up one calculation for a purely educational solution one for a purely administrative one and a third for an integrated solution. These calculations were founded on the use of a mini computer system in various configurations. They showed that there would be negligible differences in the costs respectively entailed by the three types of solution. The DIS project therefore proceeded to study the educational use of computers in schools without considering the possibility of their administrative use. Existing forecasts indicated also at that time that the cost of hardware would eventually become a less burdensome item in connection with the use of computers.

The same debate is now in progress at municipal level. School policy makers and school administrators often stipulate that the computer must be used in school administration, making this a condition for funding the procurement of equipment for classroom use. Some schools, however, have adjusted to this stipulation and integrated their administration with the educational use of computers. Some schools have common access to the computer, ie the computer is used simultaneously for administration and teaching but there are separate terminal work points available. Other schools have reserved certain days for administrative data processing. In schools which have purchased micro-computers, the administrative side has a micro-computer of its own. The latter case does not present any integration problems. The other two, understandably, have proved to be a mixed blessing. No systematic analyses have been made of experience hitherto, but the occasional instance has been reported of pupils managing to penetrate security systems in the software and destroying administrative data and programs, which has naturally been a cause of worry.

Thus it remains to make school policy makers at municipal level recognise that integration of administrative and educational use of computers has to be carefully analysed from different points of view.

1.8.9   CONTINUITY

So far we have been mainly concerned with problems surrounding the introduction of computer appreciation and utilisation in schools. The question of how to keep activities going is no less important.

There is, for example, the question of how to update teaching. Methods will have to be devised for continuously revising teaching content. This involves problems relating to both teaching materials and INSET, problems which are now discussed but have not yet been solved.

Another question concerns ways of keeping teachers motivated to provide the instruction desired. The Swedish experience is that teachers do not continue this instruction to the same extent as during the experimental phase. The new INSET model, whereby INSET is to be organised in conjunction with local development work at the individual school, may perhaps solve the problem of ensuring that teachers continue to teach computer appreciation and use computers in different subjects. The fact that the syllabi are now compulsory may also make a difference, but the need for some kind of continuous stimulus for teachers is not to be underestimated.

Finally it should be observed that, in order for those portions of teaching requiring the use of computers to function smoothly in schools, there must be an organisation which is reponsible for the computer system, its operation and development and for providing teachers and pupils with some kind of back-up in their practical use of computer equipment. There is more to it than just installing a computer.

1.8.10   THE USE OF THE COMPUTERS AS AN AID TO LEARNING

The experience gained by Swedish schools of CAL has mostly been geared to research within the PRINCESS project. Since this project has not yet been completed, only the approach adopted to CAL will be presented, together with research methods and experience of the same.

PRINCESS is concerned to see whether, and if so how, education can be improved by the use of computer aids. A model of a system for computer-based education is being developed and continously evaluated.

The pedagogical approach in PRINCESS can be summarised as follows:

- Knowledge is derived from the experience gained while performing activities.

- The student must be able to control the activity.

PRINCESS has focused its research on general computer aids for storage/retrieval, processing and communication of data and computer aids for interactive work with subject models of different types.

The PRINCESS approach to computer-based learning entails particular requirements concerning such courses. An interactive program used in a course of this kind should:

- Make operations on non-trivial models available, eg work with analytical models, information retrieval and simulation.

- Be easy to use.

- Be easy to modify and develop, from a subject viewpoint as well as in terms of pedagogical approach and in concrete interactions.

- Be executable with different types of input and output facilities.

A system of computer-based education used in schools are in principle regarded as shown in the following picture.

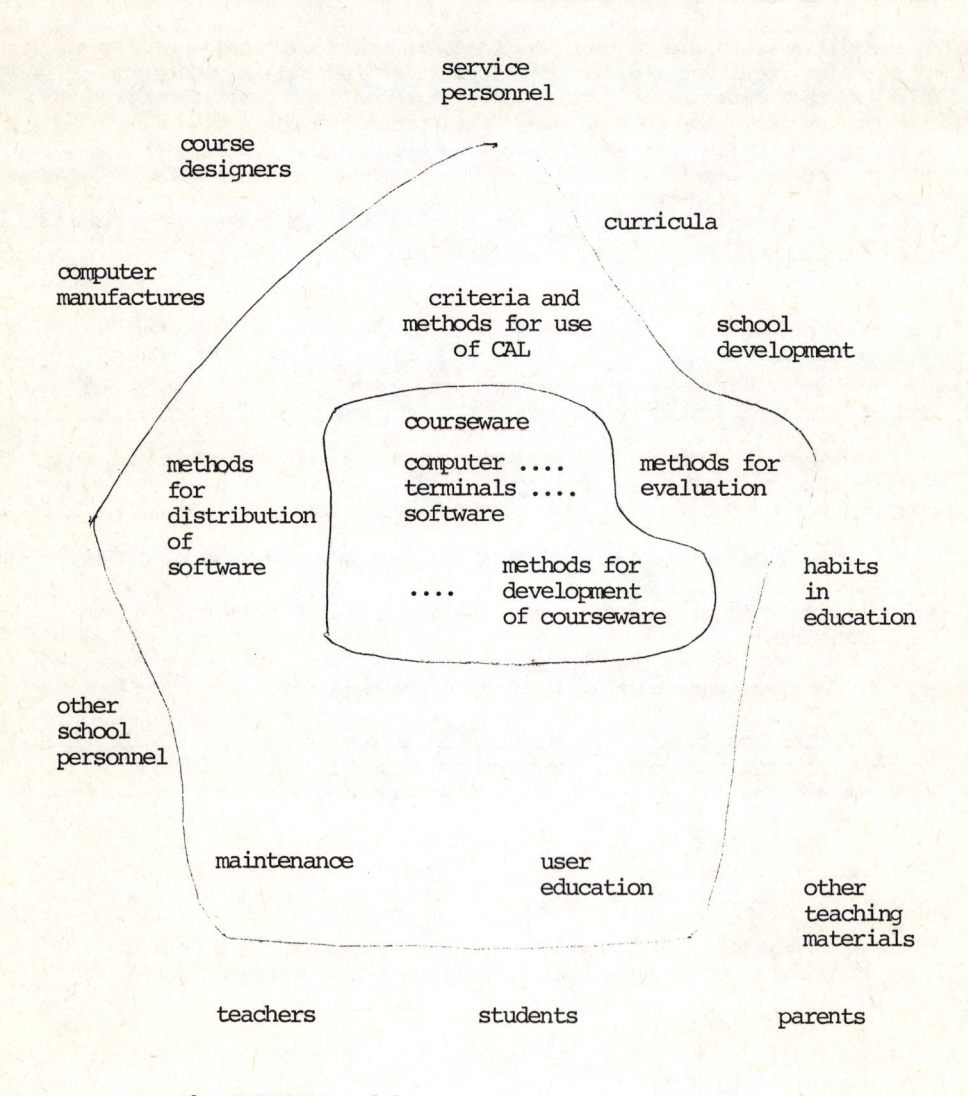

service personnel

course designers

curricula

computer manufactures

criteria and methods for use of CAL

school development

courseware
computer ....
terminals ....
software

methods for distribution of software

methods for evaluation

.... methods for development of courseware

habits in education

other school personnel

maintenance

user education

other teaching materials

teachers

students

parents

The PRINCESS model

90

Research includes all parts of a system shown in the picture, of computer-assisted instruction (CAI). The definitive results will be available for presentation after a final round of experimentation in 1982, during which most teachers and pupils in one school will be involved in CAI.

The research is interdisciplinary, and the approach can be characterised in terms of systems thinking, the conception that pedagogical requirements must influence the technique, and the principle that the people involved must participate in systems development. Furthermore, the development of methods and tools must be interleaved with empirical studies.

The research approach (which is necessary for this type of research) has caused some problems, such as the following:

- Empirical work is time consuming.

- The interdisciplinary approach causes co-ordination problems.

- Part of the work is means-oriented rather than goal-oriented, ie concerned with developing some of the software for the applications.

- Co-operation with users and financiers leaves less time for primary research. Sometimes concrete products had to be presented while basic research was still lacking.

- The academic environment and the application field make different demands on research activities. For instance, reports in Swedish must be the principal means of disseminating results.

- Demand for modern technology combined with a limited budget for equipment has forced the project to purchase badly supported research products.

- It is difficult to exchange equipment within the scheduled duration of a project.

1.8.11 CONCLUDING REMARKS

Sweden has developed a national policy concerning computers in schools. This policy has been discussed and determined by the Riksdag (ie the Swedish parliament) and enjoys strong political support.

But people not attending school also need to learn about computers and their use. In working life, a great deal of instruction in computer appreciation has been organised under the auspices of both employers and unions.

A wide-ranging information drive concerning data questions has been addressed to the general public and has included debate publications, exhibitions, theatrical performances etc. Procedures are being framed to increase the support given to data courses arranged by adult education associations.

The National Swedish Data Policy Commission is paying close attention to education in this broader sense. The Commission is a broad-based committee whose task is to assist the government and Riksdag in data questions. One of its aims is to evolve a Swedish data policy.

PART 2: NATIONAL REPORTS

2.1 AUSTRIA
COMPUTER EQUIPMENT IN AUSTRIAN SECONDARY SCHOOLS

by

Dr Johann CZEMETSCHKA
Federal Ministry of Education
and Culture, Vienna

2.1.1   INTRODUCTION

Instruction in computer science in Austria was first given 15 years ago, first as an optional subject under the "catch-all" title of Topical Studies, then as an optional subject in its own right and nowadays as a compulsory subject in all technical schools. (Technical schools under the Federal Ministry of Education and Arts are subdivided into industrial, commercial and domestic-science schools; they differ from the related vocational schools in that the former have a longer curriculum, which permits university entry by graduates).

Schools were first inadequately supplied through a computing centre of the Ministry (which meant essentially that programs had to be submitted on mark-sensed cards), through computing centres of universities (using port-a-punch cards), through the purchase of computer time on time-sharing computers, and through the acquisition of mini-computers. The decision to comply with the recommendation of the "Seminar on Computer Science in Secondary Education" organised by OECD/CERI in Sèvres in 1970 and purchase only computers programmable in high-level languages, turned out to be most advantageous.

As equipment grew in quantity, the numerous types of hardware, the different programming languages and the frequent lack of compatibility led to difficulties in further training, in software development, and in the supply of pupils with textbooks.

Moreover, in the technical schools computers were to find their way more and more into industrial and commercial subjects, into school laboratories and offices. For the commercial schools there was an urgent need to replace the conventional accounting machines used so far, which were by then no longer either in production or in business use, by more up-to-date hardware. Another necessity was the integration of modern word-processing facilities into typing instruction.

Collaboration of the Ministry, the Provincial School Boards, and subject teachers produced medium-term investment plans, which by now have been realised in full for the commercial schools, to a large extent for the industrial schools, and in one-third of the general schools.

2.1.2 EQUIPMENT OF COMMERCIAL SCHOOLS

Hardware and software suitable for courses in data processing, accounting, and word processing were solicited through public invitation of tenders in compliance with GATT regulations.

After detailed examination, microcomputers were found suitable. At each of the 100 technical commercial schools a specialist classroom (two at the larger schools) was created, housing the following equipment:

10 workplaces, each equipped with a microcomputer of 64 K-bytes capacity, including display screen and twin floppy-disc drives. Each group of five micro-computers is wired to a selector box and thence to a Tally MT 1612 RO printer. Printers are equipped with single-sheet feed for word processing.

Of the 9 provinces, 4 use Alphatronic P2 microcomputers, 4 others Philips P 2000 microcomputers, while 1 uses Commodore hardware. The accounting software (financial accounts, cost accounting and computation of wages) and the text editing and word processing software was developed by the computer companies in close co-operation with teachers.

As classes never exceed a size of twenty pupils - larger classes being split -, one workplace is available for every two pupils.

There are approximately 100 technical commercial schools in Austria, using a total of 1,300 microcomputers and 260 printers, and the computing rooms are equipped according to a common standard. This has meant an investment of over 100 million schillings within a period of three years.

8 different textbooks have been approved for data-processing instruction; selection is made by the teachers. In accounting and word-processing instruction, students also receive free suppliers manuals.

The standardisation of equipment has made software production possible at an economic cost and has also proved effective for systematic further teacher training. At present, dedicated teachers are developing software for school administration, while software for a business simulation game on the microcomputers is in the final completion stage.

2.1.3 EQUIPMENT OF INDUSTRIAL SCHOOLS

There are more than 40 technical industrial schools, using mainly multi-access systems with 6 to 10 terminals and an average memory size of 256 K-bytes. Some schools, however, prefer microcomputers or to use time-sharing terminals. The variety of specialisations precludes a policy of standardisation like that of the commercial schools. Even so, standard equipment has recently been purchased at least on the provincial level in the interest of further teacher training and of program exchange. The total investment value is estimated at approximately 40 million schillings.

Besides instruction in computer science proper, computers are also used for simulation exercises in laboratories, for computing, dimensioning and optimising components, and for exercises in process control. User software is either produced in class, or use is made of smaller industrial programs.

The Ministry's computing centre is equipped with an IBM 4341 system; the CPU has a capacity of 2 M-bytes, with approximately 30 terminals connected. The computing centre works for the administration of schools and is also available for training computer specialists (programmers, EDP managers) both at the secondary and the post-secondary levels.

There is a choice of 10 different textbooks for computer-science instruction.

2.1.4 EQUIPMENT OF GENERAL SCHOOLS

Classroom use of the computer is based on the requirements of the "visual approach" and of "encountering reality" within the context of the syllabus. Thus the accent is on evaluating experiments, on visualising imagined processes, on understanding processes in various sciences by systematic variation of the parameters of a simulation.

Computer science instruction being optional, investments at a given school depend on the interest and commitment of local teachers.

Previous work in computing centres, using mark sensed cards, lacked immediacy and was also hampered by long turn-around times. This is why the new policy provides for the purchase of microcomputers with a display screen, twin floppy-disc drives and a printer. An interface makes connection to a mainframe possible. There is considerable interest in word-processing software.

For a total of 300 general secondary schools, an annual computing investment of 5 to 6 million schillings is planned. By 1985, about 40 per cent of schools are expected to be equipped as above. At present, the scheme is completed for two provinces; 3 more are to follow by the end of 1982.

Co-operation with technical schools is also possible in many places.

Seven textbooks are approved for instruction in computer science.

2.2 BELGIUM (Dutch Language Community)

The situation in Belgium
(Dutch Language Community)

Ministry of Education
and Dutch Culture

2.2.1   MICRO-PROCESSORS IN SECONDARY EDUCATION

There is an optional "computers and programming" course for pupils in the 16 to 18 age-group, in the last two years of upper secondary schooling.

Until September 1981 various types of micro-computers were being used experimentally and occasionally, most often outside class time, by interested pupils and teachers of different subjects at both primary and secondary levels.

In the interest of order and to avoid the proliferation of software production and exchanges, the Minister of Education and Dutch Culture decided to make micro-computers an integral part of teaching. Beginning in September 1981, all state-run schools have offered a supplementary course on "computers and programming" for pupils in the 3rd level of secondary schooling, to provide an introduction to the use of specific micro-processor configurations.

A panel of experts compared existing types and an order was placed. In-service training was immediately made available for the teachers concerned and a provisional syllabus was drawn up.

2.2.2   ALSO AT THE SECONDARY LEVEL THERE IS A "COMPUTER SCIENCES" COURSE (training in programming), with more extensive facilities for using a number of programming languages: BASIC language, COBOL, FORTRAN and PASCAL; this course has been taught for ten years.

2.2.3   IN SECONDARY EDUCATION AND NON-UNIVERSITY HIGHER EDUCATION (technical courses), micro-processors are, of course, dealt with in connection with the "production processes" of quite different fields (engineering, electricity, electronics, chemistry).

2.2.4   IN NON-UNIVERSITY HIGHER EDUCATION there is also a "computer sciences" course designed to train programmer-analysts (see 2.2.2 above).

2.2.5   IN "LONG" NON-UNIVERSITY HIGHER EDUCATION (eg industrial engineering), micro-computers are being used in many courses, for laboratory and other practical work.

2.3 BELGIUM (French Language Community)

The Situation in Belgium
(French Language Community)
Prof. Guy DE LANDSHEERE and D. LECLERCQ

2.3.1   THE INTERNATIONAL BACKGROUND

In most countries the techniques of data processing have been applied in schools in three different ways.

Chronologically, the first application of computers was to management functions, a late-1950s development which consisted in using computers for the correction of tests (more often than not at some later time) and the management of pupils' files and school libraries and which used languages developed for scientific (ALGOL FORTRAN) or administrative (COBOL) purposes. This kind of application, given the generic name computer-managed instruction (CMI), did not hit the headlines when it was first introduced, but it has undergone a process of constant development and, in some pilot experiments, reached a remarkably high standard.

At almost the same time, computer-assisted instruction (CAI) was developed and immediately aroused much greater enthusiasm in educational circles than CMI. There are several reasons for this, the first undoubtedly being that simulated dialogue between a human being and a machine has something of the Promethean about it. A second reason is that, at last, technology offered a means of individualising teaching in 20th century schools, which are far from being able to provide individual tutoring. Lastly, it held out the promise of a fuller understanding of the psychological mechanisms of learning. At the time, a great deal of scientific work on psychology found practical application in CAI, eg research into operant conditioning by Skinner (Harvard), the work then being done by Minsky (MIT) and Pask (United Kingdom) on artificial intelligence or the research into problem solving being done, inter alia, by Simon (Carnegie Melton).

The uses to which CAI could be put expanded very rapidly to include tutorials, drills and practice, tailored testing, simulation, modelling, information retrieval, etc.

The last three uses were, moreover, grouped together and called computer-assisted learning (CAL). When a large part of the curriculum is based on the use of computers, the term computer-based learning (CBL) is preferred.

Finally, towards the end of the 1960s, interest focused on a third use of computers in schools: computer programming by the pupils themselves.

The birth of BASIC at Dartmouth College in 1958 and above all the appearance of micro-computers put the problem in a new light. BASIC is far and away the most widely taught language and yet, despite substantial improvements (eg BASIC PLUS EXTENDED operating on PDP11), it does not, unlike the more recently developed PASCAL, permit structured programming and is far from being an ideal language for training students in data processing (see the criticisms of LEDGARD, 1981, and PAPERT, 1981, p. 50 and p. 263). France has to its credit developments such as LSE (Langage symbolique d'Enseignement - language for science and instruction) and LOVE (Langage Orienté Vers l'Enseignement - instruction-oriented language). Even so, it is the LOGO language, developed by S PAPERT, which seems to hold out the greatest promise at the present time, particularly since it enables very young children to be introduced to data processing.

It is against the background described above that we will discuss the general trends in educational data processing in French-speaking Belgium and some of the pilot experiments being conducted there.

2.3.2   THE DOCEO SYSTEM (The University of Liège)

In 1962, the year which saw the development of the PLATO system at the University of Illinois, the Service de Mathématique Appliquée et de Traitement de l'Information (SMATI) (Applied Mathematics and Data Processing Department) produced the first DOCEO system (Latin "doceo" - I teach). It was designed to operate audiovisual peripherals (projectors) by computer (HOUZIAUX, 1965 and 1972; LEFEBVRE and HOUZIAUX, 1969). A first version (DOCEO I) made it possible to control the random projection of 16 mm films, frame by frame; the pupil entered his answer by means of a telephone dial and the computer's response was displayed by means of illuminated signals.

In 1972, a second version (DOCEO II) made it possible to control a circular slide magazine and a cassette recorder. The programme gave random access to slides and sound track. A new language was developed (LPC - Langage de Programmation des Processus Conversationnels (Conversational Programming Language)) (HOUZIAUX and others, 1978; BARTHOLOME and HOUZIAUX, 1979).

DOCEO II was used primarily by its promoters (Professors VAN CAUWENBERGHE and LEFEBVRE, of the Faculty of Medicine of the University of Liège). Its applications are varied: a number of types of anamnesis (diabetes, rheumatology, dietetics, etc), patient education, training of medical students, etc. Other departments of the university use DOCEO II including chemistry, astrophysics, geography, germanic studies and hygiene.

The laboratoire de pédagogie expérimentale headed by Professor G DE LANDSHEERE has trained teachers in the use of DOCEO II and lessons for secondary school pupils have been developed in a wide variety of fields. Other programmes have been produced on nutrition, understanding spoken English for French-speakers (JAMART and others, 1982) and French for Poles and Vietnamese (OSTERRIETH, 1982). A resolutely "multimedia" approach is used (LECLERCQ, 1980).

2.3.3   THE IMAGO CENTRE (Catholic University of Louvain)

Under the direction of Professor JONES (Department of Physics, CUL), various sequences were produced that comprised successions of audio-visual materials and computer programmes (in FORTRAN), principally in physics, biology and economics.

The project was entitled "Instruction Multimédia Assistée et Gerée par Ordinateur (IMAGO)" (Computer-Assisted and managed multimedia instruction) and gave rise to many publications (JONES, 1971; COOLS and PETEAU, 1974; DUBOIS, 1975; see also UCODI, 1977).

The inventiveness and creativity of the IMAGO project owes much to the efforts of Professor MARTEGANI. In the late 1970s the IMAGO centre was superseded by the projects derived from it in various faculties.

103

2.3.4   THE PLATO SYSTEM (ULB-VUB)

In the late 1970s the Free Universities of Brussels (Université Libre de Bruxelles (ULB) and Vrije Universiteit Brussel (VUB)) decided to make intensive use of the PLATO system developed by Control Data and the University of Illinois (Professor BITZER).

The PLATO system is characterised by high-resolution graphics a "touch-sensitive" screen and the concentration of software resources in a central computer. Several thousand hours of lessons are already available in English.

Under the direction of Professor O BEAUFAYS (ULB), American lessons have been translated and others produced in French using the TUTOR language. The accuracy of the language is the responsibility of programmers, while teachers from secondary schools in particular concentrate on presentation. Lessons in French are available in a variety of fields.

Under the direction of Professor RIGAUX (VUB), courseware has been prepared for students in secondary schools and universities and for the staff of firms.

CDC has recently developed the Micro-PLATO system, which permits the use but not the creation of lessons.

2.3.5   THE LOGO EXPERIMENTS

For a number of years French researchers (MATHIEU, 1980; BOSSUET, 1982) have taken a close interest in the work of the MIT team (PAPERT and others, 1979, and ABELSON, 1982). S PAPERT's book, Jaillissement de l'esprit (1981), has helped to increase awareness of the possibilities of the LOGO system.

In Belgium, the Laboratoire de pédagogie expérimentale at the University of Liège has, both at MIT and through direct contact with S PAPERT, followed recent developments in LOGO and gave the first major public demonstration of it at the ULB Colloquy in May 1982 (see J L HARDY, 1982). In August 1982 intensive seminars were organised for children aged 8 to 13. LOGO experiments are being started under the aegis of other bodies.

The LOGO system facilitates discovery learning, in line with PIAGET's constructivist approach. This type of learning could also be described in terms of autoregulation in five stages (HARDY, 1982, pp. 16-17 and LECLERCQ, 1979).

Experience shows that this language is at present the one most suited to providing an introduction to computing. It is an instrument of technological culture rather than a tool with specific uses, and has the advantage of being the product of a long study embracing psychology, computing and epistemology.

2.3.6   IMPACT ON EDUCATION

Micro-computers made their first appearance in schools in the mid-1970s and are now used extensively.

The description of the situation in the Dutch-speaking part of the country (see 2.2) is very largely valid for the French-speaking community too.

As in many other countries, an introductory course in computer studies has been included in the secondary school curriculum (starting in the third year of secondary school). Its aim is essentially to demystify computers and make the pupil realise that he must retain mastery over the machine so as to be of greater service to his fellow beings and not enslave them. Furthermore, computing courses exist in higher technical education and in universities and non-university higher education. In some cases terminals are linked to a central computer, particularly the Ministry of Education's, while in others micro-computers are used independently. Four regional training centres for future teachers of computing and data processing have been established.

Computers are already in common use in certain subjects and practical work (physics, mathematics, chemistry, etc).

It should, however, be noted that such projects are directed mainly at teaching computer science and that much less is done in the field of computer-assisted learning. One reason for this is that there is still not enough usable courseware designed specifically for the Belgian education system. A second is that the provision of appropriate training for teachers has hardly begun. A policy for the short-, medium- and long-term has still to be prepared; it will need to ensure that the necessary resources are available and to apply to the education system as a whole. There is reason to believe that the root of the problem lies in the fact that the cost of the basic hardware is minimal in comparison with the cost of the necessary software and teacher training.

More particularly, no decision has been made regarding standardisation of hardware and software - and this is to be welcomed, at least at the present stage. The quality of the various languages used (principally several different forms of BASIC) is far from always giving full satisfaction. There is a great danger that the distinction between those who are "good at mathematics" and those who are "weak in mathematics" will be reproduced in data processing.

CAI software and courseware intended for all levels of education are being developed in all quarters, but often prove to be unsuitable for educational use.

Clearly many Belgian teachers are coming to accept computers, but computing will also have to go some way towards meeting teachers' needs.

2.3.7   EDUCATIONAL MANAGEMENT SERVICES

The first computer-managed question bank in Belgium was set up at the Ecole Technique de la Force Aérienne (Air Force Technical School) at Saffraanberg in the very early 1970s (LECLERCQ, 1974). At present the bank contains over 20,000 multiple choice questions in French and Dutch, and the specialist centre at Saffraanberg sets and corrects several hundred tests annually at the request of the ten Belgian Air Force schools.

The computer programme is written in FORTRAN and includes a facility for correcting, inter alia, questions that require students not only to give an answer but also to indicate their degree of certainty (LECLERCQ, 1975, 1977, 1982).

Various Belgian universities have developed their own systems for correcting examinations and tests. For instance, in 1976, the University of Liège grouped into a single system called STEP (Système de Traitement des Evaluations Pédagogiques - Educational Assessment Processing System) the programmes that had been developed in various departments. STEP has a very wide variety of correction facilities and uses optical reading (DEBOT and LECLERCQ, 1980).

Various types of objectives banks (HARDY and LECLERCQ, 1981) are being set up. In particular, IEA (International Organisation for the Evaluation of Educational Achievement) has decided to set up question banks on an international level. The Laboratoire de pédagogie expérimentale of the University of Liège is at present acting as co-ordinator (LECLERCQ, 1982).

Clearly the existence of centralised question banks on the one hand and micro-computers in schools on the other may eventually lead to the development of increasingly effective methods of applying data processing to assessment.

2.3.8   CONCLUSIONS

This brief survey does not claim to cover the most recent experiments (in particular those started after 1980); rather, it sets out to show that French-speaking Belgium has taken a wide variety of initiatives whose impact on both present and future developments has been beneficial, even though restrictions on equipment for schools and on research leave something of a question mark over the future.

As a result of past investigations, it is now possible to identify overall strategies regarding the hardware, software, courseware and staff training needed in schools.

All too often educationists "asked in what teaching situations computers could be used, and not what kind of computer needed to be built or adapted or which of its capabilities could be used to help ensure teaching of the highest quality ..." (DE LANDSHEERE, 1982, p. 3).

In too many instances "computers have become the new-found instruments of teaching methods based on the logic of subject-matter and Taylorian rational appropriation strategies and not on the psychology of the learner. We have thus seen the resurgence of a kind of neo-Herbartist approach which has won all the more support among courseware sellers because it authorises the cheapest and swiftest solutions, and this - in their eyes - is necessary if they are to win markets" (DE LANDSHEERE, 1982, p. 4).

The abundance of research work may appear frightening. Yet the multiplicity of problems to be tackled calls for carefully considered solutions. For many years to come, widely differing systems will inevitably exist side by side. Constant technological advance and the falling cost of equipment mean that caution and vigilance should be the order of the day. This is not to say that we should sit back and do nothing, but that, with regard to both hardware and software, we should avoid making any irrevocable decisions.

2.3.9   BIBLIOGRAPHY

ABELSON H (1982, Logo for the Apple II, New York, McGraw-Hill.

BARTHOLOME M et HOUZIAUX M O (1979), SIAM-DOCEO II Instruction Manual, Université de Liège.

BOSSUET G (1982), L'ordinateur à l'école, Paris, PUF.

COOLS M et PETEAU M (1974), Un programme de stimulation inventive: STIM 5, Revue Française d'Automatique, Informatique et Recherche opérationnelle, vol. 3.

DEBOT F et LECLERCQ D (1978), Système de Traitement automatique d'Evaluation Pédagogique (STEP) - Guide introductif, Université de Liège.

DE LANDSHEERE G (1982), Education et ordinateur, Communication au Colloque "Enseignement assisté par ordinateur" organisé par l'Université Libre de Bruxelles, le 7 mai 1982, 17 p.

DUBOIS Th (1975), Méthodes d'évaluation et de gestion dans les systèmes didactiques multimédia, thèse de doctorat en sciences appliquées, Université Catholique de Louvain.

HARDY J L et LECLERCQ D (1980), Une banque d'objectifs gérée par ordinateur comme base d'un curriculum organisé par unités capitalisables, in Revue de la Direction générale de l'Organisation des Etudes, 15e année, No. 9.

HARDY J L (1982), LOGO, Un système informatique évolué au service d'une pédagogie évoluée, Université de Liège, série LPC 82-05-42, 51 p.
Laboratoire de pédagogie expérimentale.

HOUZIAUX M O (1965), Les fonctions didactiques de DOCEO, in Actes du XII Colloque de l'AIPELF, Université de Caen, pp 47-71.

HOUZIAUX M O (1972), Vers l'enseignement assisté par ordinateur, Paris, PUF.

HOUZIAUX M O, GODART C, LAVIGNE M, BARTHOLOME M, LUYCKS A, LEFEBVRE P (1978), Une expérience d'enseignement assisté par ordinateur chez des patients diabétiques insulinodépendants, Scientia Paedagogica Experimentalis, 15, pp 215-250.

JAMART F, LECLERCQ D, HOUZIAUX M O, LIBERT D, DELAITE P (1982), Understanding Spoken English (USE). Utilisation d'un système audiovisuel assisté par ordinateur pour l'entraînement à la compréhension de l'anglais oral, Université de Liège.

JONES A (1971), Une expérience d'enseignement assisté par ordinateur, Rapport OCDE-CERI.

LECLERCQ D (1974), Banques de questions et indice de certitude. Options docimologiques adaptées a l'enseignement secondaire (1re partie), Education, No. 149, Décembre, pp 49-59.

LECLERCQ D (1976), La fonction régulatrice de l'évaluation vue sous l'angle de l'implication de l'étudiant, in Education, No. 159.

LECLERCQ D (1977a), Sequential adaptative tailored testing and confidence marking, in VANDERKAMP, LANGERAK & DE GRUYTER, Psychometrics for Educational Debates: Proceedings of the Third International Symposium on Education Testing, p 306 (Leyden).

LECLERCQ D et PERRE F (1979), Une expérience de dossier automatisé d'étudiant, Conférence présentée a la 4e Conférence de l'ATEE, Pont-à-Mousson, 4-7 septembre 1979.

LECLERCQ D, Confidence marking: its use in testing. Pergamon, Oxford, à paraître en 1982.

LEDGARD (1981), *Proverbes de programmation*.

LEFEBVRE P et HOUZIAUX M O (1969), Anamnèse assistée par ordinateur en diabétologie, Resultats préliminaires, *Revue Médicale de Liège*, 24, pp 803-809.

OSTERRIETH S (1982), *L'enseignement assisté par ordinateur dans l'apprentissage du français par les immigrés*. Etude exploratoire. Mémoire de licence en sciences de l'éducation, Université de Liège.

MATHIEU F (1980), *Apprentissage autonome*, Université de Paris VIII, RT-7/80.

NEWELL et SIMON (1961), Computer Simulation of Human Thinking, *Science*, 134.

PAPERT S, WATT D, DISESSA A et WEIR S (1979), *Final Report of the Brookline LOGO project*, MIT Artificial Intelligence Memo 545.

PAPERT S (1981), *Jaillissement de l'esprit, Ordinateurs et apprentissage*, Paris, Flammarion.

CODI (1977), *Dossier sur l'ordinateur dans l'enseignement en Belgique*, Unité de Coordination pour la Documentation sur l'Informatique, Centre IMAGO, Louvain-la-Neuve.

2.4 CYPRUS
INTRODUCTION OF COMPUTERS IN SECONDARY SCHOOLS

by

Mr Nicos HADJINICOLAS
Ministry of Education,
Nicosia

2.4.1 INTRODUCTION

The 20th century has witnessed unbelievable acceleration in Technological progress. One of the areas that have been the subject of the fastest progress, is that of Computers.

Computers are put to a multitude of different uses and are the workhorses of almost every branch of Science, Commerce and Administration.

Cyprus, unavoidably, could not remain unaffected by the latest developments in this field. Computers were introduced in the private sector, as well as in the government service, for keeping records, accounting, billing, and to a smaller extent for research purposes and industrial applications.

This development created a demand for properly trained computer technicians. Responding to this demand, the Department of Technical Education of the Ministry of Education, decided to investigate the possibility of introducing a computer related specialisation in the Technical Schools of Cyprus.

2.4.2 HISTORY OF PREPARATORY WORK

Having taken the decision to investigate the possibility of introducing a computer related specialisation, Dr. G Philokyprou, Head of the Department of Computer Science, of Athens University was invited to Cyprus, to submit a report on the subject.

In his report, submitted in January 1982, under the heading "Computers in the Schools of Cyprus", Dr. Philokyprou investigated the problem of the introduction of Computers into the Secondary Schools.

The case for training computer technicians was studied in detail and it was recommended that top priority must be given to it.

2.4.3 DECISION FOR THE INTRODUCTION OF A COMPUTER TECHNICIANS COURSE

Following Dr. Philokyprou's recommendations, a series of meetings of a committee, under the chairmanship of the Director of Technical Education, took place in March and April 1982, with the aim of studying thoroughly the recommendations put forward, and to propose a course of action. This committee, on which all sectors of the government were represented, decided in favour of the experimental introduction in one Technical School, of a computer technicians course.

2.4.4 INTRODUCTION - SYLLABUSES

After the decision of the above mentioned committee, in May 1982, the Council of Ministers approved the operation of a three year course for computer technicians, as from September 1982, in one of the Technical Schools.

During the three years of training, the students will receive a general education, as well as practical training.

The table below shows the subjects that will be taught each year, as well as the hours per week for each subject.

Subject	1st year	2nd year	3rd year
Religious Instruction	1	1	1
History-Civics	1	1	1
Greek Language	4	4	4
English Language	4	4	4
Physical Education	2	2	2
Mathematics	5	6	6
Physics/chemistry	5	5	5
Electrical Engineering	6	2	4
Engineering Drawing	3	2	-
Binary Arithmetic and Boolean Algebra	3	-	-
Digital Electronics	-	5	-
Microelectronics	-	-	4
Electrical Installations Workshop	3	-	-
Electronics Lab.	3	4	3
Basic Structure of Computer) Lab. and machine code language)	-	4	-
Computer programming	-	-	4

The last two subjects involve the use of a mini computer.

2.4.5 TRAINING OF PERSONNEL

The introduction of such a new specialisation imposed the demand for training teachers qualified to teach the highly specialised subjects involved. To this end, the head of Computer Science, of Waltham Forest College of London, visited Cyprus and submitted a report.

2.5 DENMARK
PRESENT STATE OF RESEARCH AND EVALUATION OF COMPUTER SCIENCE AND COMPUTER-BASED TEACHING IN DANISH SECONDARY SCHOOLS

by

Dr. Jannik JOHANSEN
Ministry of Education,
Copenhagen

2.5.1 INTRODUCTION

The Danish secondary school "Gymnasium" is a three-year school. It follows immediately after the nine-years compulsory primary school. In 1981, 30% of all young Danish people aged 16 years attended secondary school.

Older students, who may have some job experience, have the choice of attending the Higher Preparatory Courses for a period of two years. As with secondary schools, these courses give access to higher education at, for example, university.

Adult students may take one or more subjects at Single Subject Higher Preparatory Classes.

2.5.2 EARLY EXPERIMENTS

Educational experiments in computer science are based upon a 1972 report from the Ministry of Education, report No. 666. This report deals with access to computer studies at all levels of education. On this basis, computer science was introduced experimentally from 1975 to 1981. These experiments, however, for a number of reasons did not attract many students and teachers. Some found the subject too hardware-oriented and the courses did not enable the students to write their own programs. After that, the Ministry of Education in a circular to all secondary schools dated October 1980 stated that an experiment of integrating computer science and computer-based teaching into social science and natural science and other subjects was to be carried out.

2.5.3 CURRENT PRACTICE

In order to give students a broad and general education enabling them to become critical users of computers and to judge the social consequences of the use of computers, this circular proposes the first two steps of the current three-step approach:

1. First, a basic course of about 30 lessons;

2. After that, integration of computer science methods in the social and natural science courses;

3. As a third step, computer science taught to particularly motivated students as a special subject.

Some experiments along these lines are already in progress (1), but it is too early to give an evaluation.

Computer science is still taught as a special subject at Single Subject Preparatory Classes, where an integration is not technically possible. The number of periods was recently increased from two to four lessons weekly. The number of schools participating in the experiment increased from 12 in 1981-82 to 22 in 1982-83. A curriculum is under preparation in the Ministry of Education.

A recent report on hardware concludes that about 90% of Danish secondary schools have some kind of computer capacity, predominantly microcomputers averaging 3.5 micros per school.

The most frequently used computer language is the Danish dialect COMAL, but PASCAL is often preferred by teachers for its higher speed in computer-based teaching programmes. A special language, designed for teachers and invented at the Aarhus Dental University is at this moment being implemented at some schools (2).

The Ministry of Education will closely follow the efforts of producing software for the secondary schools. Just now, a number of initiatives are being taken locally by groups of teachers but no central initiative has as yet been taken.

Due to economic reasons it has not been possible to systematise the education of teachers involved in computer science, but the Ministry has, whenever possible, supported local initiatives in co-operation with the Danish Union of Secondary School Teachers.

---

(1) For preliminary reports on these experiments please contact the following:

Ms Birthe Olsen, Christianshavs Gymnasium, Prinsessegade 35, DK-1422 Copenhagen K; Mr Gert Jacobsen, Aabenraa Statsskole, Forst Alle 14-20, DK-6200 Aabenraa; Mr Martin Lund, Sct Knuds Gymnasium, Laessøegade 154, DK-5230 Odense M.

(2) For further information please contact:
Mr Arne Jepsen, Århus Tandlaegehøjskole, Vennelyst Boulevard, DK-8000 Århus C.

2.6 FINLAND
THE USE OF MICROCOMPUTERS IN SECONDARY SCHOOLS

by

Prof. Jukka LEHTINEN
Department of Education,
University of Tampere

2.6.1   GENERAL

It is only in recent years that micro-computers have been purchased by secondary schools. The central educational authorities have defined the criteria for the acquisition of equipment to be adopted by the municipalities and other school authorities that receive state aid for this purpose. At present it is estimated that two hundred micro-computers are in use, but the number is increasing steadily.

2.6.2   TEACHING IN DATA PROCESSING IN SCHOOLS

The use of micro-computers in schools has started with the teaching of automatic data processing (ADP). The aims of this course in upper secondary schools have been defined as follows:

- to prepare the student for life in a society where ADP is becoming increasingly important,

- to create the student's cognitive basis for understanding ADP tasks, and using computers in an appropriate way,

- to give the students the basic knowledge to understand the modelling nature of computer science, and teach him/her the necessary discipline of logical reasoning,

- to teach the students the central features of Algol, and provide them with the knowledge and skills required to use Algol.

The ADP courses do not prepare for a specific profession.

2.6.3   COMPUTER-BASED EDUCATION

Computers have been used in the teaching of many subjects. The problem is to find suitable programs. English programs are available for many machines, but the value of these is limited, as the students' mother tongue is either Finnish or Swedish. Teachers and the authors of study material have still not had the opportunity to prepare Finnish programs.

As a solution to this problem, the possibility of translating the English programs has been considered. It is usually not enough merely to translate the programs, but they have to be adapted to the weights and measures, habits and whole culture of the country. The Finnish National Fund for Research and Development (SITRA) has in co-operation with the Technical Research Centre of Finland launched a project to evaluate the micro-computers, and the available foreign programs with a view to translating these. Likewise criteria for good teaching programs will be developed, which will hopefully make the production of Finnish programs easier. The translation problem is naturally affected by the complex copyright provisions.

The Department of Education of the University of Tampere has started to prepare a series of study programs to be used by an insurance company for staff training. The programs are created using PLATO-system terminals, which are connected to the main frame at the University of Umeå in Sweden. The programs will eventually be translated into micro-TUTOR language, so that the insurance company may use them on their micro-PLATO equipment. In connection with the project some postgraduate teacher trainee students will have the opportunity to learn how to develop programs.

2.6.4   FINAL REMARKS

The use of computers will no doubt become increasingly frequent. In what ways the computers will be used depends on technological developments and new operational conditions. In Finland one supplier has attached a voice synthesiser to a micro-computer, and the equipment has been used in special education courses. If in the near future it becomes possible to use videodiscs in micro-computers, this will increase considerably the scope of utilisation, and eventually reduce the use of other teaching material; the use of textbooks will decrease and that of computers and auxiliary equipments will grow.

2.7 FRANCE

INFORMATION PROCESSING IN FRENCH SECONDARY SCHOOLS

by

Mr Pierre MULLER
National Institute for Educational
Research, Paris

2.7.1 OBJECTIVES

The experiment to introduce information processing into secondary schools was launched in 1970. The intention was to promote a general understanding of computers and their uses, the aim being "not to teach information processing but to teach that it exists, discuss what it can and cannot do, and consider its limitations and economic implications" (1).

This objective was often called "familiarisation" and was coupled with the idea that its realisation could also foster a process of educational renewal by bringing secondary education into touch with the contemporary world and persuading teachers "to take a critical look at what they were teaching".

The strategy adopted for achieving these two objectives simultaneously was the introduction of information processing through other subjects rather than the creation of a new subject, with emphasis on the intellectual process rather than on a body of technical knowledge.

2.7.2 METHODS

Information processing could be integrated into the different subjects only by teachers with two sets of skills: a thorough knowledge of one such subject and a sufficient understanding of information processing to enable them at least to decide where it might be possible to introduce this science into their teaching. It was therefore necessary, as a first step, to train an adequate number of such teachers, who were previously very few and far between, except in mathematics.

---

(1) W MERCOUROFF, L'expérience des 58 lycées, in Education et information, No. 1, April/May 1980, pp 10-15.

After their in-depth training course, the teachers returned to their own schools where they became officially responsible for "familiarising" their pupils and colleagues with the uses of information processing. To this end, they were given special facilities: time (in the form of a lighter teaching timetable), equipment and a suitable programming language.

To monitor and co-ordinate these teachers' work, a special unit was set up in 1971 at the Institut National de Recherche Pédagogique (INRP) (National Educational Research Institute) - the Section Informatique et Education (Education and Information Processing Unit) - which organised both single-subject and interdisciplinary research groups and centralised and disseminated information, particularly software for use in the classroom.

2.7.3 EVALUATION

A major turning point in the experimental introduction of information processing into secondary schools came in 1976 when the Ministry of Education decided to stop equipping schools with mini-computers and providing in-depth training for teachers. The Ministry argued that it was neither financially nor technologically feasible at that time to generalise the scheme and that, in any case, the equipment already installed and the pool of teachers trained were easily enough to carry out a thorough experiment.

The Direction des lycées (Secondary Schools Directorate) then gave the INRP the new task of evaluation, the intention being that its finding should provide a basis for deciding whether the scheme should be generalised. The work was to be spread over four years and to result in a report being published.

Strictly speaking, evaluation would have necessitated the definition of highly precise objectives, rigorous experimental conditions (selection of pilot classes, for instance) and suitable instruments for assessment. But the initial objectives were very general and the 1976 decision had not clarified them but merely given greater emphasis to the idea of a teaching tool and relegated familiarisation to second place.

Furthermore, the field of study was vast: 58 schools, over one thousand teachers, all general and some technical subjects, all secondary school classes from the first form to the sixth form and themes covering all aspects of the school curriculum. In practice, therefore, a whole series of evaluations should have been carried out in order to cover the experiment in all its diversity, but this was something which, in any event, the limited staff of the Section Informatique et Education could not do.

We accordingly decided to confine our work to observation with a view to describing as fully and accurately as possible the structure of the experiment and the range of activities implemented. Four areas of investigation were established: the functioning of the data processing centres; material produced; benefit derived by teachers from information processing; benefit derived by pupils from information processing. By analysing the information gathered over the four years of the evaluation, we were able to present a tentative overall assessment in the report submitted to the Director of Secondary Schools in May 1981, the main points of which are summarised below.

2.7.4   FUNCTIONING OF DATA PROCESSING CENTRES

The functioning of the schools' data processing centres may be regarded as a successful example of "self-sufficiency", since the teaching teams organised and carried out themselves all the work of management and use without the help of technicians.

Taking all the schools together, the computers were used in three broadly balanced ways: in lessons (36% of total time), clubs and individual use (37%) and use without pupils (27%). Local situations varied widely, however.

As far as lessons were concerned, a study of the use made of the computer in the different subjects offers a number of surprises. Although, as might have been expected, mathematics came well in the lead, arts subjects and languages may nevertheless be considered to have done well, particularly when one bears in mind that not all teams had teachers of these subjects whereas all included at least one mathematics teacher. By taking the average number of sessions per school, it is possible to give a rapid summary of the position of the different subjects with regard to information processing and so to identify three broad categories: a high density of use (34 to 40 sessions) in mathematics, languages and arts subjects where drill exercises are possible and could be used at lower secondary level; an average density (20 to 24 sessions) in physical sciences and economics, which were not taught at lower secondary level or in all types of school; moreover, some changes had been made to the physical sciences syllabus; a low density (10 to 12 sessions) in natural sciences and history/geography, where it is difficult to use drill exercises and where the number of teachers trained and given lighter timetables was particularly low.

2.7.5   SOFTWARE

The teachers did not confine themselves to managing and running the data processing centres. They also did a great deal of work in the research and production field, the results of which were centralised by the INRP and subsequently circulated among all the schools taking part in the experiment. Over 7,000 pages of teaching material were published in this way and 400 computer programmes were supplied on request.

The computer programmes were studied systematically with the help of an analysis grid designed by the inter-disciplinary evaluation group. It was thus possible, using pedagogical and technical criteria common to all subjects, to assess not only the particular characteristics of each subject but also to discern the general trends of computer-assisted education at secondary level.

It should be pointed out first of all that lesson writing with the aid of a conventional author language was not very common, even though a computer-assisted instruction (CAI) system of this type exists. The explanation undoubtedly lies partly in the low memory capacity available, particularly in the first few years, and partly in the fact that most teachers did not want to be replaced by a computer for the whole or a part of their classroom time.

Nearly all the programs therefore related to a specific subject or field and were designed to be integrated into the teaching of a subject at a precise point. A study of them cannot be separated from a study of the teaching situation for which they were intended, since some were specifically designed to provide an introduction to the concepts and methods used while others concentrated on exploitation of data supplied.

The programmes prepared in this way can be classified into five categories:

- tutorial instruction, presenting information or lesson sequences and requiring frequent answers from the pupil;

- drill exercises for checking knowledge of facts, techniques (applying rules, solving equations, etc) and methods;

- simulation exercises, providing the results of the functioning of a model (simulating real conditions) on the basis of values attributed to the different parameters and of answers supplied by the pupils;

- programmes for processing and/or utilising data banks which use the computer primarily for its powerful calculating capacity and potential for processing a large amount of data;

- games.

These types of programme were not represented equally in all subjects: drill exercises were particularly common in languages, arts subjects and chemistry, while physics gave greater emphasis to simulation and history and geography worked more on programmes for processing; mathematical programmes were almost evenly divided between processing and drills and natural science programmes between processing and simulation.

2.7.6   TEACHERS AND PUPILS

Lastly, we wanted to see how pupils and teachers reacted to the introduction of this new tool, the computer, into the daily life of

the classroom. In carrying out this study, it would have been
impossible to look at all the classes in the 58 schools involved.
Furthermore, if we were to have sufficient information, the computer
had to be used systematically and in all subjects. We therefore
turned to teams of teachers in 8 schools and asked each of them to
teach a particular class. The information gathered during the two
years the experiment lasted helped us to form a clearer picture of
the teaching methods adopted by the teachers and of the pupils'
motivation. It must be pointed out, however, that the classes
involved were ordinary ones following the official timetables
and syllabuses and that the time spent in front of computer
consoles did not exceed 10% of teaching time.

Analysis of a questionnaire to which pupils replied twice in the
year (December and June) revealed that motivation remained excellent.
The number opposed to the experiment was small (4%) and certainly
no higher than the number of pupils who reject the school system
anyway. The reasons given in December were, in order, the play
aspect associated with operating the machine, the feeling of greater
freedom and the impression of working efficiently. In June the
play aspect was regarded as less important than the impression of
freedom, whilst the idea of efficiency was gaining ground.

The pupils' recognition of these qualities of computer work did
not blind them to its limitations. They did not think that teachers
could be replaced by machines. The programmes' shortcomings did not
escape their notice: certain exercises were too repetitive, there
was a lack of flexibility in the analysis of errors, progress was too
slow because of unwieldy question-and-answer routines.

For their part, teachers saw their approach to teaching changed
by computers. The constraints of the computer obliged them to carry
out a detailed review of content and reorganise the presentation
of facts, and they found this had several advantages: remembering
everything, seeking greater coherence, clarifying content,
systematically monitoring pupils' progress. They thus had the
impression that they were transmitting knowledge more effectively.
But the advantages as regards method were even more appreciated: the
use of information processing offered a better means of inculcating
methods of work, particularly since it was possible to break a process
down into its different stages - the use of analysitial methods and
the introduction of algorithms with or without flowcharts were
considered very helpful. Above all, the new methods involved in
simulation and the use of data banks could scarcely have been
contemplated without computers.

The introduction of information processing had an impact not only
on what was taught but also on the educational environment. As we
saw in connection with programs, account had to be taken of what
might happen before and after a session on the computer. During the
sessions themselves the teacher's role was clearly not what it
usually was: because he was released from a part of his work,
the teacher had the impression of being more available to assist those

pupils who sought his help and thereby of becoming their ally against the machine.

The computer room was a different place where relations between teachers and between pupils and teachers were different. It frequently happened that several teachers were in the room at the same time, perhaps to carry out an experiment, and the pupils then asked any one of them for help when they came up against a problem. They appreciated the teamwork which the use of a common tool had led the teachers to develop: and this teamwork was multidisciplinary, something rare enough in the French education system to warrant special mention.

The teachers who took part in these experiments nevertheless do not see the computer as a pedagogical panacea, for they realise that it cannot solve all the problems arising in the education system.

2.8 IRELAND

THE PRESENT STATE OF RESEARCH, DEVELOPMENT AND EVALUATION

Department of Education,
Dublin

2.8.1   BACKGROUND

The first in-service course for teachers on computer studies was organised by the Department of Education in the summer of 1970. The course lasted for one week and used BASIC as the programming language. Every year since then the number of in-service courses has increased so that in 1980 some 15 courses were held at the various levels - beginners, intermediate and advanced.

The interest in computer studies, first awakened at these courses, motivated many teachers to seek further knowledge at universities and at other third level institutions. And so post-graduate courses leading to further degrees over a two-year period together with diploma courses over a one-year period were eagerly received. Today many new recruits to the teaching profession have computer science in their basic degrees.

The repercussions of all this activity at teacher level were soon felt in the classroom. Teachers were naturally anxious to experiment with the new technology in order to give an added dimension to their pupils' education. In the mid 1970s, however, there were no micro-computers in schools and so recourse had to be made to the main frame computers in industry and at 3rd level institutions by means of batch mode. About this time also the Department of Education set up a small project team to evaluate existing texts and pedagogical aids to computer related learning. The report of the team stimulated the best qualified teachers to produce their own texts and the results of this work are seen in our schools today.

2.8.2   THE MICRO IN SCHOOLS

Prior to 1980 some schools had purchased micro-computers out of their own resources and some had network systems in operation. In 1980 the government decided that there should be a micro-computer in every secondary school and over Ir£1,000,000 was set aside for this purpose. As yet not every school has a computer but it is expected that some extra money will be made available shortly to complete the task.

2.8.3 PROJECT 1 CURRICULUM DEVELOPMENT PROJECT

The first step in setting up a computer studies course is to supply the hardware. The second is to select a suitable language. The programming language recommended must be easy to learn, be well structured so as to reflect sound pedagogical principles and be sufficiently flexible for use in a school context. PASCAL satisfies some of these objectives and is being taught at present in some schools. It is felt, however, that for the generality of pupils the demands imposed by this language are too great. BASIC, though easy to learn, lacks the modular structure and its GOTO command has come under severe criticism. COMAL, being a superset of BASIC, having procedures which are easier to teach than those of PASCAL and using well defined methods of sequence selection and iteration would appear to be well suited as the obligatory language. The coding language, however, is but the final process in solving the problem. The algorithm is the solution and of course this must be structured.

To lay down the guidelines and a modus operandi for the teaching and the development of structured algorithms a curriculum development project team has been formed. The research work of the team is being tested in a school environment by teachers not on the team and this is being done as an ongoing process. Some tentative evaluation was also carried out at the in-service courses for teachers and in general the reaction has been favourable. The final report will illustrate structured diagrams in the context of sequencing, selection and iteration. The many examples will be coded in the three languages - BASIC, COMAL, PASCAL - for comparison purposes and to assist the evaluation procedures. The results of this evaluation will be made available to the syllabus committee which will meet shortly to make proposals on the content and methods of examination for the new subject computer studies.

2.8.4 PROJECT 2 RESEARCH PROJECT AT TRINITY COLLEGE

The majority of Irish schools have an Apple Micro-computer. Being a 6502 machine, it cannot take COMAL immediately since COMAL is written for CP/M. To convert the Apple to take CP/M a Z/80 card was supplied as part of the package to schools. This means that not only can the Apple now take COMAL but it can also use the many facilities of the CP/M such as PIP and STAT, for example. The package delivered to schools included PASCAL, PILOT, ASSEMBLER, APPLE PLOT, APPLE POST, APPLE WRITER, together with manuals for CP/M and COMAL.

The conversion from a 6502 to a Z/80 is seen only as a temporary but necessary measure. The purpose of the research project is to develop software to enable the 6502 to take COMAL without the necessity of having to provide the additional finances for the supply of the Z/80 cards. Already a version of COMAL without the procedure parameters is available from the research team for use on the PDP 11 mini-computers at the regional technical colleges and it is expected that a full version will shortly be available for the micros.

2.8.5   FUTURE DEVELOPMENTS

Computer studies is not as yet a full subject on the curriculum of secondary schools although it is an option in the Mathematics syllabus of the Leaving Certificate. As I have said above, a syllabus committee will shortly begin work on a syllabus at two levels and it is expected to have the new subject on the curriculum in 1985. In the meantime those pupils who take the option in the Mathematics syllabus are monitored by the Department inspectors and statements of competency are issued to successful candidates. There is a body of opinion which favours the retention of this option even when computer studies becomes a full subject.

In the final analysis it is expected that:

1. there will be a non-examination subject for the 12-15 age group;

2. there will be an examination subject at ordinary and at higher level for the 18 year old pupils;

3. there will be a vocationally oriented subject for pupils of technical schools;

4. there will be a subject suitably tailored for the adult education programme.

2.9 NETHERLANDS

COMPUTERS IN EDUCATION

by

Mr Jaap AKKERMANS and
Mr Jef MOONEN

The present practices with computers in Dutch schools will be summarised by type of school. Especially for elementary and general secondary education it holds that no complete overview is available.

2.9.1 GENERAL EDUCATION

1. Primary Education (grades 1-6)

In addition to a few private initiatives there are some R & D (research and development) projects designed to build up experience with and understanding of the possibilities of computers in primary education. A few projects are in special education and in schools for cultural minorities.

2. Lower Secondary Education (grades 7-9 or 10)

In the various types of school within general secondary education at this moment there are no developments which could be called "learning about information technology" or computer literacy. In some lower vocational schools there are some developments (eg in the graphic schools computers are used for word-processing). Further, 13% of the lower business administration schools have microcomputers.

3. Upper General Secondary Education (grades 10-12)

There is not a co-ordinated development in these schools, but there are many initiatives in individual schools. Some schools are presenting computer science or programming as an appreciation course, but these courses are not part of the official examination programme. In some of these schools besides appreciation courses in computer science/programming, the originators are also using the computer as an aid in their teaching.

Appreciation courses in computer science/programming have existed in several schools for many years. Both curriculum and computer facilities are often provided by the Educational Computing

Centre (ECC) of the University of Utrecht, a centre grown out of the former IOWO-group for research and curriculum development in modern mathematics. In 1980/81 the ECC served 260 (ca. 6 1/2%) secondary schools (mainly pre-university schools). In the mid-seventies (in the pre-micro-computer era) it was too expensive for most of the secondary schools to have their own hardware. As a service to the schools and to minimise the costs of computer use by individual schools ECC was founded. The main purpose of this centre was to process the programs (on punch cards) of pupils who took part in optional programming courses. Moreover, advice from the ECC is available for schools wanting help and guidance in the introduction and the use of computers. The need to provide computer facilities will diminish as now many schools have one or more micro-computers, either financed by the school itself or by the municipality. It is rather difficult to give any figures for the number of micro-computers obtained by schools in this way. It is clear that many different types are being used, with little consideration for co-ordination and compatability.

2.9.2   MIDDLE VOCATIONAL EDUCATION

At present the emphasis is on computer science education in the technical vocational schools and in the business administration vocational schools. We will discuss these two separately.

1.   Middle Technical Schools (MTS)

Ten years ago computer science was taught for the first time in a few schools. From 1981/82 onwards computer science is being taught in the first year of each MTS (one hour a week). This time is taken from the mathematics courses. Furthermore, in every technical specialisation one or more courses in the 2nd, 3rd and 4th years include work on computer applications. Besides, to fulfil the need for computer technicians during 1982/83 four schools will experiment with a 5th year which will be dedicated to computer technology. The Dutch computer industry has great interest in this experiment. We hope that the school will be able to resist the temptation to educate for specific jobs in specific industries instead of educating for professional qualifications.

2.   Middle Business Administration School (MBAS)

Automation has increased enormously in business administration. So, since the early seventies one sees initiatives within this type of school to prepare students for data processing. At present in every MBAS attention is paid to the use of computer and peripherals as part of courses in "practical professional preparation". At present a national study group in co-operation with 50 MBAS is working on a curriculum for computer science for these schools, while the government has recently given equipment to these schools. From 1982/83 computer science will be a separate course in MBAS, but linked with the courses in "practical professional preparation".

3. Remaining middle vocational education

From the two most important remaining school types, the middle home-economics school and the middle social welfare school, no developments can be reported. A proposal to create a Middle Vocational School for Informatics - with a four year curriculum - has been rejected by the government.

2.9.3   HIGHER PROFESSIONAL EDUCATION (HPE)

In the Netherlands there are some colleges of HPE with departments of computer science. Two directions must be distinguished: technical automation (in 5 colleges) and administrative applications of computer science (in 6 colleges). Moreover one college teaches about the design of computer systems.

The quality of teaching programmes in computer science departments is generally well thought of: graduates can find jobs quite easily. There are sufficient places (especially for data processing) within these departments. Some experts think that this under-use of capacity is a consequence of prejudices about computers and automation which are found in our society. A relatively small number of women are attending these courses.

In every college of higher technical education, higher business administration college and higher agricultural college computer science is taught in almost every year of all courses.

All these colleges are co-operating in the buying, management and the maintaining of their equipment. A special foundation has been created by the Ministry of Education for this purpose.

In other areas of HPE the study of computer science is almost non-existent.

2.9.4   UNIVERSITIES

Since the middle of the sixties computer science (including programming) has been taught in all Dutch universities. Since the early seventies it has been possible to choose a major course module in Computer Science, either with emphasis on hardware (within Departments of Electrotechnical Engineering) or with an emphasis on programming and software development (usually within Departments of Mathematics). Since September 1981 in the Netherlands 4 separate Departments of Computer Science have existed. These 4 Departments are in different regions and in each region at least two universities are co-operating.

In 1981/82 a total of 600 first year students started Computer Science courses. The estimate for 1982/83 is more than 850 students. Furthermore, in many Departments of natural and social sciences programming is taught as an indispensible and supportive part of courses. 13 Dutch universities have access to large computer facilities.

Besides the role of computer science as a teaching subject in its own right and the computer's use as a powerful calculator, some universities have initiated R & D projects in Computer Aided Instruction during the last decade. These projects have had a marginal or non-existent impact on teaching habits within the universities. Some people argue that on economic grounds the use of computers as a teaching aid in higher education should be recommended.

Policies supporting such use would presume coherent efforts in all of the 13 universities, and special efforts by the Open University, which is to open in the near future. Such efforts are absent at the time of writing. The spin-off from academic institutions to secondary schools - either in the fields of academic computer science curricula or CAI - is small at present: the Educational Computing Centre of the University of Utrecht (see 2.9.1) is an exception.

2.9.5   TEACHER TRAINING

Virtually all teachers in the Netherlands are educated in special colleges of HPE. The exceptions are the teachers in the upper general education (upper grades of pre-university schools and higher general education), who are educated within the Universities first as subject specialists. Afterwards they may obtain a teaching certificate by attending a few special courses.

We have no certificate for teaching computer science/programming in the secondary schools. At present students who are studying mathematics, science, engineering or economics either at the universities or at the teacher training institutes for secondary education are also becoming familiar with computer science and programming. Graduates of these departments are usually teaching these subjects in general secondary education and vocational education. At this moment there are no teaching programmes for computer science in the teacher training colleges for the primary schools.

Finally, in the Netherlands (as in most other countries) there is no compulsory in-service training for teachers. However, in-service courses in informatics/computer science are offered by several institutions and by user-associations. Teachers may take part in these courses on a voluntary basis.

2.10 PORTUGAL

COMPUTER STUDIES

Ministry of Education and Culture

2.10.1   COMPUTER STUDIES AT SCHOOL

a.   <u>Basic elements for all students</u>

In Portugal, secondary school teaching does not, so far, comprise any fundamental discipline based on computer studies, which would enable students to acquire a global vision and/or at least a superficial knowledge about computers and about the benefit they could derive from such studies during the period of compulsory education, which will soon be prolonged up to nine years.

b.   <u>Computer studies as either a compulsory subject or an optional one</u>

In 1973 a subject called "supplementary teaching of computer studies" was added to the so-called "supplementary courses" which offered to pupils the possibility of becoming acquainted with the new technologies. In addition to general notions, this course included specific notions on computer techniques. The programme was conceived as follows:

- <u>in the first year</u>: basic notions on computers and computer techniques and introduction to practical work with computers;

- programming techniques;

- <u>in the second year</u>: elements of programming with COBOL and/or FORTRAN;

- systems analysis.

Later on, after the reform of supplementary courses (Decree No. 140-A78 of 22 June 1978, confirmed by Decree N. 135-1/79), specialised vocational training in computer studies was introduced within the context of economical and social studies.

Such specialised training was spread over a two-year course. The basic notions of computer studies were taught as follows:

- <u>10th year</u>: introduction to computer studies and computers;

- programming techniques;

- <u>11th year</u>: programming languages;

- systems analysis.

Pupils having passed the above-mentioned training may register for a final one-year vocational course (twelfth year at school) for future programmers based on the following subjects:

- <u>12th year</u>: practical programming;

- enquiry systems and utilities;

- computer applications;

- mathematics applied to computer studies.

At this level of education the course on "book-keeping techniques" has also been supplemented by the introduction of a compulsory subject: "Introduction to computer studies".

On the other hand it should be mentioned that the other courses, and in particular those offering technological training, do not have the benefit of some optional introduction into computer studies being offered.

c. <u>Computers used as a tool in other subjects</u>

Some schools already owning appropriate equipment, have done certain experiments in electronics, mechanics, physics, mathematics and civil engineering, the results of which have been published.

d. <u>Teacher education</u>

Programmes aiming at training and motivating teachers have been implemented in co-operation with private firms, particularly those on which the various departments of the ministry normally relies. For that purpose, the experts of those firms have held courses both for pupils and teachers. Moreover, some foreign experts, specialised in teaching computer studies, have been sent to Portugal where they hold courses lasting three or four days, during which time they explain the methods used in their own countries. The Portuguese Industrial Association (COPRAI) has also invited experts to give courses on computer studies.

2.10.2   MATERIAL USED

At present 31 computer terminals exist. They are connected to a time sharing computer system and provide the following:

-   MODEM (110 band);

-   printing (10 characters/second - 72 columns);

-   tape reader and punch (8 channels).

    The languages available are:

-   BASIC, FORTRAN, COBOL.

    BASIC and COBOL are used most frequently.

    There are "Users Guides: to the different languages used".

2.11 SWITZERLAND

COMPUTERS IN SWISS SECONDARY EDUCATION

by

Mr Alain BRON
Upper Secondary Education Centre,
Yverdon-les-Bains

2.11.1   INTRODUCTION

Although it has a population of only about 6 million, Switzerland is not just one country, but a confederation of 25 more or less independent states. Their independence is limited in military matters, but far-reaching in education. Of the countries represented here, Switzerland probably has the highest density of education Ministers. These Ministers who guard their independence jealously, meet regularly in conference (CDIP), either in plenary session, or by linguistic region to discuss their specific problems.

I shall briefly describe the situation as regards the teaching of computer science in the canton of Vaud, then the activities of the co-ordinating group on computers in Swiss secondary education.

2.11.2   COMPUTERS IN SECONDARY EDUCATION IN THE CANTON OF VAUD

Teachers turned their attention to the subject of computers in education in about 1970 and a number of experiments were conducted, either in conjunction with the Federal Polytechnic School, or independently after the appearance of desk-top computers. But computer science was not actually introduced in secondary education in the canton of Vaud, until after the IFIP conference in Marseille in 1975, well after its introduction in other cantons (eg Geneva and Zurich).

In 1977, the government of the canton of Vaud, mindful of the ever-increasing importance of computers in modern society - and their obvious educational value, appointed a committee on computers to study all the problems connected with the introduction and development of computer science in secondary education.

The committee, which is composed of secondary teachers and computer specialists, has two main aims: to promote basic instruction in computer science and the practical use of computers in the various branches of education. If these two aims are to be achieved, the following requirements must be satisfied:

1. clear objectives must be set,

2. every secondary school must acquire the necessary equipment,

3. the role of computers in secondary education must be defined,

4. teacher training must be encouraged and intensified,

5. the appropriate teaching aids must be available,

6. there must be a teacher in every secondary school responsible for stimulating interest in computer science.

o

o o

2.11.3 OBJECTIVES

The objectives of a computer science course are well described in CDIP report No. 29 (reference 1).

2.11.4 EQUIPMENT

With regard to equipment, secondary schools in the canton of Vaud fall into two categories:

- 26 lower secondary schools, which are dependent on their local municipality;

- 8 upper secondary schools, which are controlled directly by the canton education authorities.

As computer science is a separate branch of study in the higher commercial schools, they were the first to be equipped with mini-computers. Then, during the first half of 1981, the committee on computers made a very detailed study of possible equipment on the basis of specifications drawn up in conjunction with the heads of schools and computer science teachers. Preference was given to a decentralised arrangement and the schools can choose between the Swiss-made SMAKY micro-computers and the Norwegian mini-computers made by NORSK DATA.

Rapid progress is being made in the lower secondary schools: half of them have already experimented either with equipment of their own or with SMAKY micro-computers borrowed from the committee on computers for a few months. This practice of borrowing equipment has enabled several schools to run classes at no great expense. As a result, they have sound arguments to put forward when they request the necessary funds from their municipal authorities.

2.11.5   THE ROLE OF COMPUTERS

The study of computer science is compulsory (3 hours a week for 1 to 2 years) for commercial section pupils and optional for the rest.

Professor ERSHOV, the Russian academician, has given a new meaning to the word "literacy". He maintains that, after the GUTENBERG age, we are now entering the TELEMATICS (computer and telecommunications) age and that the late 20th century illiterates will be those who are unable to use a computer! Without taking this literally, our aim is that all pupils should be receiving basic instruction in computer science within a few years. We face certain difficulties, of which I shall mention only two at this stage:

- the fact that it is inconceivable to introduce a new subject;
- the fact that there is systematic opposition to computer science within the teaching profession, eg on the part of some mathematicians.

2.11.6   TEACHER TRAINING

The teaching of computer science and the use of computers for educational purposes are inconceivable without teacher training.

The canton's further training centre has been offering local further training courses for some years. As the department recently came out in favour of the more and more widespread introduction of computer science at both upper and lower secondary levels, the problem of systematic teacher training on a large scale currently arises. Thus, as from next year:

1. all new teachers, in the literary as well as in the scientific and commercial branches, will learn how to use computers as a teaching aid as part of their course at the secondary teacher training college;

2. the secondary teacher training college will offer some students who show a particular interest in computers the opportunity of undergoing more advanced training to enable them to give basic instruction in computer science in all branches of secondary education.

2.11.7   TEACHING AIDS

By the use of computers for educational purposes, we mean their use as a teaching aid in the same way as television, the blackboard or the microscope.

In our school (the CESSNOV, Yverdon), the biologists were the first to use computers as a teaching aid.

As it is not always possible in biology to conduct real experiments, computers are used for simulations based on models as already defined in 1973 by Professor Hebenstreit of France.

Although our biology teachers use computers mainly during practical sessions (the pupils are at the terminal), other uses are possible. For teaching basic accountancy, one colleague uses a package developed by the canton of Vaud, in which a video screen associated with a micro-system replaces the blackboard.

Note that a teaching package is usually in three parts (reference 5):

1. a computer program (usually available on a floppy disc);

2. a handbook for students, to put them in the picture, remind them of a few basic concepts, explain the procedure and set them questions;

3. a handbook for the teacher comprising a description of the program, operating instructions, recommendations of a methodological nature etc.

The package may also include a leaflet containing basic information on the subject studied and the model used.

The Committee on Computers has some 20 packages available for use by teachers. This small data-bank consists largely of packages that have been donated. The canton of Geneva, which is a few years ahead of us in this field, has helped us a lot.

I should just like to say a few words about the use of computers in school management. The CESSNOV is one of Switzerland's leaders in this field. Beginnings and ends of term would be impossible without the help of a computer (keeping pupil records, running the library, drawing up timetables, word processing etc). Of the 14 work stations currently available (12 fixed and 2 portable), 4 are used permanently by the administration.

2.11.8   COMPUTERS IN SWISS GENERAL SECONDARY EDUCATION

The situation varies enormously from one canton to another. In Berne, Basle and Zurich, the study of computer science is compulsory for the type C "maturité" (advanced-level school-leaving examination), and the canton of Ticino is introducing an optional course. Geneva has no compulsory course as yet, but optional courses are highly developed there and computers are used as a teaching aid much more extensively than in other cantons.

The co-ordinating group on computers, which is composed of secondary and university teachers, was set up in 1975 to study the introduction of computers in secondary education. In 1978 it made an initial proposal which is described in CDIP Information Bulletin No. 13: a compulsory 24-hour introductory course in computer science for all "maturité" pupils (reference 2). Such a course would have an intrinsic value as regards the pupils' general education and would make it possible for computers to be used afterwards as a teaching aid in all kinds of subjects. Aware of the difficulties inherent in its plan, which was realistic despite being reduced to the bare minimum, the group asked for permission to experiment with a 24-hour course. The proposal was accepted by the authorities and experiments were therefore conducted in several schools in the French and German speaking parts of Switzerland. With the support and encouragement of the Swiss Secondary Teachers' Association and the Swiss Further Training Centre, three teams experimented with the recommendations and prepared teaching materials:

1. a team from Zurich: M E Hui and C Jung (24 hours of classes plus 24 hours of exercises with PASCAL)

2. a team from Basle: M H Maag and M Vowe (24 hours of classes and applications with BASIC)

3. a team from the French-speaking cantons: M J-C Diethelm and P Zabey from Geneva, M P-A Grezet from Neuchâtel and myself (24 hours of classes and exercises with BASIC).

Published this year, the CDIP's report 29 (reference 1) describes the results obtained and makes a more forceful case for this introductory course in computer science to be extended. Note that a member of parliament has tabled a motion with the Federal Council in this connection and that an answer is expected this year (1982).

The group's activities are not confined to the teaching of computer science. It also assists the further training centre in organising its many courses in the subject.

In addition to bilingual courses, every year since 1975 the co-ordinating group has held a 2-day seminar in Interlaken for those responsible for the teaching of computer science in Switzerland (this year Professor Papert will be discussing his theories).

The group also takes part in teaching package exchanges, although we do encounter some difficulties as regards portability (language: German-French-Italian, programming language: BASIC, and the computers dialects are not always compatible).

Let us not forget the important role of information. In addition to the Interlaken seminars and the Yverdon meetings, which provide direct information, we have a magazine "INTERFACE" (reference 3) which reports on experiments currently in progress, assists in the choice of equipment and describes new packages.

2.11.9   REFERENCES

1. The introduction of computer science in secondary education, interim report. CDIP No. 29, February 1982.

2. The introduction of computer science in secondary education. CDIP No. 13, July 1978.

3. INTERFACE. "The computer in secondary education", Lucerne further training centre bulletin.

4. INFORMATICS IN THE SECONDARY SCHOOL EDUCATION OF THE CANTON OF VAUD. Claude Desgraz. Computer in education, part 2, WCCE, 1981.

5. RAT package distributed by the canton of Vaud.

PART 3: BACKGROUND PAPERS

3.1 PROVISIONAL LIST OF ONGOING RESEARCH (Nov 1982)

prepared by the Secretariat,
Council of Europe

3.1.1   INTERNATIONAL ORGANISATIONS

EUROPEAN COMMUNITIES

Directorate of Education/DG V
Commission of the European Communities
Square de Meeûs 8
B-1040 BRUXELLES

Contact person: M André KIRCHBERGER

- The Commission is currently preparing a communication to the Council on the impact of the new information technologies on employment, working conditions, and education and training systems. This will embody proposals for future activities in this field both at member states and at Community levels.

During 1981, the Commission has initiated four interrelated preparatory studies to establish an information base on current developments in Community countries relating to the introduction of the new information technologies into education and training systems, with particular reference to curriculum development, teacher training, the production of materials and research and development in the educational sector. It is also particularly interested in examining the potential of the new information technologies in the teaching and training of the handicapped.

The titles of the four studies are:

1. Establishment of information base;

2. Feasibility study on the establishment of a system of specialised information arrangements;

3. Comparative study of selected initiatives in the member states (England and Wales, Scotland, France, Bavaria);

4. Application to the teaching and training of the handicapped.

The Commission has established an ad hoc Group of National Correspondants from the competent authorities in the educational field in the member states to advise it in the preparation of its proposals to the Council for future action at Community level.

ORGANISATION FOR ECONOMIC CO-OPERATION AND DEVELOPMENT (OECD)

Directorate for social affairs, manpower and education/
Direction des affaires sociales de la main d'oeuvre et de l'education

Division education and training/Division education et formation

Centre for Educational Research and Innovation (CERI)

2 rue André-Pascal
F-75775 PARIS CEDEX 16

Contact persons: - CERI: M Pierre DUGUET, M Pierre LADERRIERE
                   - ET Division: M Kenneth PANKHURST

- Preparatory work on the role of the educational system with regard to the development of the new technologies in our society. (Travaux préparatoires sur le rôle du système éducatif face au développement des nouvelles technologies dans la société.)

Examination of major trends and policies with regard to the introduction of the new technologies in the educational system. (Examen des grandes tendances et politiques de l'introduction des nouvelles technologies dans le système éducatif.)

The Education Committee will undertake a study on the future development of education in changing social, economic and technological conditions in OECD countries. The technology context will feature prominently in this work.

In addition, the impact of technological change on skills and training requirements will be taken up in the work on vocational education and training under the auspices of the Joint Working Party in this area which has been set up between the Education Committee and the Manpower and Social Affairs Committee.

The CERI Governing Board has agreed to a major new project on new technologies and education which would focus on:
(i) examination of major trends and policies; (ii) role of educational institutions; (iii) conditions under which the new technologies may be adapted to the educational system.

EUROPEAN CULTURAL FOUNDATION

Institute of Education and Social Policy
p/a Université de Paris IX-Dauphine
Place du Maréchal de Lattre de Tassigny
F-75116 PARIS

Since September 1981, the Institute, on behalf of the Directorate-General for Science Policy of the Netherlands National Ministry of Education, has been carrying out a project on the use of computers (in particular micro-computers) in education in France, the United Kingdom, Denmark, the Federal Republic of Germany, and the United States. In each of these countries, a study is being conducted by a qualified specialist, and the Institute is to prepare a comparative overview of these national studies before May 1982. In addition, a group of Dutch experts accompanied by the Director of the Institute of Education, is undertaking short study visits in the above-mentioned countries, in order to discuss problems concerning the use of computers in education with official representatives responsible for national policy in this field.

The main emphasis of the project, and of all the studies on which it is based, is on the achievements of these policies so far, on the difficulties they have encountered, and on solutions and policies proposed for the future by the authorities and education systems of the five countries concerned.

It is intended that the Institute's report should be used by the Netherlands Government in the preparation of its own fresh policies in this area.

ASSOCIATION FOR TEACHER EDUCATION IN EUROPE (ATEE)

President: Professor Dr. F W BUSCH
Universität Oldenburg
Schilfweg 5
D-2902 RASTEDE 1

Secretariat: 51 rue de la Concorde
B-1050 BRUXELLES

and in particular its group studying new information technologies.

Contact person: Mr Rhys GWYN, Faculty of Community Studies,
Manchester Polytechnic,
Didsbury School of Education,
799 Wilmslow Road,
GB - MANCHESTER M20 8RR

ATEE has published an overview report on the new information technologies and education, implications for teacher education, a country report for Ireland and a compendium of training courses in the new technologies offered to teachers in the United Kingdom, see bibliography.

The 7th ATEE Conference (Birmingham 6-10 September 1982) had information technology and teacher education as its sub-themes.

FIPESO

(Fédération internationale des professeurs de l'enseignement secondaire)

Secrétariat général: 7 rue de Villersexel
                       F-75007 PARIS

Congress on "The new information and communication technologies and secondary education" (Les nouvelles technologies d'information et de communication et l'enseignement secondaire), Annecy (France), 28 July - 3 August 1982.

INTERNATIONAL COUNCIL FOR EDUCATIONAL MEDIA (ICEM)/
CONSEIL INTERNATIONAL DES MOYENS D'ENSEIGNEMENT (CIME)

29 rue d'Ulm
F-75230 PARIS CEDEX 05

- Research into the use of microelectronics in education in France, Israel, Japan and other countries.

INTERNATIONAL FEDERATION FOR INFORMATION PROCESSING (IFIP)

IFIP has ten technical committees (TC). The Chairman of the Committee on Education (TC 3) is:

M J HEBENSTREIT
Professeur à l'Ecole Supérieure d'Electricité,
Plateau de Moulon,
F-91190 GIF-SUR-YVETTE

TC 3 has set up several working parties. Working Group 3.1 (Chairman: F LOVIS, United Kingdom) looks after computers in secondary education. Working Group 3.3 (Chairman: S SHARP, USA) looks after computer-assisted instruction (CAI). Working Group 3.4 (Chairman: P RAYMONT, United Kingdom), looks after computers in vocational education.

TC 3 is organising - at regular intervals - the World Conference on Computers in Education (1970 Amsterdam, 1975 Marseilles, 1981 Lausanne), whereas the working parties organise working conferences such as the conference on "Micros in Education" University of Lancaster, March 1982 (organiser: Computers in Higher Education, Department of Mathematics, University of Lancaster, GB-LANCASTER LA1 4YL).

WORLD CONFERENCE OF ORGANISATIONS OF THE TEACHING PROFESSION (WCOTP)

5 avenue du Moulin
CH-1110 MORGES/Suisse

- Study of the implications of the new technologies for the role of teachers.

3.2.2 COUNTRIES

AUSTRIA

Mag Alfred BERGER, Österreichisches Schulrechenzentrum, A-1050 WIEN

Mag Johann BRANDL, Bundesgymnasium X, A-1030 WIEN

Prof. Dr. Manfred BROCKHAUS, Institut für Informationstechnik, Technische Universität Wien, A-1040 WIEN

Bundesministerium für Unterrich und Kunst, Postfach 65, A-1014 WIEN

- Development of learning objectives for microelectronics in upper secondary technical and commercial schools and an inquiry among teachers about the usefulness of these learning objectives.

  (Contact person: Ministerialrat Dr. Helmut AIGNER)

Dipl. Ing. Josef A DIRNBERGER, Institut für Informationssysteme, Technische Universität Wien, Argentinierstr. 8 A-1040 WIEN

- Co-author of a study on the present situation of microelectronics (Informatik) teaching at Austrian secondary schools.

Professor Dr. W DÖRFLER, Institut für Mathematik, Universität für Bildungswissenschaften, Keltengasse 67, A-9020 KLAGENFURT

- The impact of microelectronics on the teaching of mathematics at school (probability calculations)

Gymnasium der Gesellschaft Jesu Kalksburg, Promenadeweg 3, A-1237 WIEN
Director: Dr. E SCHMUTS

- Pilot experiment with microelectronics as part of general education for all pupils.

Mag Hans JAKOB, Höhere Technische Bundeslehranstalt Braunau, A-5280 BRAUNAU

Dipl.-Ing. Franz LICHTENBERGER, Institut für Mathematik, Johannes-Kepler-Universität Linz, A-4045 LINZ

Univ. Prof. Dipl. Ing. Dr. Adolf MELEZINEK, Universität für Bildungswissenschaften Klagenfurt, Institut für Unterrichtstechnologie, Universitätsstrasse 65, A-9020 KLAGENFURT.

Research team: Dipl. Ing. Werner BEYERLE
Univ. Ass. Dipl. Ing. Hartmut WEIDNER
Dipl. Ing. Martin WEISSENBÖCK

Research into teaching of microelectronics and its use at school. (What systems and computers are being used? What possibilities do they offer for schools?)

Mag Walter NEUPER, Akademisches Gymnasium Salzburg, A-5020 SALZBURG

Österreichische Computergesellschaft (Austrian Computer Society) Fachgruppe "Informatik in der Schule" (Working Party "Microelectronics at School")

c/o Dr. Helmut SCHAUER (Chairman), Institut für Informationssysteme, Technische Universität Wien, Argentinierstr. 8, A-1040 WIEN

- Study on the situation of microelectronics teaching at Austrian secondary schools;

- Study on the importance of microelectronics teaching at Austrian secondary schools with regard to later vocational practice.

- Meeting on microelectronics at school, Passau (Bavaria), spring 1979. German title: "Informatik in der Schule".

Prof. Dr. Ernst REICHL, Lehrkanzel für Informationssysteme, Johannes-Kepler-Universität, Linz, A-4045 LINZ

Dr. Helmut SCHAUER, Institut für Informationssysteme, Technische Universität Wien, Argentinierstr. 8, A-1040 WIEN

- Austrian representative for the Technical Committee "Education" of the International Federation for Information Processing;

- Chairman of the Working Party "Microelectronics at School" (Informatik in der Schule) of the Austrian Computer Society (Österreichische Computergesellschaft)

Dr. Klaus SCHEDLER and Peter GEIGER, Österreichisches Institut Bildung und Wirtschaft, Indenplatz 3/4, A-1010 WIEN.

Research into training implications of use of microprocessors in industry and administration.

Dr. E SCHMUTS, Direktor, Gymnasium der Gesellschaft Jesu Kalksburg, Promenadenweg 3, A-1237 WIEN.

Research into microelectronics as general education for pupils (pilot experiment).

Prof. Dr. Arno SCHULZ, Institut für Statistik und Informatik, Johannes-Kepler-Universität Linz, A-4045 LINZ

Frau Mag. Doris STEGBUCHNER, 2 Bundesgymnasium Salzburg, A-5020 SALZBURG

Dr. Hans STEGBUCHNER, Institut für Mathematik, Universität Salzburg, A-5020 SALZBURG

Mag Alfred VOGEL, Höhere Techn. Bundeslehranstalt, A-3250 WIESELBURG

BELGIUM

Mr MERTENS, Inspector of Educational Technology, Hezelaarsdreef 23, B-2280 GROBBENDAEL

MINISTERIE VAN NATIONALE OPVOEDING EN NEDERLANDSE CULTUUR
Rijksadministratief Centrum, Arcadengebouw, B-1010 BRUSSELS

(Contact person: M R ROOSE, Secrétaire Général)

- Evaluation of the teaching of computer studies by the network of inspectors.

The teaching of computer studies is evaluated by the heads of the institutions which had a department of computer studies and the competent inspectors. The inspectors make an effort to follow the evolution of computer studies and its implications for the employment market. They constantly adapt the teaching materials and teaching methods, with the help of out-of-school experts.

M J VAN DER HAEGHEN, Inspecteur (Ministère de l'Education Nationale), 26-28 Boulevard de Berlaymont, B-1000 BRUXELLES

DENMARK

Lektor Peter BOLLERSLEV, Røjlevangen 40, DK-2630 TAASTRUP

- Danish member of the Committee "Computers in Secondary Education" of the International Federation for Information Processing (IFIP).

Bøige CHRISTENSEN, TØNDER

Mr O Bjørn PETERSEN, V Voldgade 113, DK-1503 KØBENHAVN V

Knud Hassing POVISEN, DK-AALBORG

- Experiments with introduction into electronic data-processing at lower secondary education, involving four communal schools (Sofiendalskolen, Gistrup Skole, Gl. Hasseris Skole, Gug Skole).

Erling SMITH, Aarhus University, DK-AARHUS.

UNDERVISNINGSMINISTERIET

Frederiksholmskanal 25D, DK-1220 KØBENHAVN K

(Contact person: Director Werner RASMUSSEN)

- Evaluation of experience with computers at Danish schools.

UDVALGET VEDR UDDANNELSESFORSKNING, Forskningsrådsinitiativerne, Universitetsparken 5, DK-2100 KØBENHAVN Ø

(Joint Committee of the Danish Social Sciences Research Council and the Humanities Research Council set up to stimulate educational research)

Contact person: Mr Tom Ploug OLSEN

Research on the future information-technological society and the school/educational system (primary and lower secondary education).

FRANCE

Agence de la Coopération Culturelle et Technique, Centre d'Information et d'Echanges-Télévision, 19 avenue de Messine, F-75008 PARIS

- Bibliography about programmes instruction.

Edmond-Antoine DECAMPS, Professeur à la Faculté des Sciences de Rennes, Directeur de l'Institut de Préparation aux Enseignements du Second Degré, Sciences et Philosophie, Campus de Beaulieu, 9 rue Jean Macé, F-35042 RENNES

- Research into the implications of the new technologies for teacher education.

Maurice FAUQUET, 10 rue des Acacias, Lozère, F-99120 PALAISEAU

- Chairman of the group for teacher education and audiovisual aids of the Association for Teacher Education in Europe (ATEE)/

Président du Groupe pour la formation des enseignants à et pour l'audiovisuel, Association pour la formation des enseignants en Europe.

Monsieur J HEBENSTREIT, Professeur à l'Ecole Supérieure d'Electricité, Plateau du Moulon, F-91190 GIF-SUR-YVETTE

Institut National de Recherche Pédagogique, Services des études et recherches pédagogiques, rue Gabriel Péri, F-92120 MONTROUGE

- Microelectronics in secondary education (L'informatique dans l'enseignement secondaire): microelectronics as an intellectual approach (démarche intellectuelle) in the various subjects taught at upper secondary level as well as the use of computers as learning aids.

    (See Project No. 2462, EUDISED R & D Bulletin No. 10; Research team: Christian LAFOND, Michelle BOUNAY, Pierre MULLER. Research Director: Jacques PERRIAULT)

LE JOURNAL DE LA FORMATION CONTINUE, 2 rue d'Amsterdam, F-75009 PARIS.

Colloquy on microelectronics, computer-assisted learning and continued education (Colloque micro-informatique, enseignement assisté par ordinateur, audiovisuel, télématique et formation continue), Paris, 24-25 June 1982.

Responsible person: M Jean-Pierre FARGETTE, author of the book "Enseignement Ordinateur".

Ministère de l'Education Nationale, 110 rue de Grenelle, F-75857 PARIS

Contact persons: Mr P POULAIN and Mme C NORA, Direction des Affaires internationales

- Action "10,000 micro-computers", ie plan to equip the 12,000 French lycees with an average of eight microcomputers per school between 1979 and 1984. Delivery is functioning more or less according to plan but the 12-day voluntary information courses for teachers have proved to be unsuitable. They have therefore been stopped by the Ministry and are replaced by a new plan, providing for voluntary introductory courses of 80-100 hours for teachers at each school which is equipped with micro-computers. The course will deal with all aspects of the new medium.

Source: EURODIDAC FORUM 3/81

M Jean-Joseph SCHEFFKNECHT, Agence Nationale pour le développement de l'éducation permanente (ADEP), Tour Franklin, F-92081 PARIS-LA DEFENSE

SOFEDIR - rue du ler mai, F-91120 PALAISEAU

- Evaluation of experience with computers in 58 French lycées
  (L'école et l'informatique, l'expérience des 58 lycées en France).

M Harold WERTZ, Dépt. Informatique, Université de Paris VIII,
2 rue de la Liberté, F-93 526 SAINT DENIS.

- Research into the use of computers at school in France.

FEDERAL REPUBLIC OF GERMANY

Akademie für Informatik und Unterrichtstechnologie e.V.,
Weingartstrasse 59, D-4040 NEUSS (Academy for Microelectronics and
Educational Technology)

- <u>In-service training of teachers</u>: up to 5,000 so far.

    On behalf of the districts and certain institutions responsible
    for in-service training of teachers, the academy organises
    training courses (1 day, 3 days, 1 week).

    The programme is centred around

    - logics of programming computers;

    - computer languages BASIC, COBOL and PASCAL;

    - workshops about computer languages;

    - structured prgoramming;

    - applied microelectronics (angewandte Informatik).

    The courses take place either at the University Computer Centre
    or at one of the other schools in the area of Cologne or
    Düsseldorf. All courses focus on practical exercises. Hardware:
    modern computers equipped with typewriter and screen. Teaching
    staff: teacher trainers specialised in microelectronics and -
    for certain themes - people from industry.

    These courses are meant for teachers of all types of schools where
    microelectronics has been introduced as a subject in its own right.
    There are also courses for teachers at technical schools training
    computer specialists: these teachers are offered training in
    teaching methods (didactics).

    There is also a one-year course offering <u>basic training for future
    teachers</u> at technical schools training computer specialists.

ARBEITSKREIS "INFORMATIK" DER GESELLSCHAFT FÜR DIDAKTIK DER MATHEMATIK (working party on Microelectronics of the Society for the Teaching of Mathematics)

c/o Prof. Dr. K-D GRAF, Freie Universität Berlin (see under G)

- Proposals for microelectronics (contents and methods) as an element of mathematics at lower secondary level as well as a university subject for future teachers of mathematics.

Prof. Dr. Wolfgang ARLT,
Institut für Datenverarbeitung in den Unterrichtswissenschaften,
Pädagogische Hochschule Berlin,
Malteser Strasse 74-100,
D-1000 BERLIN (WEST)

Pilot project ECIS: Development of curriculum elements for computer studies at lower secondary school.

Studiendirektor Rüdeger BAUMANN, In den Stuken 16, D-2120 LÜNEBURG

- Use of computers and in particular the computer language BASIC in mathematics teaching at upper secondary (Gymnasium) level.

Bayerisches Staatsministerium für Unterricht und Kultus, Brieffach, D-8000 MÜNCHEN 1

Contact person: Ministerialrat Dr. Eberhard RUPPRECHT

- Evaluation of experience with computers in Bavarian schools.

BERUFSFÖRDERUNGSZENTRUM ESSEN EV (BFZ)
Projektgruppe MFA,
Altenessener Strasse 80/84,
D-4300 ESSEN 12

- Responsibility for a pilot project using microelectronics in the training of qualified (skilled) workmen.

Bernhard BORG, Berufsbildende Schule BBS I, Winsener Str. 57, D-3040 SOLTAU

- Contact person for research and development with regard to the use of computers and the teaching of microelectronics in vocational/technical and in particular in commercial education, sponsored by the Germany Computer Society (Gesellschaft für Informatik e.V.)

Activities: see under Gesellschaft für Informatik e.V.

Dr. Ulrich BOSLER, Institut für die Pädagogik der Naturwissenschaften, Olshausenstrasse 40-60, D-2300 KIEL 1

Bernhard BROCKMANN,
Zentralstelle für Programmierten Unterricht und
Computer im Unterricht,
Schertlinstrasse 7,
D-8900 AUGSBURG

- Member of the Working Party on Computers in Education
  (Arbeitsgruppe Computer im Unterricht) of the German Society
  for Education and Information (Gesellschaft für Pädagogik und
  Information).

BUNDESINSTITUT FÜR BERUFSBILDUNG, Fehrbelliner Platz 3, D-1000 BERLIN (WEST) 31

- The impact of microprocessing technologies on the process of
  qualifying for a career in the fields of metal and electro-
  technics (media, teaching methods, structural proposals)
  (Auswirkungen der Mikroprozessortechnologie auf den
  Qualifikationsprozess in den Berfufsfeldern Metall und
  Elektrotechnik - Medien, Vermittlungsformen,
  Strukturierungsvorschläge).

  Research team: BIEHLER-BANDISCH, BUCHHOLZ, FILLER, KOLAKOVIC, LAUR;

  Research director: GUTSCHMIDT;

  Duration: September 1980 - December 1981.

BUNDESMINISTERIUM FÜR BILDUNG UND WISSENSCHAFT, Heinemannstrasse 2, D-5300 BONN 2

Contact person: Regierungsdirecktor Dr. Christian BODE

- Evaluation of experience with microelectronics teaching in the
  Federal Republic of Germany.

Dierk BUSE, Studiendirektor, Fachberater für Informatik für die
Gymnasien in Niedersachsen, Herzog-Bernd-Strasse 17 A, D-3040 SOLTAU

- Member of the Bureau of the Fachausschuss "Informatik in der
  Schule" (Microelectronics at School), described under "Gesellschaft
  für Informatik"

- Development of guidelines and curricula for the teaching of
  microelectronics (Informatik) at upper secondary school level
  (Gymnasium = grammar school);

- Elaboration of uniform examination requirements for the Abitur
  (upper secondary school leaving examination) as regards the subject
  of microelectronics (Informatik) in the Federal Republic of Germany;

- In-service training of teachers with regard to the teaching of microelectronics (Informatik) in general and technical education;

- Pilot experiment "Überregionale Erprobung und Vergleich von schulspezifischen Programmiersprachen im Informatik- und Datenverarbeitungsunterricht"
  (Supraregional testing and comparions of school-specific computer languages used in microelectronics teaching).

CHEMISCHES INSTITUT DR. FLAD, Staatl. Anerkannte Berufsfachschule für Chemisch-technische Assistenten/innen, Breitscheidstr. 127, D-7000 STUTTGART 1.

- Working Party "Computers and the Teaching of Chemistry" (Arbeitskreis "Computer im Chemieunterricht"), comprising chemistry teachers from all over the country.

- Organisation of seminars about the use of computers in the teaching of chemistry (EDV-Seminare).

Prof. Dr. Volker CLAUS, Lehrstuhl für Informatik II, RuhruniversitätBochum, Postfach 500, D-4600 DORTMUND-HOMBRUCH

Prof. Dr. E COHORS-FRESENBORG, Professor für Mathematik und ihre Didaktik, Universität Osnabrück, D-4500 OSNABRÜCK

- Introduction into the notion of functions on the basis of algorisms (Microelectronics in mathematics teaching)

Deutsches Institut für Internationale Pädagogische Forschung, Abt. Allg. u. Vgl. Erziehungswissenschaft, Postfach 90 02 80, D-6000 FRANKFURT AM MAIN 90

- Teaching language, teaching assessment and evaluation, teaching algorisms (Unterrichtssprache, Unterrichtsnotation und Unterrichtsalgorithmen)

    Research team: ECKEL and RICHTER

    Duration: January 1980-?

Universität DUISBURG, Forschungsgruppe BWL-Planung und Organisation, Lotharstrasse 65, D-4100 DUISBURG 1

- Scientific control and evaluation of a pilot experiment "Use of microelectronics in the training of qualified workmen" (Einsatz der Mikrocomputertechnik in der Facharbeiterausbildung - MFA)

    Research team: Norbert SCHEPANSKI and Christian HANDEL

    Research directors: Erich STAUDT and Norbert MEYER

    Duration: October 1980 - March 1985

FEoLL-GmbH, Forschungs- und Entwicklungszentrum für objektivierte
Lehr- und Lernverfahren, Postfach 1567, D-4790 PADERBORN - and its
Department for Micro-computers in School Education (Mikrocomputer in
der Schule)

- Research into the use of micro-computers in school education.

    Research team: HAUF, KIRST, UTERMÖHLE, WAGNER, GAUS, HERMISCH,
    BRAMKAMP, REIMANN

    Research director: Dr. L STURM

    Duration: July 1980 - December 1983

    FREIE UNIVERSITÄT BERLIN,
    Zentralinstitut für Unterrichtswissenschaften und
    Curriculumentwicklung,
    Institut für Didaktik der Mathematik und Informatik, ZI 7,
    WE 3, Malteserstrasse 74-100, D-1000 BERLIN (WEST) 46

Contact persons: Mr Bernhard KOERBER
                     Mr Dieter RIEDEL
                     Mr Ingo-Rüdiger PETERES
                     Ms Marion ROHDE

    Development of curriculum elements for computer studies at
lower secondary schools.

Dr. Günter FRIEDRICHS, Industriegewerkschaft Metall, Vorstand -
Abteilung Automation, Untermainkai 70-76, D-6000 FRANKFURT AM MAIN

- Research into the implications of microelectronics for
  education in the context of The Club of Rome.

Wolfgang FROMM, Friedrich-Leitner-Oberschule, Babelsberger Str. 24,
D-1000 BERLIN (WEST) 31

- Chairman of the Advisory Council on Microelectronics (Beirat
  für Informatik) set up by the Berlin Ministry of Education
  (Senator für Schulwesen)

    The Council is to help with the development of microelectronics
    curricula, the evaluation of experience and the examination
    of teaching material, etc.

Gesellschaft für Didaktik der Mathematik (GDM) (German Society for
the Teaching of Mathematics)

Arbeitskreis "Informatik" (Working Party on Microelectronics)

Chairman: Prof. Dr. K-D GRAF (see under GRAF)

Research and development work: see under GRAF

Gesellschaft für Informatik e.V. (German Computer Society)

- Fachausschuss Ausbildung (Educational Committee) see Prof. Dr. R GRUNZENHAUSER

- Fachgruppe "Informatik in der Schule": 300 members (Sub-committee "Microelectronics at School") see Dr. L H KLINGEN

 and its

- Arbeitsgruppe "Datenverarbeitungsunterricht in den Berufsbildenden Schulen (Working Party on Data Processing in Vocational/Technical Education) see Mr B BORG

- Themes dealt with by the Fachgruppe:

    - Microelectronics (Informatik) as a subject taught at school;
    - Microelectronics (Informatik) as an aid for the teaching of other subjects;
    - Data processing in vocational/technical education;
    - Initial and in-service education and training of teachers;
    - Computers and computer languages used at school;
    - Exchange of research results and experience;
    - Didactical aspects (how to approach the teaching of microelectronics);
    - Curricula and examinations;
    - Computer-assisted learning;
    - Use of computers for testing performance.

Arbeitskreis Informatik an kaufmännischen Berufsbildenden Schulen (Working Party on Microelectronics in Commercial Schools) see Mr B BORG

 GESELLSCHAFT FÜR MATHEMATIK UND DATENVERARBEITUNG (GMD) Postfach 1240, Schloss Birlinghoven, D-5205 ST AUGUSTIN

- Research and development with regard to the use of computers in education.

- Organisation (together with FEoLL) of a meeting on microelectronics and school (Fachtagung Mikroelektronik und Schule), 24-25 June 1982.

 GESELLSCHAFT FÜR PÄDAGOGIK UND INFORMATION e.V. (GPI) in PADERBORN (Sylter Weg 3, D-4790 PADERBORN (Society for Education and Information) and its Working Parties:

- Arbeitsgruppe Bildungsverwaltung und Schulorganisation (BSO) (Working Party on Educational Administration and School Organisation)

Chairman: Studienrat L SAREYKA (see under SAREYKA)

- Organisation of a symposium on computers at school, Neuss, 20-21 November 1980 (use of computers for school management, but to some extent also for teaching)

- Elaboration of a repertory of computers (hardware and software) used by schools in Europe

- <u>Arbeitsgruppe Computer im Unterricht</u> (Working Party on Computers in Education)

Contact person: B BROCKMANN, Schertlinstrasse 7, D-8900 AUGSBURG

- Arbeitsgruppe Lehrprogramme in Schulen (LS), (Working Party on Curricula)

    Chairman: Fritz Thayssen, Schenefelder Landstr 14, D-2000 HAMBURG 55.

Prof. Dr. K-D <u>GRAF</u>, Zentralinstitut für Unterrichtswissenschaften und Curriculumentwicklung (ZI 7), Institut für Didaktik der Mathematik und Informatik (WE 03), Fachrichtung Informatik und Kybernetik, Freie Universität Berlin, Standort Lankwitz, Malteserstrasse 74-100, D-1000 BERLIN (WEST) 46

- Microelectronics (contents and methods) and the teaching of mathematics - a paper prepared 1974.

- Microelectronics and teacher education: enquiry carried out in 1977 and 1978.

- Elaboration of material for microelectronics as a subject in teacher education.

- Proposals for microelectronics (contents and methods) as an element of mathematics at lower secondary level as well as a university subject for future teachers of mathematics, prepared by the Working Party on Microelectronics of the German Society for the Teaching of Mathematics.

- Documentation on the use of computers in mathematics (situation, trends, problems) in the Federal Republic of Germany, put together 1980 with the help of Dr. KEIL, Prof. LÖTHE and Dr. WINKELMANN.

- Colloquies on the use of microelectronics in the teaching of mathematics for school and university teachers (academic year 1981-82: practical experience and work planned at school and university level).

    (The German term "Informatik" has been translated by "microelectronics".)

Prof. R GUNZENHÄUSER, Institut für Informatik, Universität Stuttgart, Anzenbergstrasse 12, D-7000 STUTTGART 1

Vorsitzender des Fachausschusses Ausbildung der Gesellschaft für Informatik (Chairman of the Educational Committee of the German Computer Society)

- Computer-assisted learning - Strategies for the teaching of mathematics

- Research into the use of computers at school (Modellversuch IDA).

Dr. P HEYDERHOFF, Merler Allee 114, D-5300 BONN

Member of the Bureau of the Fachausschuss "Informatik in der Schule" (Microelectronics at School), described under "Gesellschaft für Informatik"

Günter HOMMEL, GMD, Postfach 1240, D-5205 ST AUGUSTIN

- Research into programme construction with abstract notions in ELAN (computer language) at secondary education.

Institut für die Pädagogik der Naturwissenschaften (IPN), Olshausenstrasse 40-60, D-2300 KIEL

- Scientific control and research evaluation of a Schleswig-Holstein pilot project "Microelectronics Course" (Projekt Informatikkurse), comprising the development and testing of teaching material for microelectronics to be taught as a subject in its own right in upper secondary education (Gymnasium, Oberstufe). The project will also examine whether the computer languages PASCAL and LOGO are suitable for use in schools.

- Editor of the quarterly periodical "LOG IN - Informatik in Schule und Ausbildung" (Microelectronics in Education and Training).

- Development of framework curricula for the use of microprocessors in vocational education.

Stefan JÄHNICHEN, Technische Universität Berlin, FG Softwaretechnik, TEL 18, Ernst Reuter-Platz 7, D-1000 BERLIN (WEST)

- Research into programme construction with abstract notions in ELAN (computer language) at secondary education.

Dipl.-Inf. Hermann JANNASCH, Erziehungswissenschaftliche Hochschule, Rheinland-Pfalz, D-6740 LANDAU

U KARL, working at the Zentralstelle für den Programmierten Unterricht und Computer im Unterricht (Centre for Computer-Assisted Instruction and Computer in Education), Schertlinstr 7, D-8900 AUGSBURG

Research evaluation of a pilot project: use of computer terminals at school.

KAUFMÄNNISCHES BERUFSBILDUNGSZENTRUM III, Stengelstrasse 29, D-6600 SAARBRÜCKEN and four other commercial schools in Saarland

- Experience with microelectronics in commercial education.

Studiendirektor Dr. Karl-August KEIL, Zentralstelle für Programmierten Unterricht und Computer im Unterricht, Schertlinstr 7, D-8900 AUGSBURG

- Member of the Bureau of the Fachausschuss "Informatik in der Schule" (Microelectronics at School), described under "Gesellschaft für Informatik";

- Evaluation of experiences with computers in mathematics teaching (see also item 5 under GRAF);

- In-service training of Bavarian teachers for computer studies;

- Advice to Bavarian schools (Inspector for Computer-Assisted Instruction);

- BUS (in-service training periodical);

- Exchange of teaching programmes.

Oberstudiendirektor Dr. L H KLINGEN, Helmholtz-Gymnasium, Billrothstrasse 2, D-5300 BONN 1

- The algorithmic branch in the teaching of mathematics at Gymnasium (grammar school) level.

- First spokesman of the Fachausschuss "Informatik in der Schule" (Sub-Committee "Microelectronics at School"), which is a sub-committee of the Educational Committee (Fachausschuss Ausbildung) of the German Computer Society (Gesellschaft für Informatik). See the list of themes dealt with by the Fachausschuss, mentioned under "Gesellschaft für Informatik".

- Evaluation of the use of computers in various subjects taught at secondary school.

  Wilfred KOCH, Technische Universität Berlin, FG Softwaretechnik, TEL 18, Ernst-Reuter-Platz 7, D-1000 BERLIN (WEST) 10.

- Research into programme construction with abstract notions in ELAN (computer language) at secondary education.

Bernhard KOERBER, Institut für Datenverarbeitung in den Unterrichtswissenschaften, Pädagogische Hochschule Berlin, Malteser Str. 74-100, D-1000 BERLIN (WEST) 46

LANDESINSTITUT SCHLESWIG-HOLSTEIN FÜR PRAXIS UND THEORIE DER SCHULE (IPTS), Schreberweg 5, D-2300 KIEL-KRONSHAGEN

- The use of computers in mathematics teaching (Oberstudiendirektor Heiko WOLGAST).

- Regional co-ordination of a pilot project "Microelectronics Course" (Projekt Informatikkurse), comprising the development and testing of teaching material for microelectronics to be taught as a subject in its own right in upper secondary education (Gymnasium, Oberstufe). The project will also examine whether the computer languages PASCAL and LOGO are suitable for use in schools.

E LEHMANN, Studiendirektor, Rückertschule, D-1000 BERLIN (WEST)

- Use of computers in the teaching of mathematics at upper secondary school level (linear algebra).

Prof. H LÖTHE, Professor für Mathematik und ihre Didaktik, Pädagogische Hochschule Esslingen, Beblinger Strasse 1-10, D-7300 ESSLINGEN

- Pilot experiments with computer language LOGO at lower secondary school level (see also item 5 under GRAF).

MINISTERIUM FÜR KULTUS, BILDUNG UND SPORT,
Projektgruppe TUK
Saaruferstrasse 32,
D-6600 SAARBRÜCKEN

Contact person: Studiendirektor B FREIDINGER

- Pilot project "The use of computer terminals in vocational education (commercial schools)".

Studiendirektor Richard NAGEL, Am Steig 3, D-7347 BAD ÜBERKINGEN

- Evaluation of experience with computers used for the teaching of chemistry at upper secondary (Gymnasium) level. At a pilot experiment at Mörike-Gymnasium in D-7320 GÖPPINGEN, the pupils write their own computer programmes in chemistry.

- Evaluation of in-service education and training of chemistry teachers interested in using computers.

NORDDEUTSCHER RUNDFUNK (NDR) - SCHULFERNSEHEN (North German Radio & Television, School Television/Radio-Télévision Allemagne de Nord - Télévision scolaire)

Dr. Helmut JENZSCH, NDR-Schulfernsehen, Gazellenkamp 54
D-2000 HAMBURG 54

- Development of a television course for schools: "Introduction into microelectronics" (Einführungskurs für Informatik).

PÄDAGOGISCHE HOCHSCHULE BERLIN,
Institut für Datenverarbeitung in den Unterrichtswissenschaften, Malteserstrasse 74-100, D-1000 BERLIN (WEST) 46.

Contact persons: ARLT, FLEISCHHUT, KOERBER, RIEDEL

Research and development with regard to the introduction of computer studies at lower secondary schools in Berlin.

Rudolf PESCHKE, Hessisches Institut für Bildungsplanung und Schulentwicklung, Bodenstedtstrasse 7, D-6200 WIESBADEN

- Research into the use of computers at school.

Studienrat Ludgerus SAREYKA, Kaufmännische Schule Neuss, Weingartstrasse 59, D-4040 NEUSS

Chairman of the Working Party on Educational Administration and School Organisation (Arbeitsgruppe "Bildungsverwaltung und Schulorganisation", BSO) of the German Society for Education and Information (Gesellschaft für Pädagogik und Information eV, gpi).

Research and development work: see under Gesellschaft für Pädagogik und Information eV.

Prof. Dr. G SCHRAGE, Professor für Mathematik und ihre Didaktik, Universität Dortmund, August-Schmidt-Strasse, D-4600 DORTMUND-EICHLINGHOFEN

- Use of computers in the teaching of statistics.

Prof. Dr. Erich STAUDT, Gesamthochschule Duisburg, FB 5, Lotharstr. 65, D-4100 DUISBURG 1 (see under "Duisburg")

Prof. Dr. Hermann STEVER, Erziehungswissenschaftl. Hochschule, Rheinland-Pfalz, D-6740 LANDAU

Prof. Dr. Werner STROMBACH, Fachhochschule Dortmund, Universität Dortmund, Hessenbank 16, D-4600 DORTMUND 50.

Working Party on Informatics and Philosophy (Arbeitskreis Informatik und Philosophie), set up in co-operation with Prof. Dr. B REUSCH of the Department of Computer Studies of the University of Dortmund.

Prof. Dr. N SZYPERSKI, GDM, Postfach 1240, D-5205 ST AUGUSTIN

- Comparative research into computer studies in various countries.

Karl ULLRICH, Oberstudiendirektor, Berufsoberschule Passau, D-8390 PASSAU

Dr. WINKELMANN, Institut für Didaktik der Mathematik, Universität Bielefeld, Postfach 8640, D-4800 BIELEFELD 1

- Documentation about literature on the teaching of mathematics including microelectronics.

Prof. Dr. A WYNANDS, Professor, Professor für Mathematik und ihre Didaktik, Universität Bonn, Liebfrauenweg 3, D-5300 BONN 1

- Algorithmic work with pocket calculators at school (mathematics).

ZENTRALSTELLE FÜR PROGRAMMIERTEN UNTERRICHT UND COMPUTER IM UNTERRICHT (Central Office for Computer-Assisted Instruction and Computers in Education)

Schertlinstrasse 7, D-8900 AUGSBURG

Research and development centre set up by the Bavarian Ministry of Education to co-ordinate developments in Bavaria with regard to computer-assisted instruction and computer studies at school. The centre also offers advice to schools.

Prof. Dr. J ZIEGENBALG, Professor für Mathematik und ihre Didaktik, Pädagogische Hochschule Reutlingen, Postfach 680, D-7410 REUTLINGEN 1

- Evaluation on the use of computers in the teaching of mathematics in lower secondary education.

GREECE

Mr Stamatios PALEOCRASSAS, Vice-President of KEME, c/o Ministry of National Education, EEC Section, Mitropoleos 15, GR-ATHENS (118).

IRELAND

Mona GARVEY, An Runai, An Roinn, Oideachais (Department of Education), Marlborough Street, Baile Atha Cliath 1, IRL-DUBLIN 1.

Research into development of software system for schools (done at Trinity College).

Development of structured algorithons for use in implementation of structured BASIC or PASCAL or COMAL.

Mr William HYLAND, Chief Statistician, Department of Education, Apollo House, Tara Street, IRL-DUBLIN 2.

ITALY

Sig. Luciano ANTOLA, ITALSIEL, DCRS-Castelletto di Settimo Milanese, Via A Tocqueville 13, I-MILANO

Prof. Mario FIERLI, Centro Europeo dell'Educazione, Villa Falconieri, I-00044 FRASCATI

Sig. Gaetano LANZARONE, ITALTEL, DCRS-Castelletto di Settimo Milanese, Via A Tocqueville 13, I-MILANO

Prof. Francesco SCHINO, Istituto Enciclopedia Italiana, Piazza Paganeica 4, I-00186 ROMA

LUXEMBOURG

Ministère de l'Education Nationale, 6 Boulevard Royal, L-LUXEMBOURG

Contact person: Mr Paul LENERT, Professeur-attaché au Ministère de l'Education Nationale

Mr Théo DUHAUTPAS, Professeur-ingénieur à l'Institut Supérieur de Technologie, rue R Coudenhove-Kalergi, L-LUXEMBOURG-KIRCHBERG

NETHERLANDS

ADVIESGROEP ONDERWIJS EN INFORMATIETECHNOLOGIE, c/o Technische Hogeschool Twente, Onderafdeling Toegepaste Onderwijskunde, Postbus 217, NL-7500 AE ENSCHEDE.

Advisory Committee to the Dutch Minister of Education and Science (Chairman: Prof. Dr. Tj. PLOMP).

CENTRUM VOOR ONDERWIJS EN INFORMATIETECHNOLOGIE, Technische Hogeschool Twente, Postbus 217, NL-7500.AE ENSCHEDE

Recently founded centre with advisory and co-ordinative tasks.

Dr. A DIRKZWAGER, Vakgroep Psychologische Functieleer, De Boelelaan 1115, NL-1081 HV AMSTERDAM.

Research on interactive use of computers in education, especially primary schools

Karl KLEINE, Katholieke Universiteit Nijmegen, Afd.
Informatie Toernooiveld, NL-6525 ED NIJMEGEN.

- Research into programme construction with abstract notions in ELAN (computer language) at secondary school.

Dr. M LEIBLUM and Dr. F GASTKEMPER, Catholic University, IOWO, NL-NIJMEGEN

Research into computers and education

MINISTERIE VAN ONDERWIJS EN WETENSCHAPPEN, Directoraat Generaal voor Wetenschapsbeleid, Postbus 20601, NL-2500 EP's GRAVENHAGE

Contact person: Dr. Jaap N L AKKERMANS

- Comparative study on the use of computers in education in France, the United Kingdom, Denmark, the Federal Republic of Germany and the United States. This study is performed by the Institut d'Education of the Fondation Européenne de la Culture (for further information: see international organisations). A final report of this study is expected to be available in June 1982.

- Study on opinions of research workers about (required background research for) the use of computers in education. Study performed by Prof. Dr. E M UHLENBECK and Prof. Dr. N G de BRUIJN. Report available: June 1982.

MINISTERIE VAN ONDERWIJS EN WETENSCHAPPEN, Werkgroep Onderwijs en Informatietechnologie, c/o Directoraat Generaal voor Voortgezet Onderwijs, Postbus 20551, NL-2500 EN DEN HAAG

Project group preparing a Dutch policy document on information technologies and education.

Chairman: Dr. A M L van WIERINGEN

Contact person: Drs. P W DOOP

MINISTRY FOR SCIENCE POLICY, Advisory Group on the Social Effects of Microelectronics, NL-DEN HAAG

Chairman: Prof. G W RATHENAU

NEDERLANDS GENOOTSCHAP VOOR INFORMATICA (NGI), Sectie Educatie, c/o Mw R LUCAS, Paulus Potterstraat 40, NL-1071 DB AMSTERDAM

Prof. Dr. Tjeerd PLOMP, Twente University of Technology, Department of Educational Science, PO Box 217, NL-7500 A E ENSCHEDE

Information centre on educational and information technology
(operational 1983)

STICHTING TEACHIP, c/o Dr. H C van HUMMEL, P C Hooftlaan 46,
NL-3705 AJ ZEIST

Dr. G VONK, Vakgroep Onderzoek Wiskunde Onderwijs & Onderwijs
Computer Centrum, Rijksuniversiteit Utrecht, Tiberdreef 4,
NL-3561 GC UTRECHT

Curriculum development on computer science

VERENIGNING VOOR ONDERWIJS EN COMPUTER (VOC), c/o Mevr. W Romeyn,
St. Jacobstraat 14, NL-3511 BS UTRECHT

    Drs. Tom J VAN WEERT, Ubbo Emmius, Postbus 2056,
    NL-9704 CB GRONINGEN

- Evaluation of computer studies at Dutch schools.

SPAIN

    Mr E GARCIA CAMARERO,
    Centro de Calculo de la Universidad Complutense,
    Avenida Complutense s/n,
    E-MADRID-3.

- Research into the use of computers at secondary schools.
  (See also references at the end of his paper, item 1.6.)

Ramon PUIG DE LA BELLACASA, Fundación para el Desarrollo de la
Función Social de las Comunicaciones (FUNDESCO), Serrano, 187,
E-MADRID-2.

- Research into education (special education) and the new
  technologies.

SWITZERLAND

    Pierre BANDERET,

    Université de Neuchâtel,
    Centre de calcul electronique,
    Rue de Chantemerle 20,
    Ch-2000 NEUCHATEL

- Research into the use of computers at Swiss secondary schools.

ERZIEHUNGSDIREKTION DES KANTONS BERN, Amt für Unterrichtsforschung
und - planung, Mediendidaktische Arbeits - und Informationsstelle,
Sulgeneckstrasse 70, CH-3005 BERN.

Contact person: Mr Jörg GROSSMANN.

Project Study on Media Education (Education aux média).

Committee set up to make proposals for compulsory education curricula and teacher training. Recommendation: introduction into new media cutting across all subjects, not as a new subject in its own right.

Christian ROHRBACH, Pestalozzianum Zürich, Abteilung Programmierte Unterrichtshilfen (PU), Beckenhofstr. 31-37, CH-8035 ZÜRICH

- Evaluation and distribution of computer-based materials (évaluation et diffusion de moyens d'enseignement programmé)

SCHWEIZERISCHE KONFERENZ DER KANTONALEN ERZIEHUNGSDIREKTOREN/
CONFERENCE SUISSE DES DIRECTEURS CANTONAUX DE L'INSTRUCTION PUBLIQUE
(SWISS CONFERENCE OF CANTONAL MINISTERS OF EDUCATION)

Schweizerische Zentralstelle für die Weiterbildung der Mittelschullehrer/Swiss Centre for In-service Education of Secondary School Teachers.

Palais Wilson, 52 rue des Pâquis, CH-1211 GENEVE 14.

Co-ordination Group on Computer Studies/Koordinationsgruppe Informatik/Groupe de coordination Informatique.

WEITERBILDUNGSZENTRALE, Postfach 140, CH-6000 LUZERN 4

- Testing and promoting the project "24 Hours of Microelectronics" (24 heures d'informatique) in upper secondary education in French-speaking Switzerland (Suisse Romande).

Claude ZWEIACKER, Service de l'enseignement secondaire du Département de l'instruction publique, Château 23, CH-2000 NEUCHATEL

- Research into the introduction of pocket calculators at the end of compulsory schooling (introduction des calculatrices de poche en fin de scolarité obligatoire).

UNITED KINGDOM

ASSISTANT MASTERS AND MISTRESSES ASSOCIATION (AMMA)

AMMA's Education Committee has set up a working party to consider the curricular implications microelectronics - and computers in particular - would have for all children of compulsory school age. The working party's report concentrates on the ways in which micro-computers and their use in schools affect all teachers, not just those with specialist pre-knowledge and obvious subject applications. (See the report "Computers in school" published in "Report", March 1982.)

Members of the working party:

    Ivor BLYTHE, North West Kent College of Technology
    Alan GREENWELL, Netherhall School, Cambridge
    Jean HELPS, Bruton School for Girls, Bruton
    Anne KREEBLE, The Grange School, Aylesbury
    Glenys LORD, Peel Sixth Form College, Bury
    Rita PIERCE-PRICE, Oxhey Wood School, South Oxhey

ASSOCIATION FOR EDUCATIONAL AND TRAINING TECHNOLOGY, formerly Association for Programmed Learning and Educational Technology, BLAT Centre, BMA House, Tavistock Square, GB-LONDON WC1H 9JP

- Research into all aspects of the new technologies in school.

Mr Steve BACON, County Adviser for Computer Education, Derbyshire.

THE BRITISH COUNCIL, Courses Department, 65 Davies Street, GB-LONDON W1Y 2AA.

Organisation of a course on microcomputers in schools at Theydon Bois near London, 18-30 July 1982.

Course Director: Dr. Bill TAGG, Head of the Advisory Unit for Computer-Based Education in Hertfordshire.

    W R BRODERICK, London Borough of Havering, Educational Computer Centre, Tring Gardens, Harold Hill, GB-ROMFORD, Essex.

    Pilot project to attempt to tackle careers education at school by harnessing computer technology to the provision of careers education and guidance.

    Mr Allen CARTER, Park Campus, Moulton Park, Nene College, GB-NORTHAMPTON NN2 7AL.

    Director of a project set up to look at the way advances in micro-processor technology could most effectively be used in schools to help teachers and allow them greater flexibility in their teaching. (Machine-assisted teaching project.)

Mr Allan CARTER and Mr John SANDERSON, Park Campus, Moulton Park, Nene College, GB-NORTHAMPTON NN2 7AL

- Research into the way advances in microprocessor technology could most effectively be used in schools to help teachers and allow them greater flexibility in their teaching. Age range: 9-18.

    S J CLOSS, University of Edinburgh, Department of Business Studies, William Robertson Building, George Square, GB-EDINBURGH EH8 9JY

Pilot project to attempt to tackle careers education at school by harnessing computer technology to the provision of careers education and guidance.

Mr Peter CORTHINE, ICL, Beaumont, GB-OLD WINDSOR, Berkshire

COUNCIL FOR EDUCATIONAL TECHNOLOGY FOR THE UNITED KINGDOM,
3 Devonshire Street, GB-LONDON W1N 2BA.

Contact person: Leslie GILBERT (EEC consultant).

- Feasibility study of a European information system for microelectronics in education.

- Research into computer-assisted learning in geography.

DEPARTMENT OF EDUCATION AND SCIENCE, Schools III Division,
Elizabeth House, York Road, GB-LONDON SE1 7PH

Contact person: Staff Inspector M EDMUNDSON

- Microelectronics Education Programme (MEP): research and development with regard to all aspects of microelectronics teaching at schools, colleges and universities in the United Kingdom (except Scotland).

    Research Director: Richard FOTHERGILL

    Duration: 1980-84

Dr. Marc EISENSTADT, The Open University, Walton Hall,
GB-MILTON KEYNES MK7 6AA.

EDUCATION FOR THE INDUSTRIAL SOCIETY PROJECT, Jordanhill College of Education, 76 Southbrae Drive, GB-Glasgow G13 1PP.

Research into the use of micro-computers at secondary school.

Rosemary FRASER, College of St. Mark and St. John, Derriford Road, PLYMOUTH PL6 8BH

- A study of the use of computers in British secondary schools.

Mr Ray FRENCH, ICL, Beaumont, GB-OLD WINDSOR, Berkshire

    Mr Rhys GWYN, Faculty of Community Studies,
    Manchester Polytechnic, Didsbury College of Education,
    799 Wilmslow Road, GB-MANCHESTER M20 8RR

- Research into:

    1. European policies for new information technology and education;

2. Information technology and primary education;

3. The use of LOGO at primary level.

Barry HOLMES, St. Helen's School, GB-BLEMTISHAM, Cambs.

Responsible for a new organisation called MAPE (Micros and Primary Education) set up to promote and develop the awareness and effective use of micros as an integral part of the philosophy and practice of primary education.

Dr. Jim HOWE, Department of Artificial Intelligence, University of Edinburgh, GB-EDINBURGH.

ITMA PROJECT,
College of St. Mark and St. John,
PLYMOUTH,
Devon.

ITMA stands for "Investigations on Teaching with Microcomputers as an Aid". Training of teachers in the operation and uses of micro-computers in the classroom with a view to developing software for both primary and secondary schools.

Dr. J R G JENNINGS and Mr N M SMART, Aberdeen College of Education, Departments of Geography and Computer Education, Hilton Place, GB - ABERDEEN AB9 1FA

- Computer programmes in geography. Research developing systematically a series of specialist data files which can be used in conjunction with computer package programmes (accessible to users with no computer background).

Prof. David JOHNSON, Chelsea Centre for Science Education, University of London.

The Secretary, Education for the Industrial Society Project, JORDANHILL College of Education, 76 Southbrae Drive, GB-GLASGOW G13 1PP.

- Research into the use of microcomputers at secondary school.

Mr Beverly LABBETT, University of East Anglia, Earlham Hall, GB-NORWICH N94 7TJ

Dr. Diana LAURILLARD, The Open University, Walton Hall, GB-MILTON KEYNES MK7 6AA

Mr R E J LEWIS, Director, and
Ms Sophie McCORMICK,
Educational Computing Section,
Chelsea College,
Manresa Road, GB-LONDON SW3 6LX

Project "Computers in the Curriculum", looking at ways of using computers to help to teach particular topics in a variety of subjects including biology, chemistry, physics, geography, and economics.

Colin MABLY, School of Education and Humanities, North East London Polytechnic, Longbridge Road, DAGENHAM, Essex RM8 2AS

- Research into the significance of the microelectronics revolution for education and teacher training.

MAPE (Micros and Primary Education)
c/o Mr Barry HOLMES,
St. Helen's School,
GB-BLEMTISHAM,
Cambs.

An organisation set up to promote and develop the awareness of and effective use of micro-computers as an integral part of the philosophy and practice of primary education.

Mr M W SAGE, The Computing Service, The University,
GB-SOUTHAMPTON SO9 5NH

- Research into micro-computers in school.

Scottish Education Department, Research and Intelligence Unit, New St. Andrew's House, GB - EDINBURGH EH1 3SY

Contact person: Mr J G MORRIS, HM Chief Inspector of Schools and Director of the Unit.

SCOTTISH MICROELECTRONICS DEVELOPMENT PROGRAMME

Contact person: Mr David D WALKER, Director, Dowanhill, 74 Victoria Crescent Road, GB-GLASGOW G12 9JN

Conference/workshop at Stirling University on 14-15 June 1982. The conference is for organisers of the 68 SMDP Projects to exchange ideas and information and to demonstrate some of their developments for computers in education. The conference will also be the launching pad for a new library of "supported software" - programmes written for use in schools. Regional distribution centres from which computer software is made available have been established throughout Scotland.

Dr. Bill TAGG, Head of the Advisory Unit for Computer-Based Education in Hertfordshire.

SOUTH THAMES COLLEGE, Wandsworth Building, Wandsworth High Street, GB-LONDON SW18 2PP.

Contact person: Mr C H TEALL, Head of the Department of Educational resources.

The college offers a comprehensive programme of courses, ranging from short courses in production and the use of media to a distance-learning Diploma in Educational Technologies. These courses, meant for teachers and trainers, include micro-computing.

3.2 PROVISIONAL BIBLIOGRAPHY

prepared by the Secretariat
Council of Europe

3.2.1   INTERNATIONAL ORGANISATIONS

- COUNCIL OF EUROPE
  BP 431 R 6
  F-67006 STRASBOURG-CEDEX

1. Parliamentary Assembly, Effects on employment of the large-scale introduction of microprocessors, Committee on Economic Affairs and Development, Rapporteur: M VALLEIX, Committee on Science and Technology, Rapporteur: M MILLER, booklet, 15 pages (Resolution 717 (1980) + Doc. 4466), Strasbourg, 1980.

2. Steering Committee for Social Affairs, 10th meeting, Strasbourg, 5-9 October 1981. "Effects of the development of microtechnology on the organisation of work and on employment, especially of women", doc CDSO (81) 33 of 21 September 1981.

- UNESCO/IBE

  Conférence internationale de l'Education, 38e session, 10-19 novembre 1981, doc ED/BIE/CONFINTED 38/Réf 3 du 31 août 1981, "Enseignement et technologies nouvelles", pages 7-10.

- OECD/CERI

1. "L'enseignement de l'informatique à l'école secondaire" (Computer sciences in secondary education), rapport d'un séminaire organisé par l'OCDE avec la collaboration de la Direction de la Coopération du Ministère français de l'Education Nationale, Sèvres, 9-14 mars 1970, 268 pages, Paris 1971.

2. "L'utilisation de l'ordinateur pour l'enseignement des matières figurant au programme de l'école secondaire" (The use of the computer in teaching secondary school subjects),

Paris, OCDE, 1976, 81 pages.

3. "Governing Board. Planning of future projects. Education and New Technologies", Note by the Secretariat. Mimeographed document CERI/CD (81) 15 of 22 October 1981, 14 pages.

- EUROPEAN COMMUNITIES
  Commission of the European Communities
  Directorate of Education/DG V-C
  200 rue de la Loi, B-1049 BRUXELLES

1. Information paper "Education and the new information technologies", Interim Report, 9 July 1981, mimeographed document, 21 pages.

2. Education and the information technologies, report on the first meeting of national correspondents, Brussels, 26-27 March 1981, mimeographed document, 6 pages, Brussels, 4 May 1981.

3. "Les nouvelles technologies de l'information et la formation professionnelle: nouvelles initiatives communautaires pour la période 1983-87 - Communication de la Commission au Conseil." (The new information technologies and vocational education: new Community initiatives for the period 1983-87 - communication of the Commission to the Council), doc COM (82) 296 final du 3.6.1982, 27 pages.

- EUROPEAN CULTURAL FOUNDATION, European Institute of Education and Social Policy (c/o Université Paris IX-Dauphine, Pl. Ml. de Lattre de Tassigny, F-75116 PARIS): "Computers in Education", Interim Report for the Ministry of Education and Science, The Hague, by Ladislav CERYCH, document reference: Annex I to IE (82) C 2 of March 1982, not published so far.

- ASSOCIATION FOR TEACHER EDUCATION IN EUROPE (ATEE)
  (Bureau: 51 rue de la Concorde, B-1050 BRUXELLES)

1. Pierre PERUSSE, Edmond-Antoine DECAMPS et Françoise PECOT, "Utilisation conjointe du milieu et des ressources technologiques pour la formation des maîtres" (combined use of environment and technological resources for teacher education) in: Revue ATEE Journal 3 (1980) p 119, 113, Elsevier Scientific Publishing Company, Amsterdam.

2. "Information technology and teacher education: perspectives on development", drafted by Rhys Gwyn on behalf of the ATEE Information Technology and Teachers Education Working Group, Brussels, 1982, (130 pages).

3. "Information technology and education: a context for development" by Rhys Gwyn, in European Journal of Teacher Education, Vol 5, Nos. 1-2, 1982.

4. L'appropriation de l'Outil Ordinateur par les Enseignants en Formation" par Gérard Bossuet, (Use of computers by teacher trainees), European Journal of Teacher Education, Vol 5, Nos. 1-2, 1982.

5. "Microelectronics and Teacher Education: A Compendium", a compendium of UK courses on teacher education.

6. "The new information technologies and education, implications for teacher education" by Rhys GWYN, an overview report written for the Commission of the European Communities and published by ATEE.

7. "The new information technologies and education, implications for teacher education. Country report 1: Ireland" by Elizabeth OLDHAM.

8. "New information technologies in education in Germany", advisory report to the Ministry of Education and Science, The Hague, Netherlands, written by Prof. Peter GORNY, University of Oldenburg, on behalf of ATEE, May 1982, 62 pages.

- BACCALAUREAT INTERNATIONAL, "Guide général du Baccalauréat International, Sessions d'examens 1982, 1983, 1984". "Etudes informatiques" (page 219).

- EURODIDAC FORUM, No. 8/1981, page 8: "Information processing in schools/L'informatique à l'école/Informatik in der Schule".

- FEDERATION INTERNATIONALE DES PROFESSEURS DE L'ENSEIGNEMENT SECONDAIRE OFFICIEL (FIPESO) INTERNATIONAL FEDERATION OF SECONDARY TEACHERS

1. Special issue of FIPESO's International Bulletin (No. 142, June 1982)/Numéro spécial du Bulletin International de la FIPESO (No. 142 - juin 1982).

   Country reports about computers at secondary schools: Federal Republic of Germany, England, Austria, Belgium, Denmark, Spain, France, Ireland, Italy, Japan, Malta, Norway, New Zealand, Netherlands, Sweden, Switzerland, Yugoslavia (to prepare FIPESO's Congress on new information and communication technologies and secondary education, Annecy, 30 July - 3 August 1982).

2. New information and communication technologies and secondary education, Resolution from the 52nd Congress of FIPESO (Annecy 1982), 6 pages.

- FEDERATION INTERNATIONALE SYNDICALE DE L'ENSEIGNEMENT (FISE)/
  WORLD FEDERATION OF TEACHERS' UNIONS

  FISE Statement for the Educational Research Workshop in
  Frascati, November 1982, 2 pages.

- INTERNATIONAL FEDERATION FOR INFORMATION PROCESSING (IFIP)
  (c/o Prof. M J HEBENSTREIT, Ecole Supérieure d'Electricité,
  Plateau du Moulon, F-91190 GIF-SUR-YVETTE)

1. Proceedings of the Working Conference on "Micro-computers in
   secondary education" (North Holland, keynote address,
   pp 1-14, 1980).

2. "Programme construction with abstract notions in ELAN",
   preprint for the 3rd World Conference on Computers in
   Education, Author: Karl KLEINE, Nijmegen.

- Institut international de communication et Association Téléqual.
  "Le mariage du siècle: éducation et informatique" (The
  marriage of the century: education and microelectronics.)
  Colloque, Centre Pompidou, Paris, 25 novembre 1980,
  compte rendu: ARDITTI (C): "L'informatique à l'école"
  in Le Monde, 27 novembre 1980, p 15.

- WCCE 81 - IFIP, troisième conférence mondiale sur l'informatique
  et l'enseignement (Third World Conference on Microelectronics
  and Education), Lausanne, 27-31 juillet 1981 (avec le soutien
  de l'UNESCO et du Bureau intergouvernemental pour
  l'informatique).

3.2.2   COUNTRIES

ARGENTINA

- Horiacio C REGGINI, "Irrupción de las computadoras en la educación" (Appearance of computers in education in: IIE, Revista del Instituto de Investigaciones Educativas (Buenos Aires), No. 35, April 1982, pages 19-35.

AUSTRIA

- Helmut AIGNER, "Elektronische Datenverarbeitung für Techniker - Theorie und Praxis" (Electronic Data Processing for future technicians - Theory and Practice)

  in:

  Schriftenreihe Ingenieurpädagogik, Hochschule für Bildungswissenschaften, Klagenfurt, Band 3, Referate des 3. Intern. Symposiums "Ingenieurpädagogik 74". Verlag Johannes Heyn, Klagenfurt 1975, ISBN 3 85366 141 6.

- BUNDESMINISTERIUM FÜR UNTERRICHT UND KUNST

1. Lehrzielbank für das berufsbildende Schulwesen (Learning objectives in vocational education)

   Elektronische Datenverarbeitung für höhere technische Lehranstalten (Microelectronics for upper secondary technical schools)

   Experimentalfassung, 1 Teil und 2 Teil (FORTRAN), Wien (Vienna) 1976.

2. Lehrzielbank für das berufsbildende Schulwesen (translation: see above)

Datenverarbeitung für Handelsakademien
(Data processing in commercial colleges), Wien (Vienna)
Nachdruck 1977.

- BUNDESMINISTERIUM FÜR WISSENSCHAFT UND FORSCHUNG

   "Elektronische Datenverarbeitung im wissenschaftlich-
   akademischen Bereich - Stand-Entwicklung-Ausblick"
   (Computers in higher education and research)

   with a reference to teacher training for microelectronics
   in Klagenfurt, Wien, December 1980. 91 pages. BMWF,
   Abt. I/11, Freyung 1, 1-1014 WIEN.

- Josef DIRNBERGER, Willibald DÖRFLER, Paul TAVOLATO:

   "Zur Situation des EDV-Unterrichts an den höheren Schulen"

   (The situation of microelectronics teaching at secondary
   school level in Austria: legal situation, curricula,
   teaching material, technical equipment, problems of teacher
   training)

   Technische Universität Wien, Institut für Informationssysteme
   (Argentinierstr. 8, A-1040 Wien), Institutsbericht No. 9,
   January/janvier 1979.

- Willibald DÖRFLER, Harald GAUGG, Hans Günter SCHANZNIG and
  Elmar VOLGGER,

   "Die Bedeutung der EDV-Ausbildung an den höheren Schulen
   Österreichs für die berufliche Praxis"

   (The importance of microelectronics teaching at Austrian
   secondary schools with regard to later vocational practice)

   Technische Universität Wien, Institut für Informationssysteme
   (Argentinierstr. 8, A-1040 Wien), Institutsbericht No. 12,
   October 1980.

   The study is based on an enquiry among school leavers and
   managers in industry.

- Walter HAHSLER, "Einführung in die Datenverarbeitung"
   (Introduction into Data Processing), Berufspädagogisches
   Institut des Bundes in Wien, Wien 1982.

- ibf-SPEKTRUM (Reichsratstr. 17, A-1010 WIEN)

1. "NASA-Satellit beliefert Schulen" (NASA-Satellite giving data
   to schools in England) in ibf-spektrum of 1 August 1981.

2. "Erster Bildschirmtext-Terminal Mitteleuropas in Graz"
    (First Central European Videotext Terminal in Graz) in:
    ibf-spektrum of 1 August 1981.

3. "Computer kommt per Post ins Haus" (Computer by mail) in:
    ibf-spektrum of 15 September 1981.

4. A note on minicomputers for an Upper Austrian commercial
    school in Steyr in: ibf-spektrum of 15 November 1981.

5. "Auf Gedeih und Verderb. Mikroelektronik und Gesellschaft",
    Club of Rome (An article on the importance of microelectronics
    for schools) in: ibf-spektrum No. 396 of 1 March 1982.

6. "Für die Mikroelektronik gerüstet" (Ready for microelectronics)
    in: ibf-spektrum of 1 May 1982.

-   Dr. Adolf MELEZINEK, Institut für Unterrrichtstechnologie,
    Mediendidaktik und Ingenieurpädagogik der Österreichischen
    Universitäten, "Microelektronik im Bildungswesen"
    (Microelectronics in Education), study on behalf of the
    Federal Ministry of Science and Research in Vienna,
    Klagenfurt, November 1981.

-   ÖSTERREICHISCHE COMPUTERGESELLSCHAFT, Tagung "Informatik in
    der Schule", Passau, Frühjahr 1979, Tagungsband in der
    Schriftenreihe der Österreichischen Computergesellschaft im
    R Oldenbourg Verlag 272 pages.

    (Papers from a colloquy on microelectronics at school,
    held in Passau in spring 1979)

-   WISSENSCHAFTLICHE NACHRICHTEN, Informationsblätter zur
    Fortbildung von Lehrern an höheren Schulen (Science News,
    Journal for the Further Education on Secondary School Teachers),
    published by the Ministry of Education (Bundesministerium
    für Unterricht und Kunst, Postfach 65, A-1014 WIEN);
    No. 59 April 1982, "Algebraisch arbeitende Computer"
    (Computers doing algebra), page 30.

DENMARK

-   Knud Hassing POVISEN, "EDB på vej i folkeskolen?"
    (Microelectronics to be introduced into elementary schools,
    lower secondary education?) in: Folkeskolen,
    26 November 1981, 98 Aargang, No. 48, udgivet af Danmarks
    Laererforening.

FRANCE

-   ACTES du Colloque "Education et Informatique", pp 27-31
    "Le rôle de l'informatique dans l'éducation" (Institut
    international de Communications, Paris 1980) (Proceedings of

the Colloquy on Education and Computer Studies, pp 27-31:
"The role of computers in education", published 1980 by the
International Communications Institute in Paris).

- ACTES du Colloque "Informatique et enseignement", organisé par
  La Croix, le 20 mai 1981 (Papers of the Colloquy on
  Microelectronics and Education, organised by the periodical
  La Croix on 20 May 1981) - à paraître à ISP, 3 rue de l'Abbaye,
  F-75006 PARIS. Compte rendu de ce colloque in La Croix,
  28-29 mai 1981 (3 rue Bayard, F-75393 Paris Cedex 08).

- "ACTES du Colloque international Informatique et Société" 1979
  (Papers of the International Colloquy on Computers and Society),
  Paris, La Documentation Française 1980, 5 vol (Volume 3 about
  "Information processing, tele-processing and daily life"
  deals with several questions of microelectronics at school.

- C ARDITTI, "L'informatique à l'école" (Microelectronics at
  school) in Le Monde, 27 novembre 1980 (compte rendu d'un
  colloque/report on a colloquy) page 15.

- G BARBEY, "L'enseignement assisté par ordinateur", Paris,
  Casterman, 1971.

- Patrick BENQUET, "L'informatique à l'école" (Microelectronics
  at school), une enquête in Le Monde de l'Education,
  janvier 1981, pp 44-49.

- CAHIERS PEDAGOGIQUES, No. 198 of November 1981: "Et
  l'informatique ..." (And what about computer studies?).

- CENTRE D'INFORMATION ET D'ECHANGES-TELEVISION,
  Sophia KASSAR-BODSON et Quang-Nam THAI,

  "Télédocumentation: l'enseignement programmé"
  (Teledocumentation: programmed instruction)

  A bibliography, Paris 1980, 23 pages.
  (Agence de Coopération Culturelle et Technique,
  19 avenue de Messine, F-75008 PARIS).

- CERCLE DE RECHERCHE ET D'ACTION PEDAGOGIQUES (CRAP)

  Revue Cahiers Pédagogiques (66 chaussée d'Antin,
  F-75009 Paris), numéro spécial "Et l'informatique ..."
  (And what about microelectronics ...), No. 198, novembre 1981,
  40 pages. Themes: training problems, use of computers in
  different subjects such as History, Maths, Physics,
  Modern Languages, etc.

- 3e Colloque canadien de Technologie pédagogique, pp 77-91,
  Vancouver, février 1980 "L'enseignement assisté par ordinateur
  en France - Etat de l'art et perspectives" (3rd Canadian

- Educational Technology Colloquy, pp 77-91 of the proceedings, Vancouver, February 1980: "Computer-assisted teaching in France: state of affairs and perspectives").

- "COMPUTER", No. 7, vol 13, pp 17-21 (USA, July 1980): "10,000 micro-computers for French secondary schools"/10,000 micro-ordinateurs pour les écoles secondaires en France).

- P DAUTREY et C LAFOND, "Recherches en vue de réalisation de programmes de simulation exploitables en système conversationnel et expérimentation" (Research into the launching of simulation programmes which may be used in conversation systems and pilot experiments), Colloque international, DGRST-CNRS, in: Informatique et sciences humaines, Marseille, 11-13 décembre 1975. See also/voir aussi: EUDISED R & D Bulletin No. 10, project 2462.

- Pierre PERUSSE, Edmond-Antoine DECAMPS et Françoise PECOT, "Utilisation conjointe du milieu et des ressources technologiques pour la formation des maîtres" (Combined use of environment and technological resources for teacher education) in: Revue ATEE Journal 3 (1980) p 119) 133, Elsevier Scientific Publishing Company, Amsterdam.

- LA DOCUMENTATION FRANCAISE (8 avenue de l'Opera, 75001 PARIS)

1. Rapport SIMON, "L'Education et l'informatisation de la société" (Education and the computerisation of society), 1981, 276 pages, 2 annexes (appendices):

    Annexe 1: "Les voies de développement. Contributions des groupes de travail" (Ways of development. Contributions of the working parties), 1981, 338 pages;

    Annexe 2: "Les expériences par pays" (country reports), 1981, 308 pages.

2. Robert SCHWARTZ, "Informatique et éducation" (Computer studies and education).

3. "Les ordinateurs à l'école. Pourquoi?

- L'Education et l'informatisation de la société" (Why computers at school?

- Education and the computerised society). Annexe 1.

4. Numerous other publications on society and the new technologies in general.

- L'EDUCATION, 18 décembre 1980, pp 8-12: "Microprocesseurs" (Micro-computers).

- "EDUCATION COMPUTING", December 1981 (British journal/ Périodе britannique): "Computers in education in France" (L'informatique dans les écoles françaises).

- "EDUCATION ET INFORMATIQUE" (revue), Paris (Nathan)

No. 1 "Les problèmes généraux de l'informatique dans l'enseignement" (General problems of microelectronics at school)

No. 2 "L'informatique chez les littéraires" (Microelectronics in the humanities)

No. 3 "La simulation sur l'ordinateur" (Simulation on the computer)

No. 4 "Les jeux informatisés" (Computerised games).

Vol 1, No. 2, pp 34-36, juin 1981: "Quelques conseils aux débutants in EAO" (A few suggestions for beginners in computer-assisted learning);

No. 3, mai 1981: "L'utilisation de la simulation en EAO" (The use of simulation games in computer-assisted learning).

- EDUCATION 2000 (3 rue de l'Abbaye, F-75006 Paris)

1. Numéro spécial "Ordinateurs à tous les étages" (Computers at all levels), No. 16, printemps 1980.

2. Numéro spécial "Informatique au présent" (Microelectronics at present), No. 19, mai 1981.

- Maurice FAUQUET, "Pour une formation des enseignants à et pour l'audiovisuel" (In favour of teacher education with a view to using audiovisual aids) in: Revue ATEE Journal, 3 (1980), pp 7-23, Elsevier Scientific Publishing Company Amsterdam.

- FEDERATION DE L'EDUCATION NATIONALE, "Informatique et éducation permanente" (Information processing and permanent education), Colloque, Paris, 22-23 octobre 1980. Compte rendu CANS (R) in Le Monde, 25 octobre 1980, p 10.

- F GALLOUEDEC, Philippe LEMOINE, e a, "Les enjeux culturels de l'informatisation" (Cultural implications of computerisation), Paris, La Documentation Française 1981.

- Daniel GRAS, "The French Experiment" (L'expérience française) a report about computers in French lycées in: Educational Media International, The official quarterly journal of the International Council for Educational Media, No. 3/1981, pp 8-17.

- "L'INFORMATIQUE dans la classe" (Microelectronics at school) in l'Ecole et la Nation, No. 298, janvier 1980, pp 37-44.

- L'INFORMATIQUE DANS L'ENSEIGNEMENT (revue), INRP,
  Section Informatique et Enseignement, 91 rue Gabriel Péri,
  F-92120 Montrouge, 14 regular and 2 special issues/
  14 numéros ordinaires et 2 numéros spéciaux.

- INSPECTION GENERALE: "Apprivoiser l'ordinateur" (To feed the
  computer), compte rendu des journées d'étude de l'Inspection
  Générale en Education et technologies modernes,
  14-17 octobre 1980, in l'Education, 23 octobre 1980.

- INSTITUT NATIONAL DE RECHERCHE PEDAGOGIQUE (INRP)

1. "L'informatique dans l'enseignement secondaire" (Microelectronics
   in secondary education), numéro spécial décembre 1976 du
   Bulletin de Liaison. Service des études et recherches
   pédagogiques, section "informatique et enseignement,
   91 rue Gabriel Péri, F-92120 MONTROUGE".

2. "Pratique active de l'informatique par l'enfant" (Children
   actively engaged in computer processing), INRP, Recherches
   pédagogiques, No. 111, Paris 1981, Brochure No. 2411,
   69 pages.

3. "Dix ans d'informatique dans l'enseignement secondaire",
   1970-1980. (Ten years of computer studies in secondary
   education: 1970-1980.)

- "MICROPROCESSEURS" in l'Education, 18 décembre 1980, pp 8-12.

- MINISTERE DE L'EDUCATION NATIONALE

1. Direction des lycées, "L'informatique au lycée" (Microelectronics
   at the lycée), CRDP, Lyon, 1980, 125 pages.

2. "Présents et futurs de l'audiovisuel en éducation - Les
   fondements d'une nouvelle politique" (Audiovisual aids at
   school now and in the future - Fundamentals of a new policy),
   rapport du groupe Jacques TREFFEL à M le ministre de
   l'Education, février 1981, La Documentation Française,
   Paris 1981, 199 pages. (The booklet also treats problems of
   computer use at school.)

- LE MONDE (Dossiers et Documents), "la Télématique", No. 77,
  janvier 1981.

- S NORA et A MINC, "Informatisation de la société: rapport à
  Monsieur le Président de la République (Computerisation of
  society: a report to the President of the Republic), Paris,
  La Documentation Française, 1978, 163 pages.

- La revue POUR (14 rue des Arts, F-31000 TOULOUSE),

    Numéro spécial "Education et communication, au temps des machines ... L'informatique ..." (Special issue: "Education and communication in a period of machines ... Electronic data processing ..."), Septembre/octobre 1981, No. 79, 102 pages.

- SCHWARTZ - voir LA DOCUMENTATION FRANCAISE

- Science et Vie,

    "La révolution télématique" (The teleprocessing revolution), No. 128, hors série, septembre 1979, 162 pages.

- Jean-Claude SIMON

    "L'éducation et l'informatisation de la société: Rapport au Président de la République" (Education and computerisation of society: a report to the President of the Republic), Paris, La Documentation Française, 1980, 276 pages.

    "L'éducation et l'informatisation de la société: Rapport au Président de la République" (Education and computerisation of society: a report to the President of the Republic), annexes, Les expériences par pays: Québec, Etats-Unis, France, Japon, Rép Féd d'Allemagne et Royaume-Uni. (Appendices, country reports for Quebec, USA, France, the Fed Rep of Germany, Japan and the UK), La Documentation Française, Paris 1981, ISBN 2-11-000628-5, 305 pages.

    See also: LA DOCUMENTATION FRANCAISE

- SNES (1 rue de Courty, F-75007 PARIS CEDEX 07)

    "L'informatique dans l'enseignement" (Microelectronics in education), Paris, 1981, 112 pages.

- SOFEDIR, "L'école et l'informatique, l'expérience des 58 lycées en France" (School and microelectronics, The experience of the 58 French lycées), brochure, 1979, 72 pages.

    (To be ordered from: SOFEDIR, rue du 1er mai, F-91120 PALAISEAU.)

- Jacques TREFFEL, "Présents et futurs de l'audiovisuel en éducation - les fondements d'une nouvelle politique" (Audiovisual aids in education now and in the future - fundamentals of a new policy), rapport du groupe Jacques TREFFEL à M le ministre de l'Education, février 1981, La Documentation Française, Paris 1981, 199 pages (The booklet also deals with computers at schools).

- Harold WERTZ, "Informatik und Schule in Frankreich"
  (Computer and school in France/L'informatique et l'école en France) in: LOG IN, Informatik in Schule und Ausbildung, 1/1981, Heft 2.

FEDERAL REPUBLIC OF GERMANY

ARBEITSKREIS "INFORMATIK"
der Gesellschaft für Didaktik der Mathematik

(Working Party on Microelectronics of the German Society for the Teaching of Mathematics)

- "Stellungnahme der Gesellschaft für Didaktik der Mathematik (GDM) zur Einbeziehung von Inhalten und Methoden der Informatik in den Mathematikunterricht der Sekundarstufe I und in die Hochschulausbildung von Mathematiklehrern",
  July 1981

  (Proposals for microelectronics (contents and methods) as an element of mathematics at lower secondary level as well as a university subject for future teachers of mathematics)

  Copies may be obtained from

  Prof. Dr. K-D GRAF, Freie Universität Berlin, ZI 7-WE 03, Malteserstr. 74-100, D-1000 BERLIN (WEST) 46.

- Wolfgang ARLT, "Einführung: Mikroelektronik in der Sek. I" (Microelectronics in lower secondary education; an introduction), working paper prepared for the meeting on "Mikroelektronik und Schule", Birlinghoven, 24-25 June 1982, organised by GDM and FEoLL.

- Rüdeger BAUMANN

1. "Computereinsatz im Mathematikunterricht: Bericht über einen Grundkurs 'Stochastik mit BASIC'"

   (Use of computers in the teaching of mathematics, Report on a basic course "Stochastics with BASIC (computer language)" in: Lehrmittel aktuell, volume 7, 1981, No. 6, page 32.

2. "BASIC-Einführung in das Programmieren", Klett-Verlag, Stuttgart 1980.

3. "BASIC - Aufgabensammlung", Klett-Verlag, Stuttgart 1981.

- BERUFSFÖRDERUNGSZENTRUM ESSEN e V (Altenessener Str. 80084, D-4300 ESSEN 12), "INFO", a bulletin describing pilot experiments with the use of computers in the training of skilled workmen.

- Ulrich BOSLER and Klaus-Henning HANSEN (Hrsg)

1. "Mikroelektronik, sozialer Wandel und Bildung" (Microelectronics, social change and education) Institut für die Pädagogik der Naturwissenschaften, Kiel,

    Bericht über eine Fachtagung in Lüdenscheid, 31.Januar - 1.Februar 1980, veranstaltet vom Bundesminister für Bildung und Wissenschaft unter Beteiligung des Bundesministers für Forschung und Technologie, dem Minister für Wissenschaft und Forschung des Landes Nordrhein-Westfalen und dem Kultusminister des Landes Nordrhein-Westfalen.

    (Report on an expert meeting organised at Lüdenscheid from 31 January - 2 February 1980 by the Federal Minister of Education and Science - in co-operation with the Federal Minister of Research and Technology -, the Minister of Science and Research of North Rhine-Westphalia and the Minister of Education of North Rhine-Westphalia.)

    Beltz Verlag, Weinheim und Basel (Postfach 1120, D-6940 WEINHEIM), ISBN 3-407-69-122x 1980 374 pages.

2. "Microcomputers and Education - a Survey of Activities in West Germany Today" (to be obtained from IPN, Olshausenstr 40-60, D-2300 Kiel)

- Ulrich BOSLER and Bernhard KOERBER, "Mikroelektronik und das Schulfach Informatik" (Microelectronics and computer studies as a school subject) in: LOG IN 1. Jahrgang (1981), Heft 3, pages 25-28.

- BUS Nr 6: "Computernutzung an bayerischen Schulen", Erfahrungen, Informationen. (Computer use at Bavarian schools), Zentralstelle für programmierten Unterricht und Computer im Unterricht, (Periodical appearing twice a year). Bayerischer Schulbuchverlag, Hubertusstr 4, D-8000 MÜNCHEN 19.

- Dierk BUSE

1. "Lehrerfort- und Weiterbildung für den Bereich Informatik/ Datenverarbeitung in Niedersachsen" (Continued education and in-service training of teachers with regard to microelectronics and data processing in Lower Saxony)

    in:

    LOG IN - Informatik in Schule und Ausbildung, Heft 1/1981.

2. "Informatik in der gymnasialen Oberstufe" (Microelectronics in upper secondary education) in: Neue Unterrichtspraxis, No. 4/1978, Schroedel Verlag Hannover.

3. "Informatik - Ansätze zu einer Didaktik" (Microelectronics-Attempts to conceive a new approach in teaching) in: Handlexikon zur Didaktik der Schulfächer, Ehrenwirthverlag München 1981.

4. "Erste Erfahrungen mit Informatik als Abiturprüfungsfach in Niedersachsen" (First experience with microelectronics as a subject in the upper secondary school leaving examination in Lower Saxony) in: 11.Jahrestagung der Gesellschaft für Informatik, Informatikfachberichte, Springer-Verlag Berlin 1981.

- CHEMISCHES INSTITUT DR. FLAD (Breitscheidstr 127, D-7000 STUTTGART 1): editor of the journal "Der Benzolring", dealing - among other matters - with the use of computers in chemistry teaching)

- Volker CLAUS, "Anwendung der Mikroelektronik in der Sekundarstufe 1" (Microelectronics in lower secondary education), working paper prepared for the meeting on "Mikroelektronik und Schule", Birlinghoven, 24-25 June 1982, organised by GDM and FEoLL.

- Peter J DRESCH, "Informatik und Mikroelektronik in der Sekundarstufe 1" (Computer studies and microelectronics in lower secondary education), working paper prepared for the meeting on "Mikroelektronik und Schule", at Birlinghoven, 24-25 June 1982, organised by GDM and FEoLL.

- FEoLL and GMD, "Kurzbeschreibung der ausgestellten Modellversuche" (Summary description of pilot experiments with computers at school in the Federal Republic of Germany), document prepared for the meeting on microelectronics and school, Birlinghoven, 24-25 June 1982 (to be ordered from FEoLL, address: see 3.1 List of Research)

- FREIE UNIVERSITÄT BERLIN, Zentralinstitut für Unterrichtswissenschaften und Curriculumentwicklung, Institut für Didaktik der Mathematik und Informatik (ZI 7, WE 3), Malteserstr 74-100, D-1000 BERLIN (WEST) 46:

1. "Abschlussbericht zum Modellversuch ECIS, Entwicklung von Curriculumelementen für den Informatikunterricht in der Sekundarstufe I (1 Phase)" (Final report on the pilot project "development of curriculum elements for computer studies at lower secondary school", first phase), 2 volumes, 31 December 1979, reprinted 1982. Editor: Dieter RIEDEL.

2. "4. Kolloquium, Informatikunterricht in der Berliner Schule-Erfahrungen und Perspektiven, Berlin, 3. und 4.Juni 1981" (4th Colloquy, Computer Studies at Schools in Berlin, Experience and Prospects, Berlin 3-4 June 1981), Tagungsunterlagen (Colloquy papers) by Karl-Heinz RÖDIGER and Marion ROHDE, 36 pages.

3. "Simulation eines Ökosystems - Unterrichtsmaterialien, Schülerinformation und Material für die Hand des Lehrers" (Simulation of an environmental system by computer - teaching materials, information for pupils and their teachers), 31 Juli 1981, author: Ingo RÜDIGER-PETERS.

- Karl FREY (Hrsg), Institut für die Pädagogik der Naturwissenschaften (IPN):

    "Curriculum-Konferenz: Gebiet Mikroprozessor" (Curriculum Conference: Sector Microprocessor/Conférence sur les programmes scolaires en matière de micro-processeurs) 184 pages, Schmidt & Klaunig, Ringstr 19, D-2300 KIEL 1.

- Günter FRIEDRICHS, The coming decade of danger and opportunity, Club of Rome Conference, 3-6 October 1979, Berlin, "Microelectronics - A new dimension of technological change and automation" (L'informatique - Une nouvelle dimension de changement technique et de l'automatisation), doc. No. IT 31-01-79, 14E, 27pp. The Club of Rome/Deutsche Stiftung für internationale Entwicklung.

- Hans Rainer FRIEDRICH: voir/see MEYER

- Prof. Dr. K-D GRAF, Freie Universität Berlin

1. "Beiträge zum Mathematikunterricht 1974 - Vorträge auf der 8. Bundestagung für Didaktik der Mathematik vom 12.bis 15. März 1974 in Berlin"

    (Microelectronics (contents and methods) and the teaching of mathematics, a paper presented at the 8th meeting of the German Society for the Teaching of Mathematics, Berlin, 12-15 March 1974)

    Hermann Schroedel Verlag KG, Hannover.

2. "Zum Stand der Informatik-Ausbildung für Lehramtsstudenten"

    (Microelectronics and teacher education - results of an enquiry carried out in 1977 and 1978)

    in:

    Zentralblatt für Didaktik der Mathematik, No. 11/79/2.

3. "Informatik - Eine Einführung in Grundlagen und Methoden"

    (Microelectronics - An introduction into its basic elements and methods)

    A book written for future mathematics teachers.

    Herder-Verlag Freiburg 1981.

4. "Computer use in mathematics education - present situation, intentions, and problems in the Federal Republic of Germany"

    Paper prepared for the 4th International Congress on Mathematics Education 1980 in Berkeley, California,

    in:

    Internat. Journal Math Educ Sci Technol, 1981, vol 12, No. 5, pages 503-523.

    German version:

    "Computereinsatz im Mathematikunterricht - Stand, Intentionen und Probleme in der Bundesrepublik Deutschland"

    in:

    Zentralblatt für Didaktik der Mathematik 1981, pages 31-40.

- Peter GORNY

1. "New information technologies in education in Germany", Advisory report to the Ministry of Education and Science, The Hague, Netherlands, published by the Association for Teacher Education in Europe (ATEE, 51 rue de la Concorde, B-1050 BRUXELLES), 62 pages, May 1982.

2. "Schulen in der Bundesrepublik produzieren informationstechnologische Analphabeten" (German schools produce computer illiteracy) in: "UNI-INFO" 1 + 2/1982, 15.1.1982, Universität Oldenburg.

- Ulrich GUNTRAM, "Das Buch aus dem Kathodenstrahl - Wenn der Computer den Text 'verarbeitet'" (Computer-printed books), in: Deutsche Universitätszeitung 1981, pp 675-677.

- Helge HABERMEHL, "Computer in der Realschule?" (Computer at the middle school (Realschule)?) in: Die Realschule, No. 7/8-1981, pp 421-435.

- K HAEFNER

1. "Studien zu Schulrechnern" (Studies about school computers) in: FEoLL working paper, Paderborn 1980.

2. "Die neue Bildungskrise-Herausforderung der Informationstechnik an Bildung und Ausbildung" (The new educational crisis - implications of information technologies for education and training), Birkhäuser Verlag GmbH, Postfach 131036, D-7000. STUTTGART 13, ISBN 3-7643-1342-0, 1982, ca 260 pages.

- Klaus-Henning HANSEN

1. "Steuerung eines Aufzugsmodells mit einem Mikroprozessor"
   (Use of a micro-computer for steering a lift) in:
   "Der Physikunterricht", 14 Jahrgang (1980), Heft 3,
   pages 43-57.

2. "Technik, elektronische Datenverarbeitung und soziale
   Entscheidung. Gesellschaftliche Organisation von
   Naturwissenschaft und Technik als Thema der Bildung
   (Technology, electronic data processing and social decisions.
   Social organisation of natural sciences and technology as a theme
   of education). Soon to be published as an IPN - publication.

3. "Mikroelektronik-Labor für die Schule-Ein Lernort für
   die Schule-Ein Lernort für den naturwissenschaftlich-
   technischen Unterricht" (Microelectronics laboratory at school -
   a learning place for the natural sciences and technology)
   in: LOG IN, 1 Jahrgang (1981), Heft 3, pages 35-37.

4. See also: BOSLER and IPN KIEL.

- Annemarie HAUF, "Das Fallbeispiel des elektronischen
  Taschenrechners: Was können wir für den Einsatz des
  Mikrocomputers im Schulbereich daraus lernen?" (The case of
  electronic pocket calculators: what can we learn from them as
  regards the use of micro-computers at school?) in: LOG IN,
  1 Jahrgang (1981), Heft 3.

  The article contains a comprehensive bibliography of German
  literature about pocket calculators.

- HESSISCHES INSTITUT FÜR BILDUNGSPLANUNG UND SCHULENTWICKLUNG
  a Wiesbaden (Bodenstedtstr 7, D-6200 WIESBADEN), editor of
  the periodical "Schule und Datenverarbeitung in Hessen"
  (School and Computer Studies in Hessen).

- Gerhard HOFMANN, "Informatik an der Realschule - ein
  zusätzliches Bildungsangebot". (Computer studies at Realschule
  (middle school) - a supplementary offer.) Schulreport Juli 1982/
  Heft 3, Tatsachen und Meinungen zur aktuellen Bildungspolitik.

- "INFORMATIK-AKTIVITÄTEN"

  A periodical issued by the Working Party on Microelectronics in
  Commercial Schools (Arbeitskreis "Informatik an Kaufmännischen
  Berufsbildenden Schulen") of the German Computer Society
  (Gesellschaft für Informatik e V)

  The periodical provides information on microelectronics in
  commercial schools, eg on curricula.

To be ordered from:
HIBS, Postfach 3105, D-6200 WIESBADEN.

- <u>INFORMATIONEN BILDUNG WISSENSCHAFT</u>,

1. No. 8/1981, "EUMEL mit ELAN - Elektronische Datenverarbeitung an beruflichen Schulen (im Saarland)" (Microelectronics in vocational education, Saarland).

2. No. 9/1982

   Bundesministerium für Bildung und Wissenschaft, "Mikroelektronik und Bildung". (Microelectronics and training).

- <u>Institut für die Pädagogik der Naturwissenschaften:</u>

see under BOSLER and FREY/voir BOSLER et FREY

1. Editor of the periodical "LOG-IN - Informatik in Schule und Ausbildung" (Microelectronics in Education and Training, see: LOG-IN.

2. "Rahmencurriculum zum Gebiet Mikroprozessor für die berufliche Bildung" (Framework curriculum for the use of microprocessors in vocational education), Beilage (Supplement) zu LOG IN, 1 Jahrgang (1981), Heft 3.

- U <u>KARL</u>, "Wissenschaftliche Begleitung zum Modellversuch: Einsatz von Computerterminals an der Schule". (Research evaluation of a pilot project: introduction of computer terminals at school.) Zentralstelle für programmierten Unterricht und Computer im Unterricht. Schertlinstr. 7, D-8900 AUGSBURG. Augsburg 1979.

- K KEIDEL/K A KEIL, "Einführung in das Programmieren, ein <u>Lehrprogramm</u>", (Introduction into programming: a teaching programme). Bayerischer Schulbuch-Verlag. Hubertusstr. 4, D-8000 MÜNCHEN 19.

- Karl-August <u>KEIL</u>,

1. "The general introduction of computer into Bavarian schools." Computer in education IFIP, 1981.

2. "Computer an der Schule im Wandel", (computers at school are changing) in: Informatik-Fachberichte GI-11, Jahrestagung Springer-Verlag Berlin 1981;

3. "10 Jahre Informatik am Gymnasium", (10 years computer studies in high school) from Schulreport Juli 1982/Heft 3, Tatsachen und Meinungen zur aktuellen Bildungspolitik in BAYERN;

4. "Die Multifunktionalität des Computers in der Schule", (The various possible functions of computers in school) in Visodata 80 Dokumentation;

5. "Das Projekt Computer-unterstützter Unterricht Augsburg", (Pilot-project Augsburg: Computer-Assisted Instruction), Augsburg 1976.

   See also K KEIDEL/K A KEIL

- Leo H <u>KLINGEN</u>, "Computerbegleiteter Fachunterricht" (Computer-assisted instruction in different subjects) in: LOG IN, 1 Jahrgang (1981), Heft 4, page 2, 41-43.

- Bernhard <u>KOERBER</u>: see BOSLER.

- B <u>KRETSCHMER</u>, "Lehrpläne kaufmännischer Berufsschulen" (microelectronics curricula in commercial schools)

   in: "Informatik-Aktivitäten", Heft 1, 1981.

   (See also under "Informatik-Aktivitäten")

- Studiendirektor Harald <u>KUKUK</u> (Berufliche Schule 4, Nürnberg):

   "Zur Organisation des EDV-Einsatzes in Schulen" (Organisationsschema) (How to organise the use of computers at school - an organisation model)

   in: Schulmanagement No. 6/1981, December 1981, pages 52-54.

- <u>Kultusministerium Niedersachsen</u>

   (Ministry of Education of Lower Saxony)
   Postfach, D-3000 HANNOVER

1. "Empfehlungen zur Ausstattung von Schulen mit Rechnern für den Unterricht in den Fächern Informatik, Organisation/ Datenverarbeitung und Fachkunde des Sekundarbereichs II"

   (Recommendations about school computer equipment for the teaching of microelectronics, organisation and data procession, and other technical subjects at upper secondary education)

   in:

   Schulverwaltungsblatt Niedersachsen (1980, SVBl 6/80)

2. "Niedersächsischer Modellversuch: Mikroprozessoren in der Metallausbildung" (Lower Saxony: Pilot experiment with computers in vocational training, metal industry) in: Veröffentlichungen der Kultusministerkonferenz,

Dokumentationsdienst Bildungswesen 11/81, Luchterhand Verlag,
Juni 1981, ISSN 0343-3439.

- Kultusministerkonferenze

    Einheitliche Prüfungsanforderungen in der Abiturprüfung,
    Informatik, Beschluss vom 23.2.1981,

    (Conference of German Ministers of Education, Uniform Upper
    Secondary School Examination Requirements, Microelectronics,
    Resolution of 23 February 1981), 48 pages.

    Hermann Luchterhand Verlag GmbH & Co KG, Postfach 1780,
    D-5450 NEUWIED, Art-Nr 52970.

- H G LANGEWIESCHE, "Kurzbeschreibung des Beitrags
    'Bestandsaufnahme Sekundarstufe II'" (Computer at upper
    secondary schools in the Federal Republic of Germany),
    paper written for the meeting on "Mikroelektronik und Schule",
    Birlinghoven, 24-25 June 1982, organised by GDM and FEoLL.

- LOG-IN - Informatik in Schule und Ausbildung (Zeitschrift)

    ("LOG IN - Microelectronics in Education and Training",
    a quarterly periodical)

    to be ordered from:

    R Oldenbourg Verlag GmbH, Postfach 801360, D-8000 MÜNCHEN 80.

    Editor: Institut für die Pädagogik der Naturwissenschaften in
              Kiel.

- W LORBEER and D WERNER, "Ein Verbundsystem von Mikrocomputern"
    (A network of micro-computers) Bus No. 4, Zentralstelle für
    Programmierten Unterricht und Computer im Unterricht.
    Augsburg 1980 (Reisinger Str. 6, D-8900 Augsburg).

- Doris LÜKE, "Neue Medien - Bildung à la carte?" (New media-
    education to select from the menu?) in: Erwachsenenbildung,
    Patmos Verlag Düsseldorf, No. 2/1981, June 1981.

- Norbert MEYER and Hans Rainer FRIEDRICH, "Mikro-
    Computertechnik in der Facharbeiterausbildung" (Micro-computers
    in the training of qualified workmen) in: "Informationen
    Bildung Wissenschaft" No. 4/1982.

- M PAULWEBER, "FEoLL-Mikrocomputer. Lehrmodell zur Demonstration
    eines mikrocomputergesteuerten Fliessbandes" (Teaching model
    illustrating how a micro-computer controls a production chain).
    FEoLL working paper 1979, Paderborn (see also under FEoLL).

- PÄDAGOGISCHE HOCHSCHULE BERLIN, Institut für Datenverarbeitung in den Unterrichtswissenschaften (Malteserstr. 74-100, D-1000 BERLIN (WEST) 46): "INFO No. 9/10, Ein Informationsblatt zur Integration der Informatik in Berliner Schulen" (INFO No. 9/10, An information bulletin about the integration of computer studies at schools in Berlin), Oktober 1979, 134 pages.

- Ingo Rüdiger PETERS: see under Freie Universität Berlin.

- Dieter RIEDEL: see under Freie Universität Berlin.

- Karl-Heinz RÖDIGER: see under Freie Universität Berlin.

- Marion ROHDE: see under Freie Universität Berlin.

- SCHLESWIG-HOLSTEINISCHER LANDTAG, 9. Wahlperiode, Drucksache 9/1060, 3 June 1981, Kleine Anfrage des Abg. NEITZEL (FDP) und Antwort der Landesregierung - Kultusminister -. Informatik-Unterricht an allgemeinbildenden Schulen, insbesondere das Projekt Informatikkurse.

   (Parliament of Schleswig-Holstein, Government reply to a request about the state of microelectronics teaching in general education and the pilot project "Microelectronics Course")

- H SCHWARTZE, "Ein Interface für den CBM 3001 zur Behandlung von Steuerungen und Regelungen im Schulunterricht" (An interface for CBM 3001 computers used for teaching purposes at school). IPN working paper, Kiel 1981.

- Prof. Dr. Werner STROMBACH

1. "Philosophische Aspekte der Informatik" (Philosophical aspects of computer studies) in: Philosophia Naturalis of 18 January 1980, Meissenheim/Glan.

2. "Philosophie und Informatik; Forschungsbericht No. 122 der Abteilung Informatik der Universität Dortmund" (Philosophy and Computer Studies; Research Report No. 122 of the Computer Studies Department of the University of Dortmund).

3. "Information und Entropie" in: Strukturierung mit Superzeichen", Paderborner Arbeitspapiere, FEoLL, Paderborn 1981.

4. "Ueber formale Grundlagen und philosophische Grenzgebiete im Informatikstudiengang an Fachhochschulen" (Formal basis and philosophical aspects in computer courses at polytechnics) in: A MELEZINEK (Hrsg/Editor), Ingenieurpädagogik der 80er Jahre, Alsbach (Bergstrasse) 1981.

- L STURM, "Anwendung der Mikroelektronik in der Sekundarstufe II" (Use of microelectronics in upper secondary education), working paper prepared for the meeting on "Mikroelektronik und Schule", Birlinghoven, 24-25 June 1982, organised by GMD and FEoLL. Paper to be ordered from FEoLL, Pohlweg 55, D-4790 PADERBORN.

- Heiko WOLGAST

    "Mathematik und Informatik - Zur Anwendung von Computern im Unterricht"

    (Mathematics and Microelectronics - The use of computers in mathematics teaching)

    in: "Der mathematische und naturwissenschaftliche Unterricht", 33 1980, No. 8, pages 450-454.

- Zentralstelle für Programmierten Unterricht und Computer Unterricht, BUS, Nr 6: "Computernutzung an bayerischen Schulen", Erfahrung, Informationen. (Use of the computer in Bavarian schools) Periodical appearing twice a year/ périodique semestriel.

IRELAND

"Cork firm wins contract for school computers" in: EURYDICE NEWSBRIEF of 1 December 1981 (based on Irish Times of 27 November 1981).

- Elizabeth OLDHAM, "The new information technologies and education, implications for teacher education, country report 1: Ireland", published by ATEE (see also ATEE).

NETHERLANDS

- Tom J VAN WEERT, "Informatikunterricht in den Niederlanden" (Computer studies in the Netherlands) in: LOG IN, Jahrgang 1 (1981), Heft 4.

SPAIN

E GARCIA CAMARERO, "Ordenadores en la Escuela Secundaria" (Computers in secondary schools, Informe sobre una experiencia, Centre de Calculo de la Universidad Complutense, Avenida Complutense s/n, E-MADRID 3.

See also bibliography under 1.6.5.

SWEDEN

The Swedish Ministry of Education and Culture, New media - Broadcast teletext, videotext, Summary of the final report presented by the Commission on New Information Technology, Stockholm 1981.

SWITZERLAND

- Marcel ARNOUX, Yves DELAY, Pierre FAVRE, Claude FORRER et Samuel GUINCHARD, "Guide d'introduction et d'utilisation des calculatrices de poche dans l'enseignement secondaire inférieur" (Handbook for the introduction of pocket calculators at lower secondary education), Département de l'Instruction Publique du Canton de Neuchâtel (Château 23, CH-2000 Neuchâtel), 1978, 46 pages.

- Pierre BANDERET, "24 Stunden Informatik, Ein praktischer Weg zur Einführung der Informatik in der Mittelschule" (24 hours of computer studies; ways and means of introducing computer studies into Swiss grammar schools) in: LOG IN, 1 Jahrgang (1981), Heft 4.

- Jörg GROSSMANN, Erziehungsdirektion des Kantons Bern, Amt für Unterrichtsforschung und -planung (Sulegeckstr. 70): "Projektstudie Medienerziehung" (Project Study on Media Education), Bern, 1981, 68 pages.

- PESTALOZZIANUM Zürich, Abteilung Programmierte Unterrichtshilfen (PU), Beckenhofstr. 31-37, CH-8035 Zürich:

1. PU-Bulletin, 2-3 issues per year, summing up evaluation results with regard to computer-based materials.

2. PU-Katalog (summary of more than 70 programmes).

3. Demonstrationsprogramm (a computerised programme informing about programmes-learning aids).

4. Reprints of articles from the specialised press.

- Luc Olivier POCHON,
"La calculatrice de poche à l'école" (Pocket calculators at school) in: Coordination No. 17, février-mars 1981.

- Daniel ROUX
EPSITEC-SYSTEM SA, Ch. Mouette
CH-1092 BELMONT

"BASIC" (a simple computer language, usable in schools, 3e édition revue, octobre 1980.

- SCHWEIZERISCHE KONFERENZ DER KANTONALEN ERZIEHUNGSDIREKTOREN, Schweizerische Zentralstelle für die Weiterbildung der Mittelschullehrer, Koordinationsgruppe Informatik: "Die Einführung der Informatik an den Mittelschulen-Zwischenbericht"

(The Introduction of Computer Studies at Secondary Schools-
Interim Report) in: Informationsbulletin/Bulletin
d'information No. 29, Genève 1982.

- SCHWEIZERISCHE KOORDINATIONSSTELLE FÜR BILDUNGSFORSCHUNG
CENTRE SUISSE DE COORDINATION POUR LA RECHERCHE EN MATIERE
D'EDUCATION

"Der Taschenrechner in der Schule - Probleme, Forschungsergebnisse
und didaktische Ansätze" (Pocket calculators at school -
problems, research results, teaching approach),
Document 80.01, October 1980.

- Weiterbildungszentrale (Postfach -40, CH-LUZERN 4)

1. "Interface", Bulletin Informatik in der Mittelschule -
L'informatique dans l'enseignement secondaire (a periodical
on microelectronics in secondary education)

2. "Vingt-quatre heures d'informatique", Avant-propos, Liste des
fascicules, Le milieu du monde: mai 1980, BDGZ.

Résultats d'une collaboration intercantonale en Suisse Romande
pour tester et promouvoir le projet des "24 heures"
d'informatique dans l'enseignement secondaire supérieur/
Results of intercantonal co-operation in French-speaking
Switzerland for the purpose of testing and promoting the
Project "24 hours of microelectronics in upper secondary
education".

- Elaine WILLIAMS, "Elektronische Kommunikation zwischen Studenten
und Lehrkräften" (Student-teacher communication via computer/
communication entre étudiants et professeur par l'intermédiaire
de l'ordinateur) in: Schweizerische Lehrerzeitung,
24 September 1981.

UNITED KINGDOM

- ACE, Editor: O ODOR, Godfrey Thomson Unit, University of
Edinburgh, Scotland. This periodical deals with research on
how micro-processors may aid the handicapped.

- A ANDERSON - see DAI

- ASSOCIATION FOR EDUCATIONAL AND TRAINING TECHNOLOGY (AETT)

1. Aspects of Educational Technology, in particular volume VI,
edited by K AUSTWICK and NDC HARRIS, Pitman Publishing, 1972,
London, 408 p, and volume XIII, edited by G Terry PAGE and
Quentin A WHITLOCK, Kogan Page, London/Nichols Publishing
Company, New York, 1979, 365 pages.

(These volumes deal with various aspects of microelectronics at school/Ces volumes examinent plusieurs questions d'informatique à l'école.)

2. Journal of AETT: "Programmes Learning & Educational Technology" (Revue de l'AETT: Enseignement géré par ordinateur & technologie éducative).

- K AUSTWICK and N D C HARRIS, "Aspects of Educational Technology VI", a report on the state of affairs (including computers at school) (un rapport sur l'état actuel y compris l'informatique à l'école) published for the 1972 Annual Conference of the Association for Programmed Learning and Educational Technology, Pitman Publishing, Pitman Press, Bath 1972, ISBN 0 273 31782, 408 pages.

- P AYRE - see A PAYNE

- J G BAILEY - see N D C HARRIS

- P G BARKER, "Some experiments in man-machine interaction relevant to computer assisted instruction" (Quelques expériences en ce qui concerne l'interaction entre l'homme et l'ordinateur, présentant un intérêt pour l'enseignement assisté par ordinateur) in: British Journal of Educational Technology, vol 13, No. 1, January 1982.

- A BEATTIE - see DAI

- K G BEAUCHAMP, "School Computer Education in Australia" (L'enseignement de l'informatique dans les écoles en Australie) in: British Journal of Educational Technology, vol 13, No. 1, January 1982.

- M BENNETT - see DAI

- Ivor BLYTHE and other members of the Microelectronics Working Party of the Education Committee of the British Association of Assistant Masters and Mistresses (AMMA), "Computers in Schools", the working party's report published in report, March 1982.

- K BOSTROM - see J R HARTLEY

- Benedict and/et J B H DU BOULAY - see DAI

- Ludwig BRAUN, "Computer-Aided Learning and the Micro-computer Revolution" in: Programmed Learning & Educational Technology, Journal of AETT, Volume 18, No. 4, November 1981, pages 223-229.

- THE BRITISH COUNCIL, Education, Medicine and Science Division (10 Spring Gardens, GB-LONDON SW1A 2BN): Science Education

Newsletter: information about computers at school.

- R E B BUDGETT, Aspects of Educational Technology, Volume XIII, "Educational Technology Twenty Years On", edited for the Association for Educational and Training Technology by G Terry PAGE and Quentin A WHITLOCK, Kogan Page, London/ Nichols Publishing Company, New York, 1979, 365 pages.

- F CASSELS - see DAI

- S J CLOSS, "Choosing careers by computer" in: Education of 23 April 1982.

- Dr. W H COCKCROFT, "Mathematics counts", Report of the Committee of Inquiry into the Teaching of Mathematics in Schools, London, Her Majesty's Stationery Office.

- COUNCIL FOR EDUCATIONAL TECHNOLOGY (CET)

    (3 Devonshire Street, GB-LONDON W1N 2BA)

1. "Computer Assisted Learning in Geography - Current trends and future prospects" by Ifan D H SHEPERD, Zena A COOPER, David R F WALKER, 254 pages, London 1980. ISBN 0-86184-012-7.

2. Working Paper 17, "A-Level Tuition and Educational Technology in Schools and Colleges", C A NICHOLS, London 1979, 83 pages, ISBN 0-902204-94-7. (Various questions of computers at school.)

3. "Microelectronics: Their implications for Education and in Training" - A Statement, London, 1978.

4. Three publications for the Microelectronics Education Programme (MEP).

    MEP Information Guide 1: Micro-computers in the primary school - a before-you-buy-guide. The book gives guidance on the factors to be considered before investing in a computing system for a school.

    MEP Information Guide 2: Five of the best computer programmes in primary schools. Each of the five case-studies introduces a specific programme and teacher experience with it.

    MEP Case-Study 1: Managing the micro-computer in the classroom. The experience of five teachers is used to summarise the factors to be considered in the classroom.

- S DELAMONT - see DAI

- DAI = <u>Department of Artificial Intelligence</u>, University of Edinburgh: Series of publications

1. Yuichiro ANZAI, "A rule-based information processing model for series extrapolation", DAI Working Paper No. 27, 1977.

2. M BENNETT, "Substitutor: A teaching programme", DAI Working Paper No. 43, 1978.

3. B DU BOULAY (with R EMANUEL), "Logo without tears", DAI Working Paper No. 11, 1975.

4. B DU BOULAY, "Teaching teachers mathematics through programming", DAI Research Paper No. 113, 1979; Int J Maths Educ Sc Technol Vol 11, No. 3, pp 347-360, 1980.

5. B DU BOULAY (with T O'SHEA), "How to work the Logo machine", DAI Occasional Paper No. 4, 1976.

6. B DU BOULAY (with T O'SHEA), "Seeing the works: a strategy for teaching interactive programming", DAI Working Party No. 28, 1977.

7. B DU BOULAY, "Learning teaching mathematics" in: Mathematics Teaching, the Bulletin of the Association of Teachers of Mathematics, No. 78, 1977.

8. J B H DU BOULAY, J A M HOWE and K JOHNSON, "Making programmes versus running programmes: micro-computers in the mathematical education of teachers" Involving Micros in Education Conference, University of Lancaster, March 1982.

9. B DU BOULAY, "Teacher transformations: student teachers programming in LOGO", DAI Research Paper No. 122, 1979, submitted to the 3rd International Conference of the International Group for the Psychology of Mathematics Education, Warwick, July 1979. Also reprinted as "Using programming to help student teachers" in <u>CHIPS NEWSLETTER</u>, Western Education and Library Board, <u>Schools Computing Centre</u>, Londonderry College of Technology, 1980.

10. Benedict DU BOULAY and Tim O'SHEA, "Teaching novices programming", DAI Research Paper No. 132, to appear in "Computing Skills and Adaptive Systems", Editor: M COOMBS, London, Academic Press.

11. B DU BOULAY and J A M HOWE, "Student teachers' attitudes to Maths: differential effects of a computer-based course" in: "Proceedings of the 3rd World Conference on Computers in Education", Editors LEWIS and TAGG, North Holland, 1981, pp 707-714.

12. Benedict DU BOULAY, Tim O'SHEA and John MONK, "The black box inside the glass box: presenting computing concepts to novices", DAI Research Paper No. 133, to appear in International Journal of Man-Machine Studies.

13. J B H DU BOULAY and J A M HOWE, "Logo building blocks: student teachers using computer-based mathematics apparatus" in: <u>Computer and Education</u> vol 6, 1982.

14. J B H DU BOULAY and J A M HOWE, "Re-learning mathematics through LOGO: helping student teachers who don't understand mathematics" in: Microcomputers in Secondary Education, editors: HOWE and ROSS, London, Kogan Page, 1981.

15. F CASSELS (with J A M HOWE), "Errors in Arithmetic", Bionics Research Report No. 5, 1971.

16. R EMANUEL, "The music box", DAI Working Paper No. 10, 1975.

17. D G HALL, "LOGO, Mathematics and Problem-Solving", DAI Working Paper No. 73.

18. J A M HOWE, "Individualising computer-assisted instruction" in: Artificial and Human Thinking, editors: ELITHORN and JONES, Elsevier, 1973.

19. J A M HOWE (with S DELAMONT), "Attitudes towards computer-assisted instruction", Bionics Research Report No. 4, 1971.

20. J A M HOWE (with D MICHIE), "Teaching children by computer" in: Scottish Educational Journal, February 1970.

21. J A M HOWE, "Computer-assisted instruction: past, present and future", CAI No. 5, 1971.

22. J A M HOWE, "Computer-assisted instruction at Edinburgh" in: Computer Education, 9 octobre 1971, pp 9-11.

23. J A M HOWE (with S DELAMONT), "Pupils' answer to computer language" in: Education in the North, No. 10, 1973.

24. J A M HOWE, "Computer Maths for Primary Children", in: Education in the North, No. 10, 1973.

25. J A M HOWE, "Learning Mathematics through Programming" in: 1981 ADCIS Conference Proceedings, Georgia, pp 109-113.

26. J A M HOWE, P M ROSS, K JOHNSON, F PLANE and R INGLIS, "Learning Mathematics in the classroom through programming second: progress report", DAI Working Paper No. 83, 1980.

27. J A M HOWE (with P J BARKER, H M NOBLE and S H SALTER), "Programming a touch screen device" in: Management Informatics, No. 3, 1974, pp 69-85.

28. J A M HOWE (with S DELAMONT), "Towards an evaluation strategy for CAI projects", Bionics Research Report No. 15, 1974.

29. J A M HOWE (with F CASSELS), "Teaching primary maths by computer", Bionics Report No. 16, 1974.

30. J A M HOWE (with J KNAPMAN, H M NOBLE, S WEIR, R M YOUNG), "Artificial intelligence and the representation of knowledge", DAI Research Report No. 5, 1975.

31. J A M HOWE, "Artificial intelligence and education" (L'intelligence artificielle et l'enseignement) - Computer-assisted learning in the UK, some case studies (editor: R HOOPER), Council for Educational Technology, London, 1975.

32. J A M HOWE (with B DU BOULAY), "Microprocessor assisted learning: turning the clock back?, PLET, No. 16, p 3, 1979.

33. J A M HOWE (with T O'SHEA and F PLANE), "Teaching mathematics through LOGO programming: an evaluation study" in: Computer-Assisted Learning - Scope, Progress and Limits, Editeurs: TAGG and LEWIS, North Holland 1980.

34. J A M HOWE, "Development stages in learning to program" in: Cognition and Memory, Editeurs KLIX and HIFFMAN, Berlin, Deutscher Verlag, 1980.

35. J A M HOWE, "Learning through model building" in: Expert Systems in the Microelectronic Age (éditeur: D MICHIE), Edinburgh, University Press, 1979. Also reprinted as "Nuts and bolts fix in learning processes" in: Practical Computing, 3, 2, pp 92) 96.

36. J A M HOWE, P M ROSS, F PLANE and K JOHNSON, "Learning mathematics in the classroom through programming", First progress report, SSRC Grant, DAI Working Paper No. 62.

37. J A M HOWE and B DU BOULAY, "Re-learning mathematics through LOGO", Second progress report, SSRC Grant, DAI Working Paper No. 63.

38. J A M HOWE, "Teaching mathematics through programming", DAI Research Paper No. 129. Also reprinted as "Sizing up a classmate named Terak", Computing, 8, 5, 1980.

39. J A M HOWE, "Some role for the computer in special education", DAI Research Paper No. 126. Computers: A Researcher's View.

Special Education: Forward Trends 7, 4, pp 17-21.

40. J A M HOWE, "Teaching handicapped children to read: A computer-based approach" in: Proceedings of the 3rd World Conference on Computers in Education, Editors LEWIS and TAGG, North Holland, 1981, pp 433-440.

41. J A M HOWE (with T O'SHEA), "Learning mathematics through LOGO", SIGCUE Bulletin, 12, 1978.

42. J A M HOWE (with T O'SHEA), "Computational metaphors for children" in: Human and Artificial Intelligence, editor: F KLIX, 1978.

43. J A M HOWE, "AI and CAI: ten years on" in: Programmed Learning and Educational Technology, vol 15, 2, 1978.

44. J A M HOWE, "A new deal? Using computers to teach children with communication difficulties" in: McGill Journal of Education (Fall Issue), vol XIV, No. 3, 1979.

45. J A M HOWE, "Designing a language programme", DAI Working Paper No. 37, 1978.

46. J A M HOWE, "Teaching and Learning as examinable processes: a role for the computer in special education", DAI Working Paper No. 38, 1978.

47. J A M HOWE (with T O'SHEA), "Learning mathematics in the classroom through programming: a proposal for research", DAI Working Paper No. 39, 1978.

48. J A M HOWE (with T O'SHEA and F PLANE), "Learning through LOGO: outlining the non-reactive evaluation study", DAI Working Paper No. 40, 1978.

49. J A M HOWE (with B DU BOULAY), "Re-learning mathematics through LOGO", DAI Working Paper No. 41, 1978.

50. J A M HOWE (with A BEATTIE, F CASSELS, J JOHNSON and A ANDERSON), "Teaching handicapped children to read in a computer-based learning environment", DAI Research Report No. 57, 1978.

51. J A M HOWE, "Artificial intelligence" in: Encyclopaedia of Educational Media Communications and Technology, MacMillan Press Ltd, 1978.

52. J A M HOWE, "Using technology to educate pupils with communication difficulties in: THE Journal, vol 15, 5, 1978.

53. J A M HOWE (with T O'SHEA), "Exploring mathematics by computer", University of Edinburgh Bulletin, vol 14, No. 2, 1977.

54. J A M HOWE and P M ROSS, "Moving LOGO into a mathematics classroom" in: Microcomputers in Secondary Education, editors: HOWE and ROSS, London: Kogan Page, 1981.

55. J A M HOWE, "Learning engineering science in school by computer", DAI Working Paper No. 65.

56. J A M HOWE, "Turning turtle", Times Educational Supplement 3340, June 1980.

57. J A M HOWE, "Using computers in special education", Computer Assisted Learning Community Meeting 1980, Seminar and Conference Report 4, London: Council for Educational Technology.

58. J A M HOWE, P M ROSS, K JOHNSON, F PLANE and R INGLIS, "Teaching mathematics through programming in the classroom", CAL81, Leeds, April, 1981.

59. J A M HOWE, "Teaching writing skills to handicapped children", Biological Engineering Science Conference on High Technology Aids for the disabled, London, October 1981.

60. J A M HOWE, "Autism: using LOGO to establish communication".

61. K JOHNSON, "The Unix Logo Interpreter", DAI Working Paper No. 52, 1979.

62. K R JOHNSON (with P M ROSS), "LOGO - A computer language for children in schools", Microprocessor Software Quarterly, Issue 5, November 1981, South West Universities Regional Computer Centre.

63. C D McARTHUR, "EMAS LOGO: user's guide and reference manual", DAI Occasional Paper No. 1, 1974.

64. H M NOBLE, "A computer-based statistics project: progress during 1972/73", CAI-14, 1973.

65. H PAIN, "A computer aid for spelling error classification in remedial teaching" in: Proceedings of the 3rd World Conference on Computers in Education, Editors: LEWIS and TAGG, North Holland, 1981, pp 297-302.

66. H PAIN, "Analysis of errors in spelling", DAI Working Paper No. 61.

67. T O'SHEA, "Artificial intelligence and computer-based education", Computer Education, No. 30, 1978.

68. T O'SHEA (with R M YOUNG), "A production rule account of children's errors in substraction", Proceedings of AISB/GI Conference on Artificial Intelligence, Hamburg, 1978.

69. P M ROSS, "Terak LOGO user's manual (for version 1-0)", DAI Occasional Paper No. 21, 1980.

70. P M ROSS, "Design of the Terak LOGO System", DAI Working Paper No. 49, 1979.

71. P M ROSS and K R JOHNSON, "A simple filespace management scheme for floppy discs", DAI Research Paper No. 136.

72. P M ROSS and J A M HOWE, "Teaching mathematics through programming: ten years on" in: Proceedings of the 3rd World Conference on Computers in Education, Editors: LEWIS and TAGG, North Holland, 1981, pp 143-148.

73. M SHARPLES, "Micro-computers and creative writing" Micro-computers in Secondary Education, editors: HOWE and ROSS, London: Kogan Page, 1981.

74. Mike SHARPLES, "A computer-written language lab", DAI Research Paper No. 134, Computer Education, No. 37, February 1981, pp 10-12.

75. M SHARPLES, "Poetry from LOGO", DAI Working Paper No. 30, 1977.

76. M SHARPLES, "Using a computer to develop written style", DAI Working Paper No. 54, 1979.

77. M SHARPLES, "A computer-based teaching scheme for creative writing" in: Proceedings of the 3rd World Conference on Computers in Education, Editors: LEWIS and TAGG, North Holland, 1981, pp 483-488.

78. Mike SHARPLES, "A computer-based language workshop", DAI Research Paper No. 135, SIGCUE Bulletin, July 1980.

79. N W STUBBS, "Some problems connected with the presentation of foreign language teaching material by computer-assisted instruction (CAI)", CAI No. 4, 1971.

80. S WEIR (with R EMANUEL), "Using LOGO to catalyse communication in an autistic child", DAI Research Report No. 15, 1976.

81. S WEIR (with R EMANUEL), "Catalysing communication in an autistic child in a LOGO-like learning environment", Proceedings of the Second Conference on Artificial Intelligence and Simulation of Behaviour, Edinburgh, 1976.

82. R YOUNG, "Strategies and the structure of cognitive skills", Strategies of Information Processing (editor: G UNDERWWORD), London Academic Press, 1978.

83. R YOUNG (with R LINZ and G PLOTKIN), "Analysis of an extended concept-learning task", Proceedings of the 5th International Joint Conference on Artificial Intelligence, Cambridge, Mass, 1977.

84. R M YOUNG, "Mixtures of strategies in structurally adaptive production systems: examples from seriation and substraction", DAI Research Report No. 33, 1977.

85. R M YOUNG, "Some experiences with OPS2 Production System Interpreter", DAI Working Paper No. 45, 1978.

86. R M YOUNG, "Production systems as models of cognitive development", Bionics Research Report No. 22, 1974.

- DEPARTMENT OF EDUCATION AND SCIENCE, Welsh Office, Department of Education for Northern Ireland,

  "Microelectronics Education Programme - The Strategy" (Programmes d'enseignement en matière d'informatique - La stratégie)

  April 1981, 11 pages.

  To be ordered from:

  The Publications Dispatch Centre, Department of Education and Science, Honeypot Lane, Canons Park, GB-STANMORE HA7 1AZ.

- EDUCATION, (published by Council and Education Press, 5 Bentinck Street, London) "Microelectronics in schools".

- R EMANUEL, see DAI.

- F FOTHERGILL and J S A ANDERSON, "Strategy for the Microelectronics Education Programme (MEP)" in: Programmed Learning & Educational Technology, Journal of AETT, Volume 18, No. 3, August 1981, pages 121-129.

- Rosemary FRASER,

  "Computer in der Secondary Education in Grossbritannien" (Computers in British Secondary Education)

  in:

  LOG IN - Informatik in Schule und Ausbildung, Heft 1/1981.

- Jan GLEN, "Exploring with the micro-computer" in: Special Education. Forward Trends" (British Journal of Special Education), vol 8, No. 3, September 1981, published by the National Council for Special Education.

- Rhys GWYN, "The new information technologies and education, implications for teacher education", an overview report written for the Commission of the European Communities and published by ATEE (see also ATEE).

- D G HALL, see DAI.

- O D W HARGIE, "Research paradigms and theoretical perspectives in microteaching", in: British Journal of Educational Technology, vol 13, No. 1, January 1982.

- N D C HARRIS and J G BAILEY, "Conceptual problems associated with the evaluation of educational technology courses" in: British Journal of Educational Technology, vol 13, No. 1, January 1982.

- J R HARTLEY and K BOSTROM, "An evaluation of micro-CAL in schools", Computer-Based Learning Unit, The University of Leeds.

- J A M HOWE, see DAI.

- B HUTCHINGS, see A PAYNE.

- R INGLIS, see DAI.

- A F IRVINE, "Secondary School Projects and the Microship", Education for the Industrial Society Project, Microelectronics Technology Group, March 1982 (Jordanhill College of Education, 76 Southbrae Drive, GB-GLASGOW G13 1PP).

- K JOHNSON, see DAI.

- R JONES, "Microcomputers: their uses in primary schools", Council for Educational Technology (CET), London?

- Marie-Madeleine KENNING and Michael KENNING, "Computer Assisted Language Teaching made easy" in: British Journal of Language Teaching, vol XIX 3, Winter 1981, p 119.

- J KNAPMAN, see DAI.

- John LEEDHAM: see K AUSTWICK.

- R LEWIS, "Computer Assisted Learning", Trends in Education, No. 2, Summer 1978.

- R LINZ, see DAI.

- Colin MABLY, "The microelectronics revolution - An assessment of its signification for education and teacher education" in: Revue ATEE Journal 3.1980, p 25, Elsevier Scientific Publishing Company, Amsterdam.

- C D MacARTHUR, see DAI.

- D MICHIE, see DAI.

- John MONK, see DAI.

- H M NOBLE, see DAI.

- P ODOR, Editor of the journal ACE, Godfrey Thomson Unit, University of Edinburgh, Old College, South Bridge, GB-EDINBURGH EH8 9YL.

  The journal edited by Mr P ODOR deals with research on how micro-processors may aid the handicapped.

- Tim O'SHEA, see DAI.

- G Terry PAGE: see R E, B BUDGETT

- H PAIN, see DAI.

- S PAPERT, "Mindstorms: Children, Computers and Powerful Ideas", in: Harvester Studies in Cognitive Science, 1981, No. 14, The Harvester Press, Brighton, 216 pages + Notes (7 pages) + Index (6 pages). Critics: "... most exciting and stimulating book on education ...".

- A PAYNE, B HUTCHINGS, P AYRE, "Computer Software for Schools" (Logiciel pour les écoles).

- F PLANE, see DAI.

- G PLOTKIN, see DAI.

- Gareth W ROBERTS, "The use of micro-computers for the teaching of modern languages" in: British Journal of Language Teaching, vol XIX, 3, Winter 1981.

- Alexander J ROMISZOWSKI,

1. "Troubleshooting in Educational Technology or, Why Projects Fail" in: Programmed Learning & Educational Technology, AETT Journal, Volume 18, No. 3, August 1981, pp 168-189.

2. "A new look at instructional design. Part II: Instructions: Integrating One's Approach" in: British Journal of Educational Technology, vol 13, No. 1, January 1982.

- P M ROSS, see DAI.

- S H SALTER, see DAI.

- SCHOOLS COUNCIL NEWS, No. 39, Summer term 1982, "Computers - a key".

- SCOTTISH MICROELECTRONICS DEVELOPMENT PROGRAMME:

1. Strategy and Implementation Paper, April 1981, 41 pages.

2. "Phase Two", a quarterly periodical reporting on educational computing in Scotland published at SMDP, Dowanhill, Glasgow.

   (Address: Dowanhill, 74 Victoria Crescent Road, GLASGOW G129 JN.)

- M SHARPLES, see DAI.

- Ifan D H SHEPERD, Zena A COOPER, David R F WALKER, "Computer Assisted Learning in Geography - Current trends and future prospects", Council for Educational Technology with the Geographical Association, 254 pages, London 1980. ISBN 0-86184-012-7.

- N W STUBBS, see DAI.

- THE TIMES EDUCATIONAL SUPPLEMENT, special issue on computers in education, 4 June 1982 (Computers in primary education, in history, language teaching, talking computer for blind students etc).

- R F TINKER, "Micro-computers in the teaching laboratory" in: The Physics Teacher, February 1981.

- S WEIR, see DAI.

- D J WHITE, "Micro-computers and the Secondary School", Education for the Industrial Society Project, Microelectronics Technology Group, March 1982. (Jordanhill College of Education, 76 Southbrae Drive, GLASGOW G13 1PP.)

- R M YOUNG, see DAI.

USA

- James W BOTKIN, "Microelectronics and intuition" in: Prospects, vol XII, No. 1, 1982.

- ERIC, Clearing House for Science, Mathematics, and Environmental Education, 1200 Chambers Road, Third Floor, Colombus, Ohio 43212, "Micro-computers and Mathematics Instruction" (ERIC/SMEAC Mathematics Fact Sheet No. 4, also listing numerous bibliographic references).

- Frederic GOLDEN (with Philip FAFLICK and J Madelein NASH), "Here Come the Microkids", in: Time, 3 May 1982, pp 46-54.

- Chen-Lin C KULIK, Barbara J SCHWALB, James A KULIK,
  "Programmed Instruction in Secondary Education: A Meta-Analysis of Evaluation Findings" in: The Journal of Educational Research, Volume 75, January/February 1982, No. 3.

- Harold E O'NEIL jr, Editor of the special issue "Computer-based instruction - A State-of-the-Art Assessment, The Educational Technology Series, Academic Press, A Subsidiary of Harcourt Brace Jovanovich Publishers.

LIST OF PARTICIPANTS

I. **DELEGATES**

   AUSTRIA

   Ministerialrat DDr. Hans CZEMETSCHKA, Leiter der Abteilungen II/6 und III/7, Bundesministerium für Unterricht und Kunst, Minoritenplatz 5, A-1014 WIEN

   BELGIUM

   Monsieur W LEURIDAN, Directeur de l'Institut "Sint-Amandus", 13 St-Michielsstraat, B-9000 GENT

   CYPRUS

   Mr Nicos HADJINICOLAS, Director of Technical Education, Ministry of Education, CY - NICOSIA

   DENMARK

   Fagkonsulent (Adviser), Mr Jannik JOHANSEN, Directorate of Upper Secondary Education, Ministry of Education, Amagertorv 14, DK-1160 KØBENHAVN K

   FEDERAL REPUBLIC OF GERMANY

   Studiendirektor Dr. Karl-August KEIL, Leiter der Zentralstelle für programmierten Unterricht und Computer im Unterricht, Schertlinstrasse 7, D-8900 AUGSBURG

   Studiendirektor Lothar SACK, Senator für Schulwesen, Jugend und Sport, Bredtschneiderstrasse 5-8, D-1000 BERLIN 19

   FINLAND

   Dr. Jukka LEHTINEN, Professor of Education, University of

Tampere, PL 607, SF-33101 TAMPERE 10

FRANCE

Monsieur Pierre MULLER, INRP, 91 rue Gabriel Péri,
F-92120 MONTROUGE

GREECE

Dr. Nikolaos ALEXANDRIS, Ministère de l'Education Nationale
et Religions, Direction des Relations d'Enseignement
internationales, Département C: Organisations Internationales,
Mitropoleos 15, GR - ATHENS

IRELAND

Mr C O CAOIMH, Senior Inspector, Postprimary Branch,
Department of Education, Floor 3, Hawkins House, IRL - DUBLIN 2

ITALY

Mr Alfio ANDRONICO, Dipartimento di Matematica, Universita
di Lecce, Strada per Arnesano, I-73100 LECCE

Mr Nadio DELAI, (CENSIS), Pza di Novella 2, I - ROMA

Mr Giovanni LARICCIA, Istituto per le Applicazione del
Calcolo, CNR, Viale del Policlinico 137, I - ROMA

MALTA

Mr Lawrence BORG, Head of Department, Mathematics Department,
New Lyceum, Msida, MALTA

NETHERLANDS

Dr. J AKKERMANS, Ministry of Education and Science,
Directorate General for Science Policy, PO Box 20601,
NL - 2500 EP THE HAGUE

PORTUGAL

Professor Antonio MARTINS BARATA, Direccao-Geral do Ensino
Secundario - ETV, Av 24 de Julho, 140, 5, P-1391 LISBOA CODEX

SPAIN

Mr Fernando Rodriguez GARRIDO (excused/excusé), Directeur,
Cabinet technique, Sous-Secrétariat de l'aménagement éducatif,
Ministère de l'Education et de la Science, Calle Alcalà 34,
E - MADRID 14

SWITZERLAND

Monsieur Alain BRON, CESSNOV, 35 rue Roger-de-Guimps,
CH-1400 YVERDON

UNITED KINGDOM

Mr M EDMUNDSON, HMI, Department of Education and Science,
Room 3/89, Elizabeth House, 39 York Road, GB - LONDON SE1 7PH

Mr P BARKER, Moray House College of Education, Holyrood Road,
GB - EDINBURGH EH8 8AQ

Mr R FOTHERGILL, Director, Microelectronics Education Programme,
Cheviot House, Coach Lane Campus, GB - NEWCASTLE UPON TYNE
NE7 7XA

II. MINISTERO DELLA PUBBLICA ISTRUZIONE - DIREZIONE GENERALE
SCAMBI CULTURALI

(Via Napoleone III n 8, I-00185 ROMA)

Mr S AVVEDUTO
Direttore Generale

Mr Felice CONDO

Mme Chiara A VACIAGO

Mme Elisabetta LA CURRUBBA

III. RAPPORTEUR AND LECTURERS

Mr William R BRODERICK (Rapporteur Général), Head of
Educational Computer Centre, Tring Gardens, Harold Hill,
GB - ROMFORD RM3 9QX, Essex

Dr. Helmut AIGNER, Ministerialrat, Bundesministerium für
Unterricht und Kunst, Minoritenplatz 5, A-1014 WIEN

Dr. Ulrich BOSLER, Institute for Science Education (IPN),
Olshausenstr. 40-60, D-2300 KIEL 1

Prof. M FIERLI, Ispettore Tecnico Periferico, Ufficio
Scolastico Interregionale del Lazio e dell'Umbria, Centro
Europeo dell' Educazione, Villa Falconieri, I-00044 FRASCATI

Don E GARCIA CAMARERO, Director del Centro de Calculo de la
Universidad Compultense, Ciudad Universitaria, E - MADRID 3

Dr. Anita KOLLERBAUR, Department of Information Processing

and Computer Science, University of Stockholm, S-106 91 STOCKHOLM

IV. OBSERVERS

UNESCO

Prof. Gotcha TCHOGOVADZE, Informatics in Education, Division of Structures, Content, Methods and Techniques in Education, UNESCO, 7 place de Fontenoy F-75700 PARIS

OECD

Mr Pierre DUGUET, Principal Administrator, Centre for Educational Research and Innovation, OECD, 2 rue André-Pascal, F-75775 PARIS CEDEX 16

COMMISSION OF THE EUROPEAN COMMUNITY

Mr André KIRCHBERGER (excused), 200 rue de la Loi, B-1049 BRUXELLES

EUROPEAN INSTITUTE OF EDUCATION AND SOCIAL POLICY

Mr Ladislav CERYCH, Director, Institut Européen d'Education et de Politique Sociale, c/o Université de Paris IX-Dauphine, Place du Maréchal de Lattre de Tassigny, F-75116 PARIS - CEDEX

FIPESO

Monsieur Guy Van LAETHEM, 57 rue Joseph Clokers, B-4410 VOTTEM (Herstal)

WCOTP

Monsieur Marc-Alain BERBERAT, Secrétaire Général Adjoint, WCOTP/CMOPE, 5 avenue du Moulin, CH-1110 MORGES

IFIP (International Federation for Information Processing)

Excused

ATEE (Association for Teacher Education in Europe)

Mr Rhys GWYN (excused), (Chairman, Working Group on New Information Technologies and Teacher Education), Manchester Polytechnic, Faculty of Community Studies, Didsbury School of Education, 799 Wilmslow Road, GB - MANCHESTER M20 8RR

FISE (World Federation of Teachers' Unions)

Mme Catherine HOSTALIER, 36 rue Parmentier, F-94210 LA VARENNE ST. HILAIRE

FEoLL-GmbH

Herr Dr. STURM, FEoLL-GmbH, Postfach 1567, D-4790 PADERBORN 1

FUNDESCO

Mr Alberto ALCAZAR IBERLUCEA, Secrétaire Général, FUNDESCO, Calle Serrano 187, E - MADRID

Mr Ignacio ITURRINO ALBENIZ, Directeur d'Education, FUNDESCO, Calle Serrano 187, E - MADRID

V. COUNCIL OF EUROPE

(BP 431 R6 - F-67006 STRASBOURG CEDEX)

Mr Michael VORBECK, Head of the Section for Educational Research and Documentation/Chef de la Section de la Documentation et de la Recherche pédagogiques

Mme Danièle IMBERT, Secretary

VI. INTERPRETERS

Mr Peter FARRELL, Via E Besta 16, I-00167 ROMA

Mlle Marta MINNOGUE, Via Dandini 3, I - ROMA

Mme Christiane TOMASSINI, Via Roccaraso 30, I-00135 ROMA

Mme Jacqueline KAPP DE FICHY, Viale Africa 50, I-00144 ROMA